THE WORLD IN US

THE WORLD IN US

LESBIAN AND GAY POETRY
OF THE NEXT WAVE

AN ANTHOLOGY

EDITED BY

Michael Lassell

AND

Elena Georgiou

ST. MARTIN'S PRESS

New York

Design by Fritz Metsch

Library of Congress Cataloging-in-Publication Data

The world in us : lesbian and gay poetry of the next wave : an anthology / edited by
Michael Lassell and Elena Georgiou—1st ed.
    p. cm.
  ISBN 0-312-20943-6
    1. Gays' writings, American.   2. American poetry—20th century.   3. Gays—
Poetry.   I. Lassell, Michael, 1947-   II. Georgiou, Elana.

PS591.G38 W67 2000
811'.54080920664—dc21

99-086683

First Edition: April 2000

10 9 8 7 6 5 4 3 2 1

CONTENTS

—≺✸≻—

INTRODUCTION

The book you hold in your hands has its roots in the active voice of poetry. It was conceived in a random moment of enthusiasm at a reading of gay and lesbian poets, one of a series curated by the Publishing Triangle, the organization of lesbians and gay men in publishing. The venue was the New York Public Library's historic Jefferson Market branch in Greenwich Village, the room that was once the city justice system's courtroom for women—in fact, the very room where the radical activities of such diverse foremothers as Mae West and Emma Goldman had been judged to be criminal. We were so impressed by the quality of the poetry we had been hearing that night, and on many other nights, that we agreed there just had to be some way to make a book full of the best poetry being written now. *The World in Us* is the result.

As we began to prepare the proposal we eventually submitted to Keith Kahla at St. Martin's Press, we came across the following:

> I see the life of North American poetry at the end of the century as a pulsing, racing convergence of tributaries—regional, ethnic, racial, social, sexual—that, rising from lost or long-blocked springs, intersect and infuse each other while reaching back to the strengths of their origins. (A metaphor, perhaps, for a future society of which poetry, in its present suspect social condition, is the precursor.)

This passage, from Adrienne Rich's award-winning *What Is Found There: Notebooks on Poetry and Politics* (W. W. Norton, 1983) brought together all our own feelings in a concisely poetic summary of "verse" at the end of the twentieth century. These words from a doyenne of the lesbian/gay/bisexual/transgendered (LGBT) community—as the locution now runs—are notable not only for their insight and wisdom but for their literary and social optimism. Rich's life and work stand as conjoined symbols for a unity of poetic and activist purpose, and the affectionate respect she has earned both in the mainstream and in her queer community are a measure of her success in communicating her aesthetic/ethic of inclusion and integration.

This passage perfectly captured our experience at that Jefferson Market Library reading nearly two years ago. What Rich wrote is what we are trying to say with our title. *The World in Us* is not just an invitation to enter the world that our minority poetry has become as the millennium turns, but a statement—one we believe is supported by the work—that by ourselves we contain the world. We hardly need a place at anyone else's table, when our own dining room is full to bursting.

Historically, the waning years of centuries have been times of unrest and uncertainty, and, this, lamentably, is as true of the last months and weeks of the twentieth century as ever before. But we choose to cast our lot with optimism—and Adrienne Rich—because two of Rich's most salient points seem particularly true of the poetry being written now inside the tribe: Queer people are meeting the uncertainties of the future with a flood of poetic energy, and the poetry is coming from as heterogeneous a group of people as the population of the country we all inhabit.

By the time Carl Morse and Joan Larkin edited the landmark *Gay and Lesbian Poetry in Our Time* for St. Martin's Press in 1988, there was already a considerable literary context for the book, openly homoerotic poetry from Sappho to Frank O'Hara, although through much of its history, our poetry has been closeted, covert, coded. By 1988, there was also far too much material for one book, even with small selections from many of the poets. Many of the writers included in *Gay and Lesbian Poetry in Our Time* were literary lions, both living and dead. Remarkably, the world of queer poetry has changed dramatically since 1988. Its personnel has changed radically, and the mood is palpably different.

It is difficult to remember a more receptive moment for poetry. The art not long ago deemed both irrelevant and unsalable has been taken down from its Dead Poets Society pedestal and is being reinvented as a viable force that speaks to a new generation. It is highly significant that the first MTV Lollapalooza tour included poetry (and openly homoerotic poetry at that) and that the New York Poetry Slam has been won by at least one unapologetically gay poet. As usual, the lesbian/bi/gay community has moved forward ahead of the times, taking to the Internet, for example, with an alacrity that gives us a disproportionate presence there and on its poetry Web sites.

While there is some satisfying kernel of truth to the hyperbole that the history of American poetry is identical to the history of queer poetry, so many outstanding poets from Walt Whitman to Allen Ginsberg having been homosexual, it is also true that many poets who share our sexuality refuse the appellation and will not consent to appear in the context of our poetry. Disappointingly, some high-profile poets declined to appear in this book, and their refusal shows there is still a sense of stigma attached to identifying oneself as a member of a sexual minority. Most of these reluctant writers are, let's say, of the pre-Stonewall generation, although others, members of racial and ethnic "minority" communities, expressed the concern that a public gay, lesbian, or even bisexual profile would undercut their work in those communities of color. There is much to be done in the new century.

Fortunately, younger poets are creating a far more open field, both for sexuality and for the literature of sexual minority, a field of unity and integration rather than exclusion and separation. There can be little doubt that the relative openness of the world of queer poetry is having an impact on the world of poetry at large.

Significantly, poetry, as the most personal of literary genres, has always appealed to our community—many of us having grown up in secrecy and isolation—and our poetry has long had a committed audience. Richard Labonté, general manager of the A Different Light bookstores, likes to tell this story: When he asks new employees for their best guess about the dollar volume of poetry sales, the uneducated estimate is invariably lower than the actual sales figure by a factor of ten. While it is difficult to remember the last poetry title that appeared on the best seller list of *The New York Times*, poetry is frequently included on such lists in lesbian and gay newspapers.

The world of queer poetry is not, at century's end, looking backward. It is looking forward, its antecedents internalized more often than cited. The reading rooms of cities with large gay populations are no longer entangled in a cobwebby sense of history or duty. Poetry is becoming less like work and more like pleasure. Readings are more than likely to be high-energy affairs, good-humored and heartfelt. This is a community of readers that knows and likes poetry. The readings, which tend to be emotionally interactive as well as extremely lively, set a tone of conversation between poet and audience—a conversation that proceeds from the written word to the spoken word and then back into the written word, as it affects the writing of others. Readings have become community-building affairs, occasions for strengthening identity and community through literature.

The slam sessions at the annual OutWrite conference, a national confab of queer writers and their readers, hold scores of listeners in their sway, even though they last late into the night.

Across the culture, poetry is more available, more present, more "normal." Enrollment in college poetry classes is increasing, and some of our best poets have even developed followings. In New York City, the Poetry in Motion program of postering subway cars with extracts from poetry past and present has been surprisingly successful in increasing the awareness of poetry. Poetry has shown up on TV's *Late Night at the Apollo,* too, making Amateur Night winners out of Jessica Care Moore and a Chicago poet who calls himself "The Boogie Man." Even Nike took up the cause, making bus stop posters of street/slam poets like "Moms de Schemer" (a regular at the historic Nuyorican Poets Café, which was cofounded, unsurprisingly, by a gay poet).

This is not to suggest that LGBT poetry at the turn of the century speaks in one voice, in one style, or even with one notion of generation. Since 1988, the broadening, more inclusive community has become one of the most diverse groups on earth, and the poetry being written by its members is staggering in its variety as well as its energy. This new queer poetry (or perhaps "postqueer" describes it more accurately) is democratic in the best sense, even though individuals may be as elitist about "private languages" as any before us. Many of the writers now emerging came of age long after the Stonewall riots reorganized the social landscape homosexuality inhabits. These young women and men are maturing in a world in which the unambiguous statement of equality has already been made. Their writing lives have had that context from the beginning.

Many of these younger people (and some of their not-so-young colleagues) are drawing on a whole new set of antecedents for their work. Movies, videos, television, and music have all found their way into poetry, in subject matter, rhythm, and form. This is a poetry with one foot at least in city streets, and lingual experiment abounds, from exercises in Spanglish to poems expressed in hip-hop vernacular. But not all young poets write like rap singers, and it was among the great surprises of the research for this book to find how many young writers are enamored of established forms and a sense of decorum that the Beats were trying to subvert.

In "Tradition and the Individual Talent" (from *The Sacred Wood*, 1920), T. S. Eliot put forth the altogether radical and thereafter normative notion that every new work of art recontextualizes every previous work of art. In other words, history works in two directions, forward and back. Virginia Woolf's *Mrs. Dalloway*, for example, is forever changed by the 1999 Pulitzer Prize–winning novel *The Hours* by Michael Cunningham (a gay man), whose book is inspired by and in a way recapitulates *Mrs. Dalloway*. The writing of today's prominent and emerging queer poets redefines not only the realm of "gay poetry" but that of all poetry (and consequently, of course, of all art, all society).

The forms of this end-of-century expression range from the most classic to those that are related more to the spoken voice and dramatic monologue than to musical (or mathematical) scansion. Although some of the poets here are self-taught and emerge from oral traditions, many have impressive academic credentials, teach at some of the country's most prestigious universities, and refer often to the world of poetry and art that has gone before.

As to the content of LGBT poetry today, it is nearly impossible to generalize, but there are common themes. Childhood and loneliness occur frequently, particularly in settings of repressive or abusive birth families, as does the establishment of families of choice. Love, as with any group of poets, is important, and the forging of primary relationships. Impossible and even imaginary loves crop up in a number of the poems in *The World in Us*. Loss and grief are also major themes, particularly in works related to AIDS and breast cancer, two killers that have devastated not only the wider population but our ranks of poets.

Politics occur regularly, too, both insider and outsider considerations of ordering the world. Ethnicity itself is a theme in much of this poetry, particularly as it relates to multiple generations of ethnicity; frequently the issues of race and sexuality come together in fresh and surprising ways.

Many of the poets here are adept at traditional forms; some are overtly experimental; some draw on prose and in particular the dramatic monologue as a poetic idiom. Some speak in gently introspective voices; others are more outwardly ironic, worldly, troubled. Personal histories that seem emblematic of the clan recur, as do poems of shared cultural icons. Some of these poets write, in part, of exclusion even inside the community.

Sex, sexual identity, and sexual expression are frequently dealt with directly as subject matter, but they also serve as metaphors for "broader" issues. In fact, it has been said that the single most important contribution of queer writing has been the liberation of the American libido, the celebration of pleasure (separate from procreation), the establishment of new patterns of sensual expression. It was writer/historian Joan Nestle, a prominent member of our clan, who remarked that, as a group, we gay and lesbian people are responsible for having written desire into history.

Making an anthology is daunting—partly because there is so much excellent work, but also because so many decisions depend on so many variables. It was clear from the beginning of the project that we wanted to include a larger sample of each poet's work than is traditional in poetry anthologies, where one or two short poems stand in for each poet's career. This meant selecting fewer poets, which was agonizing. But this book is not intended as an overview or a broad sampling of the field, but as a long, curated poetry reading in book form.

Since this is a book about the present and future of queer poetry, its thrust and instinct are intentionally nonhistorical. There are enough books that look backward at the accomplishment of this and other expired centuries. All the poets in *The World in Us* are living. This was a more difficult decision than it might seem, since premature death has been particularly cruel to some of the brightest and best of our poets of the last decade, and even more particularly to women and men of color.

All the poets live in the United States. Certainly, the world is smaller than ever before, the queer poetry community is more and more international, and great work is being written all over the globe and in many languages. But the field is far too vast to cover it all—even to find it all. We don't wish to imply that queer poetry and queer American poetry are synonymous, but lines have to be drawn somewhere and the border of our own begged, borrowed, and stolen country seemed huge enough given the diversity of our population (even though our once vaunted pluralism is increasingly maligned and underappreciated).

All the poets whose work appears here are actively writing poetry. We have chosen not to include people who, for whatever reason, are no longer writing poetry, regardless of how much or how well they have written in the past. Some writers who have been known for their poems in the past declined to be included because they are no longer or not now writing poetry. Some may take to writing poetry again, but we have confined ourselves to writers who are actively engaged in the queer poetry community. Additionally, the forty-six poets whose work follows are all, in some sense, at midcareer.

Now, "midcareer" is a subjective notion. Some of our tribe's spirit mothers and fairy godfathers may still be considered "midcareer," because they are still actively writing, but we have focused on poets who, we suspect, will write their best work in the twenty-first century. This does not mean they are all inexperienced. Most have published books (some, many books), won prestigious grants, prizes, fellowships, residencies. The range of age is roughly midtwenties to midfifties. In other words, generally speaking, it's a post–World War II crowd—in some cases, post-Vietnam (if generations are to be marked by violent global conflicts). We assume a bit of prescience here: We assume they will become (or at least have the potential to become) the next century's May Sarton and Langston Hughes, Audre Lorde and W. H. Auden. In some cases, the future of our selected poets is tied inextricably to the future of medicine, as some live with HIV and other physical conditions that may bring an end to their lives before all their writing is done.

We have chosen poets for a variety of reasons: because their work has justifiably captured widespread attention; because the shape or content of their poems sparks the imagination of others; because they are dynamic, inspirational teachers or editors; because individually they offer a missing piece of the social puzzle and together they represent the larger writing world and the larger community world(s) they inhabit. Always, the bottom line was excellence. Still, there is not enough room for everyone. For that we would need another book this size, a set or series of books.

No one who edits an anthology can pretend to be free from biases, and we admit we have them. It turned out, for example, that we both have a decided appreciation for (or tolerance of) longer poems than are usually found in anthologies. We both enjoy being moved by poetry, although we acknowledge that "moving" is not the only justifiable or meritorious purpose of poetry.

We know, of course, that there are "schools" of poetry — or rather, to oversimplify, there is "school poetry" and there is "nonschool poetry." Most dichotomies, like that of "gay" and "straight," are inherently false, but for most of this century, criticism has contended with one notion of poetry that is described by words like *Apollonian* and *academic* and *well-wrought* and *hermetic* (usually exemplified by T. S. Eliot and other erudite white men of privileged class) and another described by words like *Dionysian* and *lyrical* and *confessional* and *exuberant* (the kind of poetry written by Walt Whitman and by most of the non-white, nonmale, nonheterosexual poets of the twentieth century).

Like our contemporaries, we are of the post-Beat generation, more Whitmanesque than Eliotarian by persuasion. Like many of the poets we have included, we have a pronounced affinity for pop culture and its expressive forms. This book, you will find, contains more poems about rock musicians and movie stars than about Greek mythology. And the poets are, for the most part, candid not only about their sexual orientation but about their specific sexual agendas and activities. On the other hand, you would never know from reading some of the poems whether the poet was gay or straight, woman or man.

What generalization can be made, we think, is that the poetry being written now by the queer community is active and powerful. It is frequently, although not always, "positive." Rather than simply affirming our legitimacy, it often dares us to improve as individuals and as a community. The poetry here does not embrace isolationism or ghettoization, but attempts to engage readers of all kinds, to grab hold and shake them with the force of the poems. This is poetry written as if the lives of the poets depended on it, and in many ways, they do.

The poets of *The World in Us* are shaping their lives and the lives of others with words; their collective modus operandi is to affect everyone who comes in contact with them—perhaps effecting changes in consciousness or behavior along the way—as if each poem were a new sun that casts for each reader an unfamiliar shadow. The strategies are diverse: the poems challenge and shock, they explain and assault, they entertain and amuse. It is strong work from a group of strong individuals. It is work that is not shy about its medium or its content. It is poetry that makes visible the world in us. It is poetry of the necessary word.

MICHAEL LASSELL
ELENA GEORGIOU
New York City

In loving memory of those
gay and lesbian poets
whose lives have inspired us
as much as their words.

They are sorely missed,
but their spirits are
present in this book.

Walta Borawski
Joe Brainard
Melvin Dixon
Tim Dlugos
Allen Ginsberg
Essex Hemphill
Audre Lorde
James Merrill
Paul Monette
Pat Parker
Assotto Saint
Paul Schmidt
Donald Woods
and
our legions of others

*

MARK BIBBINS

·

WHITMAN ON THE BEACH

We sit on barstools,
two random flowers
at the edge of a pool,
baffled by our reflections
and by our thoughts
of how the inevitable
kiss goodnight will be negotiated.

When you get up
to go buy cigarettes,
I imagine what it would be like
never to see you again.

Walt Whitman recited
Shakespeare into the cold
waves at Coney Island—
sonnets floating like rafts,
line by line, toward shores
on the other side of the world.

I settle for mumbling
a few lines I had
written about you
into my cocktail.

By the time you return,
I have finished the drink
and forgotten the words.
I stir the thinning ice cubes
to see if they remember. You should
listen to what they say.
This may be your only
opportunity
to hear what I think of you.

·

BLUEBEARD

I am not certain I love him
and if I do
I am certain I do
not wish to.
He has become
as acrid and infallible
as the clouds around Venus,
invisible to a naive,
earthbound eye
cast heavenward
as dusk thickens into night.

He was a daring jewel
hanging over the mountains,
promising the comfort of
the first-star-I-see-tonight,
but when I flew to him,
he proved impenetrable
and lethal.
Still, I continue in this
foreign orbit that spun
us together into these rooms.

I wait for him
with sheets pulled up
to a face that faces the wall,
wishing I could
disappear from the bed
before he arrives,
leaving behind only a fading
patch of warmth
in the shape of my body—
a body his hands
will not remember.

I know I am not the first,
but I cannot find the others.
He will not even tell me
their names. I want to send
carrier pigeons in search
of these men,

with my story tied to
their pink and scaly ankles,
but I know the very words
would pull them down like rocks.

My notions of escape
wither each time he enters
the room and turns off the light.
I clench my just-brushed teeth,
watching his outline
grow thinner as his clothes
come off slowly in the new dark,
and the way he undresses
is the way
Bluebeard sharpens his axe.

.

GEOMETRY CLASS

Mark is a fag scratched in blue ink
        on the surface of a desk, and true

enough. Trust letters and numbers,
        if not hands that form them,

geometries of loss worked out
        on cool green skins of slate.

Clap these woolly erasers together,
        inhaling ashes of a dead theorem

as they slide down rulers of light
        slowly to the linoleum floor.

Trust what lines do to each other:
        they are creatures lacking malice.

•

MUD

Then we had just the pink carpet, the drugs kicking in, the flat soda. A *loner*, you called me, *by choice* — but that would only be part of the story — in fact, it took dozens of wrong choices to get me here. Oh, what I wouldn't give right now for a little lesbian chic. It might help me to connect these dots, touch my nose with my eyes closed, say the alphabet backwards. It also might have prevented me from botching my attempt at the resurrection — or, more accurately, reconstitution — of a boy who didn't survive long enough to try the new medications (*undetectable levels*: it seems like a reasonable aspiration). Rumor has it that to burn is not to destroy, but to rearrange. Encouraged, I gathered his ashes, mixed in water, kneading my would-be Galatea recast as a boy. Be warned, the edict Don't Try This at Home applies here: what comes is not flesh, just mud. The carpet is still recovering — it provided the surface for an illicit tango with a guy who fancies himself the incarnation of personal style, an encounter that left me sucking poison from my ankle. After a certain point (determined largely by astrological means, as well as by one's choice of hair-care products) worry becomes unseemly, a false mustache you forgot you had on. While the others were shooing ghosts from the room with rolled-up newspapers, the shadows hurried down the walls, off to yet another of their secret meetings.

•

COUNTING

While you are sleeping
in a bed tethered to the wall
by the cord
of a nurse's call button,
I count my fingers.
They outnumber the days
you have left
to spend in this room,
so I busy them with
arranging the cards
from the people who want you
to be a teddy bear
with a sprained ankle
and get well soon.
Late afternoon sun
shines through the plastic bag

that drips your drops of morphine,
and the light comes out numb
as it swims up the wall.
At the end of her shift
we serve your favorite nurse
a daiquiri in a paper cup.
She props her stockinged feet
up on your bed
and you rub them—
on her right foot
she has six toes.
She tells us this
was how she learned
to count to twenty-one.
The laughing minutes
fall away from us
like cherry blossoms,
and I want us to glue them
back onto their branches,
but you're sleeping again
and I don't want to wake you.

OLGA BROUMAS

·

FROM CARITAS

1.

Erik Satie, accused
once of formlessness, composed
a sonata titled: Composition in the Form
of a Pear. When I tell you
that it would take
more brilliance than Mozart
more melancholy precision than Brahms
to compose a sonata in the form of
your breasts, you
don't believe me. I lie
next to your infidel sleep, all night
in pain
and lonely with my silenced
pleasure. Your breasts
in their moonlit pallor
invade me, lightly, like minor
fugues. I lie
between your sapling thighs, tongue
flat on your double lips, giving
voice, giving
voice. Opulent
as a continent in the rising light, you sleep
on, indifferent
to my gushing praises.
It is as it should be. Atlantis,
Cyprus, Crete, the encircled
civilizations, serene
in their tidal basins, dolphin-
loved, didn't heed to the faint, the
riotous
praise
of the lapping sea.

3.

There are people who do not explore the in-
Sides of flowers . . .

—SANDRA HOCHMAN

With the clear
plastic speculum, transparent
and, when inserted, pink like the convex
carapace of a prawn, flashlight in hand, I
guide you
inside the small
cathedral of my cunt. The unexpected
light dazzles you. This flesh, my darling, always
invisible like the wet
side of stones, the hidden
hemisphere of the moon, startles you
with its brilliance, the little
dome a spitting
miniature of the Haghia Sophia
with its circlet of openings
to the Mediterranean Sun.
A woman-made language would
have as many synonyms for pink/light-filled/holy as
the Eskimo does
for snow. Speechless, you
shift the flashlight from
hand to hand, flickering. An orgy
of candles. Lourdes in mid-August. A flurry of
audible breaths, a seething
of holiness, and
behold
a tear
forms in the single eye, carmine
and catholic. You too, my darling, are
folded, clean
round a light-filled temple, complete
with miraculous icon, shedding
her perfect tears, in touch
with the hidden hemispheres
the dome
of our Cyclops moon.

·

ETYMOLOGY

I understand her well because I too practice love
for a living. She came for therapy which I explained
from the root *create*, as in the cognate *poem*,
and *theros*, summer harvest and heat,
and how the ancient prostitutes, *therapaenidae*,
practiced the poetry of heat. She had
enjoyed the whoring but not the pimp
she railed against
so loud in our fourth session
I ducked to keep the pressure with my thumbs
and covered my ears with her breasts to bear her decibels.
"Red tails of poison up my thighs, goddamn him.
Beat on my head all day last time I saw him,
and when the cops arrived, *Her boyfriend*
beat her up. Stopped by to see if I could help.
He had the bad luck later to blow a cop.
Tooth and heart. Isn't everything?"
No. Faith as prelude and spine.
That is a more important.
That is a larger that.

·

TRYST

The human cunt, like the eye, dilates
with pleasure. And all by joy never named

now are priceless in the magnitude of the stars.
From are to are, have to have, beat sub-eternal.

By day, I found these on the beach, for you each
day and give. By night, remind me, I have

forgotten. Action replied by action, peace by peace.
Take you in all light and lull you on a sea

of flowers whose petals have mouths, mesmerized
centerfold, upsweep toward sleep.

·

THE MASSEUSE

Always an angel rises from the figure
naked and safe between my towels
as before taboo. It's why I close
my eyes. A smell
precedes him as the heart
fills from his bowl. I bow
down to the riddle of the ear,
its embryonic sworl nestled with nodes
that calm the uncurled spine,
a maypole among organs.
Each day a stranger or almost
crosses my heart to die
from the unsayable
into the thickened beating
of those wings and we are shy.
Or frightened as with clothes
on we forget
abysmally what heaven
shares with death: what gypsy vowels
unshackled from the lips
rush the impenetrable
mind and the atlas
clicks in my trowel hands.
Crocuses on the threshold's south
side then and now. It goes on
like an egret scaling the unruly bands
of atmosphere we have agreed on
by my palms'
erratic longing of the flesh
to try. Toes crack. Hips
soften and the spine,
a seaweed in the shallow spume,
undulates like a musical
string by the struck note,
helpless with harmonics.
Rock. Cradle the perceptible
scar of the compass, sensible
stigma in a poised blind
of trust angling for reentry,
and the rain, the wind
across its face like minnows in the dark

of love schooling the light
will speak to you and you will walk
home dizzy, grazed by the gloaming and the just
illumined stars.

.

LANDSCAPE WITH NEXT OF KIN

Imagine father that you had a brother were
not an orphan singly that you had a twin
who moved away when he got married had
a kid a similar career whom you had not seen
but heard from frequently for thirty years
imagine meeting him some evening somewhere
familiar to you both not in the village but by
the sea / perhaps / you have

been talking for hours
and for many days
at ease in the proprietor's
gaze — he is young you are old he could have been
a soldier in your regiment that northern province
not so long ago / perhaps he is / you are

here this evening you and your brother seated at the damp
alloy table rusting in some seaside
Patra of the mind identical sighting
the prow of the ferry from Brindisi / perhaps / a woman

bows out from the throng
of tourists very feminine and very strong
resemblance to this man your brother you have never
married / yourself / tonight
are you sipping

the weak milk of your ouzo
having heard everything / at ease / on the other side
of the customs waiting for his daughter your
first blood kin is there anything
in the love you feel

swimming towards him as you did
nine months one heartbeat

pounding like an engine in those waters / is
there anything you won't forgive
her / him

⤙✲⤗

CHERYL BURKE

·

LIZZIE

her mascara makes butterfly patterns on my pillowcase
that I stare at intently to avoid looking her in the eye
she is the girl who talks to me in gym class
and offers to help me fix my hair
she flirts with me in a subtle manner, teases me with little
smiles and makes me feel like I shouldn't
I am confused as she reaches out to touch my hip
grabs inches of flesh in her palm and pulls me close
It is New Year's Day
I am sixteen and she is seventeen
and my body aches from too much liquor in my system and
cigarette smoke in my face
she strokes me like you're supposed to stroke a baby
gentle and controlled
she is petite, feminine and normal
giggly and soft like a woman's supposed to be
she has a boyfriend who looks intimidating and plays football
we spent last night kissing in my bed
the touch of her breast against mine made me feel inadequate
her mouth was small but welcoming
something about her makes me feel silly
but I don't know what it is

later when she is gone
the scent of her perfume is on my sheet
her voice is in my head
and I picture her seated at her boyfriend's house
eating broccoli casserole with the family
I lie in her spot on the bed
thinking about how someone could possibly like both him and me

she made me watch *Gone With the Wind* one night
I don't know what about it made her cry
I liked the Carol Burnett version better
but I didn't say anything
then we went out

only to part when she ran into her boyfriend at Friendly's
and I walked along the highway home
wondering if there was something wrong with me
not knowing that
someday this relationship would make for amusing party anecdotes
fit neatly inside a poem or two
for then it was all I knew about lust
she is a housewife in Delaware, I'm assuming,
I really don't know for sure
perhaps I shouldn't be so easy to judge
but it's probably not far from the truth
I hope she is having an affair with the woman next door
who is just as bored as she
she really was a good kisser.

·

MOTOR OIL QUEEN

Tina speaks to her friend on the phone:

So, it goes like this: Amanda went to the garage over on Union, and she was like waiting there for a while in her car, no not the Caddy, that's her brother's car, you know her car, the 1972 blue Monte Carlo with the white leather upholstery, the dice, the circle of unicorns around the door handle, yeah the one with the 8-track player, you remember, you've been in it. She gave you a ride that night, that night down in Seaside with those guys, the Puerto Rican guys from Queens, remember Christina was like freaking out because she thought she was pregnant 'cause that guy came on her stomach, yeah, yeah, and Jen's hair caught on fire, and Jean that fucking skank, she was all over that guy, the one that I liked, she knew I fucking liked him, fucking blow-job whore, walking skank pond, I'm right aren't I? the girl looks like she's fucking covered in *Sexually Transmitted Diseases*. Anyway, Amanda was at the garage and, you know how she is, she's flirtin' with the guy, he's helping another customer, eventually the other customer drives away and they're there by themselves, a beautiful Saturday spring day and there's no one else around, she says it was like a fucking ghost town. Anyway, she says there was something wrong with her steering wheel, the suspension was off, I mean the car is as old as we are, and he was in there checking it out and one things leads to another before you know it they're on top of the workbench foolin' around and of course he wants to fuck her and Amanda, you know how she is, she's always lookin' to get her pieces of the action. So anyway, they don't have any rubbers, and Amanda being the fucking moron she is, don't get me wrong I love her, I love her, she's one of my best friends, she's like a fucking sister to me, but she's an idiot, she's always buying those *Playgirl* magazines, I'm lookin' through them goin' "these guys they're a bunch of fags, they don't wanna do you, they wanna *be* you, look at them, how many guys do you know wear hot pink bikini underwear, none, right? My sister Annette is a lesbian and she lives up in the Village so I been exposed to that sort of thing, I speak from experience. Anyway, what was I talking about? Oh yeah, Amanda that fucking idiot, so like they don't have rubbers, right? So instead of just going across the street to the Cumberland Farms like a normal fucking person, she has . . .

[pause]

Wait. You can't tell anyone, you promise, all right she lets him fuck her up the ass, right there in the open on the workbench in the middle of the day right out on the highway. Yes. I was stunned, and it gets even worse, so they do it and she says he used some sort of lubricant, of course she doesn't question it. So the deed is done and over and a few days later Amanda is feeling a little weird down there so she goes down to PP and finds out she has an infection in her butt, she tells me this and I'm like you're lucky that's all you have you fucking idiot, all right I didn't call her a fucking idiot right to her face, but I was thinking it. I mean in this day and age you gotta be careful, so hopefully the infection will go away. But there's more. We were out the other night at Danny's and the minute we walked in the whole place went quiet, it was like time stopped or something and they were all just lookin' at us. The whole night we heard everybody buzzing about Amanda and motor oil, they were saying names like Pennzoil girl and motor oil queen, I mean these are her fucking friends, right? Well, apparently that guy, the ass-fucker from the garage, was going around telling everybody that he used motor oil as a lubricant, I don't know if it's true, but I guess it makes sense. Amanda was just totaled. I felt so bad so I took her home and we sat outside her house in my car and she just wouldn't stop crying, and the entire time I kept picturing her as the Tin Man in *The Wizard of Oz*, you know with the can of oil. If she only had a brain. It's not funny though, we shouldn't be laughing, I worry about her, really I do, she's like a fucking sister to me. So anyway, I gotta go. What are you wearing tonight? Yeah that sounds great. Okay hon, I'll see you there.

—<☼>—

REGIE CABICO

·

CHECK ONE

The government asks me to "check one."
I say, "How can you ask me to be one race?"

I stand proudly before you, a fierce Filipino
who knows how to belt hard gospel songs
played to African drums at a Catholic mass—
and loving the music and suffering beats
and lashes from men's eyes on the Capital streets—

Southeast D.C. with its sleepy crime.
My mother nursed patients from seven to nine
patients gray from the railroad
riding past civil rights.

I walked their tracks when I entertained
them at the chapel and made their canes pillars
of percussion to my heavy gospel—
my comedy out-loud, laughing about,
our shared stolen experiences of the South.

Would it surprise you if I told you my blood
was delivered from North off Portuguese vessels
who gave me spiritual stones and the turn in my eyes—
my father's name when they conquered the Pacific Isles.
My hair is black and thick as "negrito," growing abundant
as "sampaguita"—flowers defying civilization
like *Pilipino* pygmies that dance in the mountain.

I could give you an epic about my ways of life or my look
and you want me to fill it in "one square box."
From what integer or shape do you count existing identities,
grant loans for the mind or Crayola white census sheets—
There's no "one kind" to fill for anyone.

You tell me who I am, what gets the most money
and I'll sing that song like a one-man caravan.

I know arias from Naples, Tunis and Accra —
lullabies from welfare, food stamps and nature

and you want me to sing one song?
I have danced jigs with Jim Crow and shuffled my hips
to the sonic guitar of Clapton and Hendrix,
waltzed with dead lovers, skipped to bamboo sticks,
balleted kabuki and mimed kathakali
arrivedercied-a-rhumba and tapped Tin Pan Alley
and you want me to dance the *Bhagavad Gita*
on a box too small for a Thumbelina-thin diva?

I'll check "other."

·

MANGO POEM

Mother fetched the fruit from the mango grove
        behind closed bamboo
        ripped its paper-leather cover during midday recess,
before English class. Described their dance —
peaches, plums, cantaloupes — before my first-world
        eyes. When the sun blazed on the dust,

She let the mellifluous fluids
        fall on her assignment books.
Where the mangos were first planted, mother,
an infant, hid under gravel
swaddled by *lola*, my grandmother,
after my mother's aunt and uncle
were tied to the trunk
        and stabbed
by the Japanese. Mother and daughter living off
        fallen mangos, the bits planted in darkness,
        years before I was born.

We, a family of five, left the Philippines for
        California dodging
U.S. Customs with the forbidden fruit.
        Thinking, who'd deprive mother of her mangos.
Head down, my father denied that we had perishable
        foods and waved passports in the still air,

motioning for us
    to proceed towards the terminal.
Behind a long line of travelers,

my sisters surrounded mother
like shoji screens as she hid the newspaper-covered
    fruit between her legs. Mangos slept
in the hammock of her skirt, a brilliant batik
    billowing from the motion
of airline caddies pushing suitcases
    on metal carts.

We walked around mother like mini-airplanes,
    forming a crucifix, where she was the center.
On the plane, as we crossed time zones, Mom unwrapped
her ripe mangos, the one from the tree *lola* planted
    before she gave birth to my mother,

the daughter that left home to be a nurse
in the States,
    who'd marry a Filipino navy man
    and have three children of her own. Mother eating
the fruit, whose juices rained
    over deserts and cornfields.

·

GAMEBOY

he buys me a glass
of bass draft
& asks
if i am japanese

his remarks:
you are the perfect
combination of boy & man

are you the hip hot hung
    9 inches of fun
    seeking the slim,
    smooth, smiling
    authentically

thai-tasting
geisha-guy
on the side
macho dancer
looking for his lord & master
m. butterfly/wedding
banquet/joy fuck club?

I am not a korean dragon lady
running down avenue a
with a teapot between my legs

shouting
    where's my tip—
    gimme my trophy

you wanna play with me?
you can
just quit orientalizin'
cuz I ain't gonna
change my cotton-knit calvins
for you or my mother

if I lose

I ain't gonna fry you an emperor's meal
or throw you eurasia
or butterfly you an opera

I'm thru giving sex tours of unicef countries
3rd world is for hunger & fat sally struthers

I am not a teriyaki toy
a rice queen's dream

a bowl of soy sauce
to dip yr meat in

I've long been the *it*
in a rice queen phenomenon
that's burned faster than gin bottles
thrown at the black of my skillet

games so old as jason & hercules
men fucking my body
like fresh golden fleeces

they ride my boyhood on bikes
in the woods
then rape it & kill it
with leashes   spit words
in personal ads
(those clever written puzzles)

for fun
they blood-brother baptize
my emotions
then martyr my sisters
in the backroom basements

I'm thru with charades
I'm thru with your malice
& your riots like hopscotch
I'm not gonna fight it

I am beyond being
poker-faced/mysterious/submissive
wanted by you
or a being who's glossy
& g.q. queen gorgeous

you wanna play freeze tag
I'm frozen already
touch me
you'll swear I'm the iceman's ice monkey

hit me
& watch where the mah jong chips land

lust me
I'll soon feel the back of your hand

play with me then
if you think
the sweet that's left
to the taste in my tongue
is enough & not bitter

love me for this
I forfeit the game
remove my make-up

& call you the winner

·

ANTONIO BANDERAS IN HIS UNDERWEAR

I don't want to be overexposed.
—ANTONIO BANDERAS,
Vanity Fair, 1996

His back and clavicles are draped
        in a gossamer robe, reserved for
an Iberian Zeus.

Only his hands protrude,
        curved over an invisible
steel backing. Sitting among

a flock of palm trees, he doesn't
        mind the sun
against his chiseled brow,

nor bother with the photographer's
        lens thrust skyward.
His head tilted, a typical

model pose. Chest and loins
        exposed, he parts
his legs accepting the glare

of the heated bulbs. The constant
        pulse and click of the camera
as an unexpected sea-breeze

surreptitiously licks his calves.
        Wrapped around the ankles,
white slippers caress his

feet. Engrossed in deep
        contemplation, his right hand
twirls a red silk tassel

brushing the bronze of his
      inner right thigh. Perhaps he knows
his fans: mortal men, nymphs,

     Madonna, talking horses
and pigs alike will ooh and ahh
at the voluptuous swoop

and arch of his super star-studded
      quality, spilling full-frontal
and oh . . . so generously! He sits content.

The wealth of flesh, unseen to us,
      coyly tugging the black-lycra
   band of his briefs —
branded HOLLYWOOD.

•

ART IN ARCHITECTURE

Could
Frank Lloyd
Wright   create
better   structure
what   lies
between my
lover & me
is   where
the   similar
transcends
the   seven
wonders of
the   world
Twin Towers in white
sheets how   his slopes
against my teeth   a mini
skyscraper resting on muscle
boy rocks a   cultivated
landscape   falling
like   Babel

RAFAEL CAMPO

•

BELONGING

I went to Cuba on a raft I made
From scraps of wood, aluminum, some rope.
I knew what I was giving up, but who
Could choose his comfort over truth? Besides,
It felt so sleek and dangerous, like sharks
Or porno magazines or even thirst—
I hadn't packed or anything, and when
I saw the seagulls teetering the way
They do, I actually felt giddy. Boy,
It took forever on those swells of sea,
Like riding on a brontosaurus back
Through time. And when I finally arrived,
It wasn't even bloody! No beach of skulls
To pick over, nothing but the same damn sun,
Indifferent but oddly angry, the face
My father wore at dinnertime. I stripped
And sat there naked in an effort to
Attract some cannibals, but no one came;
I watched my raft drift slowly back to sea,
And wished I'd thought to bring a book
That told the history of my lost people.

•

FROM SONG FOR MY LOVER

VI. Our Country of Origin

I'm dreaming geographically these days.
Last night I dreamt I found our island home.
My finger traced a slick, gigantic globe
Atilt in its mahogany while days
Flashed by because I spun the world so fast.
The continents began to look obscene.
They seemed to drift apart. They seemed like stains,
Gigantically polluting stains, adrift

Upon the solitary ocean. Time,
Forever running out in my father's den
When I was just about to understand,
Had suddenly run out. The mastermind
Of every scheme was in that globe; he grinned
At me in latitudes and parallels.
Discovery, forbidden islands, hell—
To reach between your thighs was not a sin.

XI. A Medical Student Learns
Love and Death

The scalpel finds the heart. The heart is still.
The way it rests, suspended in his chest,
It seems a fruit unharvested, its flesh
Inedible but oddly tempting—swelled
A size I never will forget. My sleeves
Rolled up, I touch, I trace an artery—
A torturous, blockaded road—and free
The muscle from connective tissue sheaths
An unforgotten lover left in place.
My working hands become the fluttering
He must have felt; the lost anatomy
Of his emotions, gardens left in haste.
Past human bodies, no one has evolved.
With these deflated lungs, he's penitent,
He wants to say how love will never end.
I cut, and make from him the grave I rob.

.

FROM TEN PATIENTS, AND ANOTHER

IV. Kelly

The patient is a twelve-year-old white female.
She's gravida zero, no STDs.
She'd never even had a pelvic. One
Month nausea and vomiting. No change
In bowel habits. No fever, chills, malaise.
Her school performance has been worsening.
She states that things at home are fine.
On physical exam, she cried but was
Cooperative. Her abdomen was soft,

With normal bowel sounds and question of
A suprapubic mass, which was non-tender.
Her pelvic was remarkable for scars
At six o'clock, no hymen visible,
Some uterine enlargement. Pregnancy
Tests positive times two. She says it was
Her dad. He's sitting in the waiting room.

VII. Manuel

In Trauma 1, a gay Latino kid—
I think he's seventeen—is getting tubed
For respiratory failure. "Sleeping pills
And Tylenol," I translated for him
As he was wheeled in. His *novio*
Explained that when he'd told his folks about
It all, they threw him out. Like trash. They lived
Together underneath the overpass
Of Highway 101 for seven weeks,
The stars obstructed from their view. For cash,
They sucked off older men in Cadillacs;
A *viejita* from the neighborhood
Brought *tacos* to them secretly. Last night,
With eighteen-wheelers roaring overhead,
He whispered that he'd lost the will to live.
He pawned his crucifix to get the pills.

XI. Jane Doe #2

They found her unresponsive in the street
Beneath a lamplight I imagined made
Her seem angelic, regal even, clean.
She must have been around sixteen. She died
Who knows how many hours earlier
That day, the heroin inside her like
A vengeful dream about to be fulfilled.
Her hands were crossed about her chest, as though
Raised up in self-defense; I tried to pry
Them open to confirm the absence of
A heartbeat, but in death she was so strong,
As resolute as she was beautiful.
I traced the track marks on her arms instead,
Then pressed my thumb against her bloodless lips,

So urgent was my need to know. I felt
The quiet left by a departing soul.

.

WHAT THE BODY TOLD

Not long ago, I studied medicine.
It was terrible, what the body told.
I'd look inside another person's mouth,
And see the desolation of the world.
I'd see his genitals and think of sin.

Because my body speaks the stranger's language,
I've never understood those nods and stares.
My parents held me in their arms, and still
I think I've disappointed them; they care
And stare, they nod, they make their pilgrimage

To somewhere distant in my heart, they cry.
I look inside their other-person's mouths
And see the wet interior of souls.
It's warm and red in there—like love, with teeth.
I've studied medicine until I cried

All night. Through certain books, a truth unfolds.
Anatomy and physiology,
The tiny sensing organs of the tongue—
Each nameless cell contributing its needs.
It was fabulous, what the body told.

—<✻>—

CYRUS CASSELLS

·

NEW SONG OF SOLOMON

Look how we're wedded—
jubilant, unchecked.
The armoire mirror
is our witness:
this is a new Song of Solomon
we're fashioning;
in Tuscan niches
where our bed is green
or trophy-bright,
in shuttered
Florentine and Roman rooms,
your body has become
my refuge and intoxicant.

You've given me
rosemary, trumpet lilies, musk, God
in the hours of languor.
You've given me
calamus and cinnamon,
your hand's acumen.

I want the crush of your pelvis,
your outlaw kiss.
I want your inmost wonder,
your fierce mouth
here. And here.

·

A COURTESY, A TRENCHANT GRACE
FOR JIM GIUMENTARO (1959–1992)
AND FOR TERRY PITZNER

Leaving you,
Knowing you would likely die
While I was away,
Made me recall
The photographer's tale,
How he ventured into a realm
Of monkey temples, rickshaws,
River-pilgrims, ghats,
The numinous city of Benares,
And discovered an urchin
Toppled in a clamorous street:
No one would touch him;
Not one among the merchants
Or mendicants.
He lifted the dust-checkered child,
Swabbed his hands, the russet
Planet of his face.
You understand,
The photographer was a man
Annealed by war,
Inured to suffering,
Yet at having to leave
The frayed child
Only rupees, a little food,
He felt his surgeon's soul unclappered.

But on his return
The following day, he found
The boy of the holy, moribund flesh,
The threadbare boy,
Upright;
The city of ash and fervent pilgrim's prayer
Seemed unstainable then,
The yogi's poise by the river
More radiant—

Jim, once we lay in the lee
Of the plague's unblooming
Gusts and battleground,

On a calm bed,
The gift which at the very last
Had to stand for
All my allegiance,
My living arms' goodwill:
I cradled you,
Mindful of your shingles,
Let you doze
For an unhaggard hour:
I was giving you my bed
To die in.
And in my grief and will
To absolution for what seemed
My gargantuan failure
To keep you alive,
It was as if I was fashioning
An inmost shrine,
An evensong to be stationed
Wherever on this earth
A courtesy, a trenchant grace
Is enacted
In the smallest gesture:
Soup spoon tucked
Under a lesioned lip,
Palm-and-lotion laving
A wand-lean leg;
Above the intravenous tube,
Or through a martyrdom of flies,
A true and level gaze
Is manna,
In laboring hospices,
In compassionless, dusty streets,

In the sacred city of Benares.

·

MARATHON
FOR MELVIN DIXON
(1950–1992)

Sensuous and hilarious wit,
Nothing on this roiling, breakspirit earth
Could have readied you
For the doctor's stark edict:
There is a small window of time
To save your sight;
Choose your eyes,
And leave your lover's deathbed.

Choose, choose—
The word, keen as a scimitar.
Better to go blind, anointing
The chalice of his last breath?
Better to see, bereft
Of merciful closure?

When the simoom of contagion—
Shared world, shared semen,
Shared needle, shared blood—
Is hushed at last,
Perhaps then I'll grasp
How you outpaced the minutes,
Hectoring wings,
How you raced home from surgery,
The lapis of the bay intact,
To his blessed persistence:

Love of my life, you can ebb now;
Being-without-end,
Pass your sight into me.

•

BEAUTIFUL SIGNOR

All dreams of the soul
End in a beautiful man's or woman's body.
—WILLIAM BUTLER YEATS,
"The Phases of the Moon"

Whenever we wake,
still joined, enraptured —
at the window,
each clear night's finish
the black pulse of dominoes
dropping to land;

whenever we embrace,
haunted, upwelling,
I know
a reunion is taking place —

Hear me when I say
our love's not meant to be
an opiate:
helpmate,
you are the reachable mirror
that demands integrity,
that dares me to risk
the caravan back
to the apogee, the longed-for
arms of the Beloved —

Dusks of paperwhites,
dusks of jasmine,
intimate beyond belief

beautiful Signor

no dread of nakedness

beautiful Signor

my long ship,
my opulence,
my garland

beautiful Signor

extinguishing the beggar's tin,
the wind of longing

beautiful Signor

laving the ruined country,
the heart wedded to war

beautiful Signor

the kiln-blaze
in my body,
the turning heaven

beautiful Signor

you cover me with pollen

beautiful Signor

into your sweet mouth—

This is the taproot:
against all strictures,
desecrations,
I'll never renounce,
never relinquish
the first radiance, the first
moment you took my hand—

This is the endless wanderlust:
dervish,
yours is the April-upon-April love
that set me spinning even beyond
your eventful arms
toward the unsurpassed:

the one vast claiming heart,
the glimmering,
the beautiful and revealed Signor.

JUSTIN CHIN

·

WHY A BOY

In the dark room, lit only by the stray light
from a bathroom somewhere in the back of the house
and the blue emanation of porn from the television,
the joint is passed back and forth, the drill sergeant
is stuffing a dripping fat dildo into the recruit's ass,

the sound is turned so low that each thrust, each play-acting
wince on the boy's face sounds like a whisper in a great
library, the actors rarely ejaculate on this tape and soon
it runs out, follows the stains up the wall to the ceiling,
spatter of Crisco and shit, some homeowners stick little

luminous stars on their ceilings so that they can gaze at the
heavens as they lay on the floor, but heaven means different
things to different people and he changes the tape, another
fister, I ask him what was the biggest thing he ever had
up his ass, he scratches his beard, smoothes the hairs over

his balding head and thinks, I wish he would say something
really fantastic like A Watermelon, or Half A Cocker Spaniel,
but he says two hands, some people got bigger hands, he says
and two hands at the same time is much bigger than a foot,
the joint is done, the lines are done and the action

on the television guides us, with my arm in his ass, I feel
the rough nubs of his vertebrae, I wriggle my fingers and see
how they pop up against his old belly, feel the twist-tie
of his belly button from the inside, I look down and creeping
out of his ass, plugged by my arm, a thin stream of blood,

red as all of last year's misery flows *who's a daddy*
I put off visiting and when I finally do see him, it's not
as bad because he's put back on the weight he lost months ago
and they changed his medication and so he's not so spaced out
anymore, soon, someone will have to take care of him all day

and all of the night, and across the world in a Buddhist
hospice in Bangkok, what's left of a man tries to sleep,
the only comfort he has is the picture of his teacher, next
week, he will be left to die in a hospital because someone will
bomb the place, next week a Man will find a Boy and take him

to his heart and home and cock and wallet, and the Boy will
find something in that *who's a boy* the phone rings and I
agree to meet him because his wife is away for the day,
he says he imagines I were his little boy neighbor who would
worship his cock everyday, drink off his balls; once in a park,

a bus station, a dead end, a man told me he had a friend
in Santa Cruz who picked up street kids so he could rub
some crank in their asses and pump the boy silly, let's visit
him sometime he said and I never saw him again, and maybe
somewhere in this wide country a boy is really being fucked

by his daddy's crystal smeared dickhead *what a daddy what a boy*
wants is an unspoken agreement that parents should never ever
have to bury their children, tonight I can't sleep and my eyes
are too tired to read and the voice on the television is
hysterical ranting about how fathers are missing in our

culture, how men don't take responsibilities anymore,
how role models are missing, how homosexuality is threatening
the family that is already threatened because there are no men,
not enough men, once many years ago, we danced to a proclamation
that there were too many men and way too little time, it used

to rain men goddammit, oh prophecy that is disco, tell us
where we can find the love to love ya baby, let's just blame it
on the boogie *when a daddy when a boy* finds that everyone
around me seems to be dying and I wonder if I'm not too, seems
the whole world is dying and the speed of surviving, existing

here, now, is waiting for that final impact, that head-on collision,
the shock that may or may not break your neck, look over here,
in Goya's suite *Disasters of War*, the 81st etching shows us
the Proud Monster, a horrible beast whose regurgitating maw
pours out an avalanche of men. Oh, my Terrible Father devours

me. I want to be the hero in my own version of this story
but I am too often the monster, puking out my share

of father, grandfathers, brothers, uncles, cousins, nephews,
sons, grandsons, contributing to the shortage and it feels

like sitting in a pool of blood, like hunting for God's cum, like
watching the whole world spin like a teacup ride at Disney, like
knowing why a daddy and, if you're still here in the sound
of my voice, know why a boy.

·

COCKSUCKER'S BLUES

Beauty does not come cheap
but there are enough discount stores out
there.
Pennies turn to dimes,
dimes into nothing but hard time.
I walk the city with my eyes shut
against the flesh crawl of need,
ducking into alleyways and bookstores
lined with pathetic creatures begging for blow
and a buffed jock named Chad begging
for one more token, one more day
at a time. It's enough to keep
the saddest cocksucker happy.

You said you used to be so beautiful
that people would pay to suck you off
and you didn't even have to cum to collect
but now you would let anyone have you
you have no choice, you said,
and I agreed and tried to make you
feel like a million bucks for $4.99.

Buy your beauty:
At 10, it tastes like spit
      at 20: melted government margarine
      at 30: Elmer's glue paste
      at 40: Vaseline
don't bother going any higher,
pack your bags, and hit the road, Jack,
it'll never taste like what you paid for
no matter how high you can get.

You crowned yourself Queen of the Poppers.
Sucked so much amyl nitrate
that the vapors were the only thing
holding your tongue together,
the Tic Tac of your dependency coats your words.
Your silk suit crumpled, your body in a cold sweat
your flaccid penis tasting like stale elbow grease
your icy balls stretched into a tight bruised blue
to match your lips that have turned turquoise hours ago.
You said, you needed a few more lines to turn it up.
Damaged goods, but who isn't these days.

In Vegas at the Mirage,
Sigfried and Roy's White Tigers trapped
in a perpetual daylight, 24 hours of fake light
in a Plexiglas cage with a glittering waterfall
landscape out of *The Snow Queen*.
Poor tigers held up to the scrutiny
of the ugly sour-faced masses
decked in sequins, appliqués and wash-and-wear,
spongy folk who have lost so much currency
shoved down metal slots.
Only impotence can drive someone
to look at tigers at 3 in the morning.

At 3 in the morning,
I follow reflections and piss-stained corridors
to bedsits and broomsticks.
The first time the first time the first time.
He was a wino a bum a banker a chemist a greengrocer.
He was a lawyer a doctor a systems analyst.
His name was Rico, he wore a diamond.
He slapped me around he fucked my face
he came in my mouth when I asked him not to.
He showed me pictures of younger boys
Polaroids of bodies without heads, hands holding dicks,
fingers in arses, smooth armpits
and said I want you to be just like that.
I wanted to die when he got too mean and too rough
I wanted to kill him when he apologized
and offered a sandwich, a ride home when it was done
I wanted to swallow more, swallow more.
Maybe that wasn't the first time,
it could have been the 2nd or 3rd

it could have been every subsequent time.
it could also be nothing but a done-up jack-off lie.
Just one for my baby and one for the road.

I crawl out at dawn
into the soup of light and scarred gratitude.

A crazed Born-Again bearing a sandwich board
approaches, gives me a tract
that will save me from the evils of the material world.
Repent, he says, *repent.*
There is healing in the blood of the Lamb of Christ.

580 billion babies have died in my mouth.
580 billion more will follow, their daddies abandoning them,
like AIDS-infected darlings, in spit and in confession.
I repent nothing.

I would do much more.

I would dance barefoot on shards of your broken beauty.
I would call you Daddy in the face of my sadist master.

I would match Rod Stewart's record
12 pints and they won't have to pump it out of me,
I will choke it down and keep it down.

Ask me anything. Tell me anything.
I want all beauty to weep for me.
I wear my wounds on my tongue,
my dependency is my king,
and my immortal imperfection, my fractured wings.

UNDETECTABLE

The spacepod shrunk to microscopic
proportions with its inhabitants aboard,
injected in the vein of the terminally
ill coma patient. Traveling in the
bloodstream, we peek into the human body:
tissue, cell, organ, blood, lymph.
Every lucid hue taken away
by the black-and-white television set.
The mission: to reach the tumor,
to blast it with the specially designed
and shrunk laser gun. There are
complications, of course (why should
fiction not have a smudge of horrible reality?)
and Raquel, plucky scientist in her daring
skin-tight curve-enhancing wetsuit, swims
in blood to do something heroic,
but she is attacked by white blood cells (eek!),
envisioned by the special effects department
as crunchy foam fingers, not unlike
the white fungus delicacy of soups
in Chinatown restaurants; deed
done, more white cells attacking,
oh how will they escape? Through the eye!

Cure or Blight. Who is
the foreign body here?

There is a battle in my body. Every day
a small chunk of me is given up in this
microscopic war. Small flecks of cells,
shreds of tissue, muscle, skin, bone,
disintegrate, turn to junk, float
through my body and are pissed out.

This atom, this molecule, this bond
between them will quell the virus.
Squash it into almost nothingness,
into something so small, smaller
than it already is, so it won't show,
cannot be counted,

like ghosts and gases, its true existence
undiscovered, lurking
ready to kiss or kill. Undetectable.

Only in B-movies:
foreign body kills foreign body,
chemicals and petri dishes don't lie,
easy redemption, happy ending.

Every day, a small bit
of myself dies
in that chemical battle.
    An undetectable bit
of myself dies every day.

I get tired easily. I take more naps.
I dream less.
I smell like the medicine chest.
Some days I think I can
feel every single cell in me.
I can feel every single one
that dies.

•

EX-BOYFRIENDS NAMED MICHAEL

My mother is concerned that I haven't met a nice boy to settle down with.
She keeps asking me if I've met the right guy yet.

Well, Mom, there've been some nice guys who just didn't work
out, some guys that have broken my heart, and there've been ex-boyfriends
named Michael.

Ex-boyfriend named Michael #1 was a sheer mistake, but we make
such delightful mistakes when we are young. You're supposed to learn from
your mistakes, but heck . . .

Ex-boyfriend named Michael #2. I've washed him right out of my
colon. Just for once, I'd like to date a man and not his therapist.

Ex-boyfriend named Michael #3 said I had communication
problems, and I said, "Oh, go fuck yourself, asshole." What I should have
said was, "Honey, I am trying to understand your feelings of frustration at
our seemingly inept articulations of our emotions, but I do have some
unresolved feelings of anger towards you, so please go fuck yourself,
asshole."

But maybe there's the off chance he's right. I have never been that great at communicating. Ex-boyfriend named Michael #4: I should have known better the first time we met and went back to his apartment to fuck. His idea of fuck music was Dan Fogelberg's *Greatest Hits*. I asked him to change the CD, and he changed it to the only thing that could have been worse: *Neil Diamond Live at Madison Square Garden*.

Coming to America, indeed.

But I stuck with him and every fuck at his place was sheer hell. I tried telling him that his taste in music sucked and that I could seriously help him, but somehow I lacked the communication skills to do just that. But then I thought I loved him, and then I was young enough and foolish enough to believe that love can overcome Linda Ronstadt.

It cannot.

Ex-boyfriend named Michael #5 was suffering from a severe case of yellow fever and dumped me for little Taiwanese guy, fresh off the damn boat. Two weeks in the Yoo-Ass and the little pissant faggot manages to find his way to Café Hairdo, ready to be picked up by his American Dream of Homosexual Romance. I can just see him sitting there, legs crossed, working his non-threatening little Third World charm, offering to share his table and newspaper. I can just see them now: sharing haircare products, making mutual consensual decisions about dinner, movies, sex and their emotional well-beings. I can see them sitting on the sofa with the dictionary in their laps trying to figure out the difficult words in Barbara De Angelis's *Making Love Work* video seminar, and thinking about adopting a fox terrier named Honey. I can see them having deep, deep discussions about which one of them has a better butt:

"You do."

"You do."

"No, you do."

"Stop it! You do."

"Yours is tight and tanned."

"But yours is pert and angry."

What a pair of goddamn fucking freaks. I would just like to see them in a big car accident crashing into an oncoming truck carrying a shipment of Ginsu kitchen knives.

But hey, I'm not bitter, I'm descriptive. I'm not jaded. I just have too many ex-boyfriends named Michael.

Just once, I'd like to see everything of my life with ex-boyfriends named Michael laid out on a fat barge sent off to the landfill of affection. I'll watch the barge ferry its way through the flotsam of therapy & crabs, dish soap & bad sex, shared shirts & worry, devotion & drugs, pissed-off nights & legless drunken revelry.

I'll wave good-bye and I'll be fine.

‹✲›

CHRYSTOS

·

I SUCK

her toes, bite her arch, trail my tongue along the inside of her leg &
wait   She groans, pushes her hips toward me   I smile & return to sucking
her toes   Take my time with the back of her knees, small sucking bites
while she wiggles   Lift her thighs onto my shoulders, kneading her ass,
my finger greased as I slide along her crack, teasing   Slap her pussy as she
tries to pull me down with her knees   My tongue aching for her petals
but waiting until the moment when I feel her urgency greater than
mine   She pulls my hair in a fury of need until my lips touch her curly
wetness   I kiss her everywhere except where she wants me   Her clit fat &
erect   I bite her hair with my teeth, pulling   What do you want,
Baby?   *YOU KNOW*   No, I've never done this before you'll have to tell
me what to do   *LICK ME*   I lick her once from her cunt to her belly &
rise to suck her breasts   She pounds my shoulders, scratching my back
until I suddenly remember how to eat pussy, how much I love to eat pussy,
how I could have pussy before & after every meal & would definitely snap
up a job in the lesbian whorehouse eating pussy   My tongue is slow
looking for the path down into the lights of need   I am her pleasure,
focused   I'm erased into the fruit of her flowering, colors spinning   I
follow her through fear   through shame   through cold memories into the
valley where pleasure shimmers in a spring haze

Her voice leaping pushes sound her body bites the air in a long sobbing
scream roaring her head banging the wall her fists pounding we're an arc
of rainbow as I hang on to her thighs my nose banging   her cunt clenching
my hand so tightly it's numb & I feel her let go into that flamingo pink
sea vibrating lavender to magenta

Did you come a little bit, Baby? *Oh FUCK you*
Oh please do
As soon as you can move

·

I BOUGHT A NEW RED

dress to knock her socks off, spent all day looking for just the right combination of sleeve & drape, so I could actually knock all her clothes off   She met me at the boat dressed so sharp she cut all the boys to ribbons

Over dinner in a very crowded queer restaurant I teased her by having to catch drips of my food with my tongue, staring into her eyes, daring her to lean over & grab my breast or crotch & titillate the faggot waiters   She sat back soaking me up, enjoying my teasing tidbits, for all the world not wanting to fuck me ever   I knew better as she's kept me on my back all night since we met   I began to pout because I wasn't affecting her enough to suit me & she hadn't said a thing about my dress   Just then the waiter brought our dessert, a small cake she'd had decorated to say *Beg Me to Fuck You*, with pink roses all around the edge

I laughed so hard I tore my dress a little   The waiter smirked   I fed her roses from the cake, she licked my fingers so slowly I almost screamed   Near us some blazer dykes were very nervous & offended, so naturally she began to make loud sucking noises   Laughing, we left them to their girl scout sex & went dancing, where she kept her hand on my ass & her thigh between my legs even during the fast ones   Going home she pulled my thigh-top stockings to my knees & played with me   I'd worn no underpants especially for her   We were having such a good time she couldn't park & we laughed as she tried a third time & I blew in her ear almost causing a wreck

Then we started doing it in the front seat of her car, awkward with gear knob & wrong angles, until a cop pulled up & said sarcastically through the open window   *Do you need some assistance parking, Sir?*   She flamed as red as my dress & returned to maneuvering the car instead of me

I was so horny I could barely walk in my matching red high heels & she held my arm as we crossed to her place, pinching my nipple with her other hand & smiling her grin of anticipation   We necked on the porch to upset her nosy neighbors, who have twice complained about the noise I made coming   Then she couldn't get the lock to work & we giggled as I stood with heels in hand, my stockings full of runs & a wet spot on the back of my silk dress almost as wide as my ass   The door popped open so suddenly she fell forward & I tumbled after her, gasping   I started up the stairs heading for her bed when she caught hold of my pubic hair with her hand & pulled me back onto her until I was kneeling on the stairs as she fucked me from behind & my dress ripped some more as she took me hard, kicking the door shut with her foot, taking me out of this world until I was upside down with my head at the door & leg on the banister   Heat of her crotch as she came on me, my dress ripping right up the front as we laughed harder

The next morning her roommate said we were disgusting & we grinned with pride   The cleaners cannot repair the sweet dress & looked at me very oddly but I went out giggling & made her a pocket handkerchief with part of it, sewing rolled hems & a discreet message along one edge *PLEASE rip my dress off anytime*

·

YOU KNOW I LIKE TO BE

bossed around in the sack but honey don't you be tellin me what to do anywhere else cause you see I need to run my own time & if I want to talk & talk & talk for 3 hours on the phone with my best girlfriend you know you'd better find yourself something else to do   You do what you need to be doing & I'll do the same   My pussy is yours when I say you can have some   Otherwise she belongs to me & if I want to give her a vacation or 2 with some other fine woman, doesn't mean there's any less for you   You be vacationing your own self & I won't say a word   Possession is a drug-related offense & it offends me when anyone wants to put a dog collar on me, visible or invisible, cause I ain't no bitch   I'm my own damn woman & I like *all* kinds of trouble   But no screaming matches, no stuff about how you can't live without me because you know I ain't your lungs   I intend to redefine those 4-letter words, Miss Love & Miss Fuck, with my own body   Let's see each other when it's good & take a break when it's hard   You're not my woman & I'm not yours except when I'm coming   Doesn't mean I love your ass any less   Means I love you more than some 2-bit teenage romance, honey means I love you like a good woman should

·

I BRING YOU GREETINGS: HOW

Hey yo I'm a savage in fake braids who races
across your technicolor living room screaming smoke
This is my authentic catsup covered tomahawk from Atlanta GA
I want your dandruff
Look at me twirl around be a Bambi painting of Corn Woman
done by a white lady thief for sale in Albuquerque, cheap
Watch this brave with glycerin tears hawking
plastic garbage bags be an Indian giver
Here's me a box of oranges or sterling silver knives
with forked tongues and burnt spoons
I'm your hot fav brand of flaming hatred arrows
several different lemon cars
This is me on the denial poster in your hallway
in a house full of other people's stuff
I'm dead fish violated treaties don't let me bore
into you with this same old tired refrain of pain
How about heaped carcasses of 40,000 buffalo
so easterners could have lap robes
Thought I didn't catch that one didn't ya
Not this plastic totem pole cigar store of fear
feathered dancer for buffalo bill
How
could I forget a minute of our charming 506 year acquaintance
I slept with your grandfather for something to eat
My brother died under your poison blanket
I'm the children you stole   the breathing of millions
who are not dead
I'm the pulse of earth gagging under asphalt
which still tells lies
I'm the hungry raped Indian girl left by the road or railroad tracks
I'm the running brown woman shot from a helicopter in the amazon
Alive with history and current events and future intents
no one can bear to admit
How

IN HONOR OF JANET SPOTTED EAGLE

·

THE OKEYDOEKEY TRIBE

Historically these people have been noted for a strange dish called hamburgers, which contain no ham. They also contain no burgers, a simile for storekeepers, although many salespeople might be better ground up, especially the kind that sell to Indians at higher prices or not at all.

The Okeydoekey tribe has one of the widest ranging territories of any group known to man. They are very similar in this respect to cockroaches, ants & rats, all of whom have an identical widespread distribution. There has been much speculation about the method of their dispersal, but the currently accepted theory is that they made such a mess wherever they went that they were in constant need of new territory. Rumor has it that they plan to colonize outer space if they can find anyplace with enough resources to sell.

They celebrate all major occasions with a liquid distilled from rotted fruit or vegetables. They consume as much of this as they can in an effort to be happy. This often fails. They do not seem to have any other method of enjoying themselves. Some members have stopped using this liquid, as they find it disagreeable & go to meetings to talk about it instead.

The Okeydoekey people will, in fact, meet for almost any excuse & will often argue long into the night about who should speak first or what shape the table they sit at must be. We have long been puzzled by the importance of the table but apparently this is closely guarded information, as none of our informants could offer a clue.

We have found that when attempting to communicate with the Okeydoekey people, who are, as a general rule, very primitive, it is best to offer money first, as this is their abiding love & concern. We recommend large amounts of cash before any independent inquiry is conducted into their habits.

FOR JENNIE & JIM VANDER WALL

CHERYL CLARKE

·

PALM LEAF OF MARY MAGDALENE

Obsessed by betrayal
compelled by passion
I pull this mutant palm leaf, orange
from my childhood of palm sundays.
Weave it into a cross, pray to it,
wear it as a headband and wristband,
strap it to my ankle.
Magical as the pentecostal holy ghost.
Turning to fuchsia in afternoon light.

More than once an olive-skinned nun pulled her
skirts up for me; later bribed me with a wild
orange palm leaf; thought its color a miracle
awesome as the resurrection; whispered it was
the palm leaf of Mary Magdalene, laughed;
side to side, stroked her unfrocked breasts
and shoulders with it; tied my wrist to hers
with it and took my forgiveness.

Mary Magdalene's palm leaf to you, dearest whore.
Flash it cross your sex back and forth like a
shoe shine rag more gently with as much dedication
while I (and the one you sleep with tonight instead
of me) watch and wait for the miracle
weave it into a cross pray to it
wear it as a headband and wristband
tie your ankle to the bedpost with it
tongue of the holy ghost
palm leaf of Mary Magdalene.

·

STUCK

where i am you may also be.
— THE HERMIT

i laughed at that boy
a tropical bird trapped
in his fear of mounds of leaves
where he saw children hiding
and straight pins in his food
and driving by himself.
i laughed at him and roughly
pulled his pants and shorts down.
then, when he cried at how i
mocked him,
i pretended empathy,
so i could fuck him.
i did not want to know his demons
(or his angels).
i did not want to know my own.
i was full of appetites then
and quick poetry.
my menses flowed many days.
arrogance was my way.

i ate that boy.
i laughed so hard at that boy
placing his pleading personals
each week and waiting tables.
i was mean and capable of any
metaphor.
smoked a lot.
kept late hours.
(that boy's shower was so hot
i was scalded before i knew
the water wasn't cold.)
ego is numbing.

my blood lasts two days now.
and now i understand that boy's fear
if he drove in the country
in fall he might run over a child
hiding in a mound of leaves.

i tore through a heap myself
this year,
thought i heard the screams
of a bleeding child.
i laughed at myself
and saw the boy in my rearview
mirror crying.
for distraction
i bought a shirt
and removed seven of its eight
straight pins
the eighth was mysteriously missing.
its hole gaping at me
fish eye.

i counted the odd number of pins.
it was missing.
i felt myself choking on it.
my lover calmed me, told me
i hadn't swallowed it.
looking askance, i laughed at
her desperate reassurances
and wore the shirt.
all day i felt it sticking me
but couldn't find it
though i undressed several times.
i was afraid to eat or drink.

that night i saw the boy
on my fire escape peeping in
my window, a toucan lighting
on his shoulder.
"the pin is in you," he said.
"so is the bleeding child."

•

PASSING

i'll pass as a man today and take up public space with my urges in
the casual way he does in three-piece suit and gucci pumps big pants and
large sneakers tight jeans and steel-tipped boots read my newspapers
spread-eagled across a whole row of seats make my briefcase-boombox-
backpack into an ottoman on the seat across from me on the l.i.r.r.; and

spread my legs from here to far rockaway on the mighty i.n.d.; and when
i get sleepy or bored spreading the brim of my blue fedora on the bus to
queens hunch down cross my fat feet into the aisle and lean forward with
my arms folded into the great press of rush hour flesh, hawking, spitting,
and pissing all the way.

•

MAKE-UP

1.

If I were to paint myself for you
I'd paint my skin like a Nubian.
I'd do it at dusk by a bright fire.
I'd squat like a Nubian
genitals revealed and flaccid.
First the henna.
Then the ocher.
Then the ash.
Your breathing would quicken.

2.

I remember my mother painting herself mornings.
The exact applications of powder, rouge, mascara.
She had passions and mostly obsessions, my mother.
And peacock ink etchings staining her fingers, the
ledgers and looseleaf.
Evenings she spent before the canvas painting to
mute
the day's cadenced relentless supervision.
Make-up was her art
like the Nubian.

3.

We are all three naked:
the artist, you, me.
Let her tattoo the dream of a perfect design
the dream of sunrays.
Let her make it a perfect cicatrix.

I watch her with the needle.
You are brave as the ink takes hold,
as the blood comes to the surface.
The sun is belligerent.

•

VICKI AND DAPHNE

Being given a lover's key is an intimate gesture; without it one can figure what course the relationship will take; with it, trust is a temptation.

Blood of the cut from a serrated knife blotted by a slice of cake frosted white and garnished with a sugar molded rose the same color red as her blood set Vicki to musing on the risk she'd taken coming from an office party without warning with half a cake to persuade Daphne.

No bandages in Daphne's medicine cabinet or night table. (Daphne never had what Vicki needed when she needed it. But Vicki was an ex-Marine and compensated by being relentlessly adaptable.) So, she scissored a sanitary pad down to the size of a Curad (to her amazement Daph did have pads) and taped it round her hemorrhaging finger with Daph's last bit of Scotch tape.

Vicki's feet hurt in her business pumps. Her business suit pinched her waist and pressed her breasts. The scent of perfume and deodorant mixed with the odor emanating from her pits. She didn't want to get too comfortable. She preferred to await Daphne's pleasure. Her feet might swell or Daph might want her to book.

Vicki removes one shoe and slides the other off her burning heel. (She carries sneakers in her bag but can't really stand the way treads look with nylons.) All day she'd been driven by lust for Daphne. She'd left messages by everyone who might see or speak to Daph to tell her she wanted her.

Where is Daphne? Surely she'd be home soon so Vicki could take off her clothes and complain about her aching pussy.

Being in Daphne's apartment at 11 p.m. without warning and Daphne not home but imminent, fantasy o'ertakes Vicki.
The sound of Daph's
keys in both holes
turning noisily
the house dark
Daphne comes for Vicki where she sits
runs her hand along her nylons
and beyond
Vicki guides her hand

Her throbbing finger draws her back to the reality of her situation: fully clothed, horny, and without warning, and how would she be able to take Daph up the cunt with her middle finger bandaged bulkily? She couldn't even stand air on the wound. Could she Daphne's salty cunt? And her right hand was not so dexterous.

Does Daphne come? Vicki prepares an appropriately humble expression and the honest explanation: *Baby, I'm gonna keep on lovin you til the day I die, cuz I love the way you satisfy.*

No keys in holes.
No Daphne.
Only next door neighbor fumbling.

Without warning, Vicki feels cramps. Her ankles swell. Her finger bleeds every time she flexes. Her pussy is gamy with secretions. She wants to lie down. But Daph hates wrinkled bedclothes.

Vicki falls into a daze, limps to Daph's bed and pulls back its comforter and top sheet, limps then to an odd chest of drawers and removes a small object of comfort. After pulling her skirt to her crotch, lies face down on Daph's bed and applies it to her genitals eleven times calling Daph a whore sweetly and being Daph calling herself a bitch roughly.

Vicki sleeps deeply in suit, nylons, and one pump, awaking at 6 a.m. without warning, without Daphne returns the object to its place pulls top sheet and comforter over passion and menses stained sheets smoothes her wrinkles brushes the lint.

•

A POET'S DEATH

A poet's death and sex thoughts rode me
through the flashing December hurricane.
My day was spent traveling in circles
to get somewhere aboveground.
I had a straight-ahead goal when I woke up.
The floods altered it quite a bit.
I didn't get there.
Only got as far as the corner.
The winds and no available cabs
made me turn back.
And I was unfulfilled in the afternoon that followed.

All day long your words fought against my forgetfulness.
They became beasts with sharp bites.
In the distance cars on the FDR were sucked into the East River.
Cum residues sucked me back into thoughts of you.
And you, floating somewhere over the Guinea Coast
or some other blood-anointed place.
And you stuck in Brooklyn,
trains out.

The trains were running by the time I needed to ride
them, and, oh, what a Dutchman's ride they were
with absolutely no service to Far Rockaway.
I did not have to get out of Brooklyn either
and patiently passed the crisis underground.
My addictions tickling me through several stations.
I tried to memorize a poem by Whitman to get my mind
off sugar.

Audre, my good neighbor,
I miss your elegy,
your so-long song.
Long rhythmic lines of striking metonyms.
A raging narrative to recall your hermetic lineation.
Raw and grand images breaking splendidly
and turning to new space.
Spare like headlines or epitaphs.
My loveliest, my darkest, my most voice.
I miss my voice, my tongue, my most voluptuous lips.

You are in a different weather zone.
The airports are closed here
and everybody who's got a home
has been advised to stay in it.
Unless, like me, there is contraband you really need.
Really needy me
and denying it all the way uptown.
totally oblivious of the fact
that a thirty-eight-year-old woman
was killed in Jersey City
when struck by a gutter propelled by the winds.
You thought it might have been me.
It might've.

A poet's death and the smell of cunt
rode me like angels of hell
on the underground
today
traveling in circles
looking for
vague space somewhere
just ahead or just behind.

⟨❁⟩

JEFFERY CONWAY

·

MARLO THOMAS IN SEVEN PARTS AND EPILOGUE

1.
I sit in front of our Zenith TV, eat
peanut butter & jelly and watch as Ann
Marie puts Donald's car in gear and accelerates.
The back wheels spin and mud is flung all over
Don's face and clothes. I watch *That Girl* every day
right after *Bewitched*. I love Ann Marie's kite,
the one with her image—thick lashes, big smile,
perfect black flip.

2.
I'm standing in Studio One, West Hollywood's
largest video bar. The place is packed for
the television premiere of *Consenting Adults*,
a drama about a gay son who comes out
to his parents, starring Marlo Thomas as the mom
and Martin Sheen as the dad. I'm drinking
greyhounds and feel a bit tipsy—I laugh
out loud at the scene when the cute blond son
spills the beans to Marlo, "Mom, I'm a
homo (pause) sexual."

3.
At dinner in a small West Village restaurant,
William and Michael poke at their plates and mourn
the loss of a friend who recently died of AIDS.
They tell me he had loved his job running
Marlo Thomas's country home, and that he always
spoke quite highly of Marlo and Phil Donahue.

4.
Ann Marie shows up at my '70s party
wearing a yellow crinoline dress, holding
a yellow parasol. "Hi, Mary!" She storms
into the house and asks where she may put her things.
She changes outfits every ten minutes, screaming

each time she exits the room, "Commercial break!
Costume change!"

5.
Wayne complains on the phone.
He tells me about Tim's Thanksgiving spent
in the hospital with Rodney. Marlo and Phil
sent a feast, complete with stuffed turkey
and creamed onions. Wayne says Tim and Rodney
didn't eat a thing. I imagine
the note Marlo sent with the food, expressing
her love and regrets:
"My hair just hasn't been the same without you."

6.
I pull a postcard from the mailbox: "Greetings
from the BUFFADORA BLOW HOLE!" I turn it over—
"Hi, honey! Wish you were here!" It's from Dora.
He's been traveling for six months and having sex
with men all around the world. In a postscript
he adds, "Oh yeah, Doug died. Poor Ann Marie,
at least it was quick—ammonia city."

7.
I stare at a photograph I've pulled from
a Beakins box. Summer, 1987—my '70s party
at the house I shared with James in the Hollywood
Hills. In the photo, Ann Marie stands behind
Loni Anderson, who sits on the floor
in a feminine pose. Ann is wearing a short
black & white checkered dress with a white bib
collar, white panty hose, white gloves, and she holds
a shiny white purse. Her face is expressionless,
her black wig frozen in place: I can almost
smell the Aqua Net she sprayed that entire
evening, desperately trying to hold it together.

Epilogue:

I'm standing behind the service bar, which
I've dubbed the "Anne Frank Bar" because
I'm constantly hiding from customers, when
a man—Phil Donahue—and a woman come down
the steps and approach me. The woman says,

"We had an 8:45 reservation, is it too late?"
The innocent, hopeful look—it's Marlo!
I open my mouth, but nothing comes out at first.
Finally I stutter, "Just a minute, please,
I'll get the host." As I walk through the dining room,
thoughts shoot through my head: *Why are they*
in Cape Cod? Is she an angel or an omen?
Why is her hair so flat? Angel or omen?
When I return I say, "Your table is ready,
the host will seat you." They walk to the rear
of the dining room. I pour myself a Coke.
A few minutes later, Marlo reappears and says,
"Excuse me, where's the Ladies Room?"
I point, afraid of her all of a sudden.
She reaches for the handle and glances up
at the sign: "Restroom." She spins around
and exclaims, "Oh! They're unisex!"
She's looking at me with her eyes huge
and her mouth open in a wide smile.
I say, "Yes," and wait for a wink—like the one
she'd give at the beginning of each show,
wearing a white wedding dress, poised
in the window of some department store—
but the wink never comes, or maybe
it does and she becomes an angel
before my eyes as she did each day at noon
when I was a boy. Another second,
and she disappears behind the restroom door.

.

MODERN ENGLISH

Tonight the moon hovers in the sky
like a huge communion wafer—I can see it
through the spotted and bullet-holed windshield
of your truck as we speed along Route 6, somewhere
outside of North Truro. The radio's green glow
lights up your hand as you reach for the knob.
"Leave it there." A song I loved
ten years ago fills the cab and you
put your hand back on the wheel.
I turn and stare out my open window,
mouthing the words, "There's nothing you and I

won't do, I'll stop the world and melt with you."
We pass a moonlit inlet at the side of the road.
In the distance, beyond the black water, is a silhouette
of sand dunes, the perfect movie set backdrop
for a moment like this.

We head for Race Point, pull into the parking lot.
The engine sputters, then dies. We walk the beach
and I laugh at something you say.
You stop, turn to me—the pitch-blue sky
surrounding your face—"Don't laugh at the way
I talk." The wind kicks sand at us.
We kiss. Far out in the ocean, lightning
cracks. We decide to drive to your place.

Inside, you offer me a drink.
It's midnight—a few sips
of seltzer and I follow you
to the next room.
You light candles and more
candles. A sheer curtain blows. Dozens
of empty vases line the room. We undress
slowly, our bodies pound for what seems
like days until I collapse on top of you.

My lips make their way from your throat to
your now soft cock. "Be careful!" you say,
pulling my face close to yours. You
wipe the cum from my upper lip, I
raise my head. Above us, on top of
the dresser, a photo in a silver frame:
you and another man on a balcony,
kissing. It's the same balcony
you showed me earlier as part of your tour.
It's where you paused and mentioned a lover
who died, then changed the subject.
You revealed other things: your parents live
in Florida, you collect vases, your aunt
was born in the Ukraine, you're forty-three.

I stare at this man in the photo,
remember the wetness you tried to wipe
away. It's ten years later and there are some
things you and I won't do, ten years later

and my new favorite song,
"Bluer Than Midnight," fills my head.

·

HANGOVER

In a dark bar corner we talk for about an hour.
I drink Budweiser, he's sipping Miller Lites.
He leans over, kisses me — dark eyes, the most
handsome man I've seen — and invites me to his apartment.

In the cab he says my hands are rough, like a laborer's.
I say his are smooth, the hands of a statue.
"That's funny," he says, "I'm a sculptor."

We undress to the B side of The The's *Mind Bomb*.
I lie nude on top of him in bed. I'm drunk — slobbering as I kiss.
He says he'll get a rubber. I tell him no, I don't fuck.
He says we'll be really safe. I say no, I don't do that.
His cat jumps onto the bed, purrs. We pet her for awhile
then start to kiss again. We cum at the same time,
he pulls my body next to his without washing off.

At noon, after few hours sleep, he brings me tea
and oat bran cereal, banana sliced over top.
My head is pounding and I have a dry mouth.
I set the tray on the floor, kiss him again.
We cum a second time. The tea is cold when I reach for it
and the cat has licked the milk from my bowl.
Next to the tray on the floor I see a card
from the Spike, where we met. I turn it over — "Phil"
and a phone number, 201 area code. New Jersey?

At the door, "Thank you for having me over."
He takes an orange from the off-white fruit bowl in the kitchen,
kisses it, puts it to my lips, then slides it into my hand,
telling me to take it for the subway ride.

On the street, cold air — my eyes water.
The skin on my face is burned, his morning stubble.
I go down into the subway station at Houston and 2nd to wait for the F.
A Puerto Rican boy with dark eyes walks up, says he'll give me
$20 for the leather jacket I'm wearing. I say I bought it

in Tijuana, that I'm attached to it. He hands me a brown bag.
Inside there's a bottle of medicine for stomachache and nausea.
He asks if I think it'll work, that he feels like barfing.
"It's worth a try," I say. He says he'll buy the orange
off me for a quarter, he's hungry. As the train pulls up
I say, "You can have the orange." I step in and watch him
devour the fruit as the doors close.
The train begins to rumble into a dark tunnel.

·

WEIGHT BELT
FOR RUSSELL FALCON
B. NOV. 1955 D. MAY 1987

What I know of you I take
from three old photos buried in a leather box
in a corner of my lover's living room.
What I know of you I take
from stories, stories I receive
like communion, in silence with awe:
the first time he ever laid eyes on you
in a crowded room in New York City,
he stopped dead and couldn't move,
had to be pulled away by the shirt collar;
the time you cut his hair
at his apartment, slowly your hands
made their way from his scalp
down his nose to his lips,
the scissors fell to the floor
and you began to kiss, even though
it was forbidden—you'd been seeing his best friend.

In one photo you are achingly sexy—
you stand on a beach in a tight swimsuit,
head cocked to one side, thick build, black
hair, mustache. In another you are partner
to the one I love, sitting a step higher than him
on the porch of a P-town house.
The third I think of most often: you are emaciated
in the stark white tub
in the apartment on Sixteenth Street,
your face drained, beaded with sweat,
your dark eyes glassy marbles.

It is June and I've fled New York,
but still you find me here on the Cape.
You come to mind by design, the way
birds would appear along the path
in front of Jackie O as she strolled
the grounds of her private retreat—
the papers said her gardener secretly walked
ahead, tossing seed onto the trail.

Today I crossed the breakwater
to deserted Long Point Beach, spread my towel
and drifted asleep. I woke feeling something—
a caterpillar—crawling on my thigh.
I scooped it up with the toy shovel
I'd found earlier, carried it to the dune,
and set it free on a stalk of beach grass.
I returned to my towel and watched as the black
fuzz zigzagged back towards me,
scrunching itself up and out.
I picked it up once more,
tossing it into the dune. Again it inched
towards me. And right then
my thoughts turned to you. I shoveled
that caterpillar up, hurling it as far as I could,
then went for a swim in the icy water.

On my way home across the rocks,
I ran into a friend who stopped me
to say how lucky I am to have such a nice man.
He said, "I knew his ex, Russell.
He was the sweetest angel."
I mumbled good-bye and stormed off.

Later I biked to the gym
and put on your weight belt,
the one he gave me months ago, saying
someone should make use of it.
I slipped the silver tongue
into the hole I carve for myself each day—
a notch tighter than the one worn in by you.
I stared at my body
in the glitzy mirrors; too thin, I thought,
and pushed the dumbbells into the air.
I felt the pressure of black leather

on my sides and lower back. It held me
like a pair of strong hands, the way
your hand, veiny and soft, clutched a pen —
the day I took the belt he told me
that you began to write a lot toward the end.

DENNIS COOPER

·

AFTER SCHOOL, STREET FOOTBALL, EIGHTH GRADE

Their jeans sparkled, cut off
way above the knee, and my
friends and I would watch them
from my porch, books of poems
lost in our laps, eyes wide as
tropical fish behind our glasses.

Their football flashed from hand
to hand, tennis shoes gripped
the asphalt, sweat's spotlight on
their strong backs. We would
dream of hugging them, and crouch
later in weird rooms, and come.

Once their ball fell our way
so two of them came over, hands
on their hips, asking us to
throw it to them, which Arthur did,
badly, and they chased it back.
One turned to yell, "Thanks"

and we dreamed of his long
teeth in our necks. We
wanted them to wander over,
place deep wet underarms to
our lips, and then their white
asses, then those loud mouths.

One day one guy was very tired,
didn't move fast enough,
so a car hit him and he sprawled
fifty feet away, sexy, but he was
dead, blood like lipstick, then
those great boys stood together

on the sidewalk and we joined them,
mixing in like one big friendship
to the cops, who asked if we were,
and those boys were too sad to counter.
We'd known his name, Tim, and how
he'd turned to thank us nicely

but now he was under a sheet
anonymous as God, the big boys crying,
spitting words, and we stunned
like intellectuals get, our high
voices soft as the tinkling of a
chandelier on a ceiling too high to see.

·

TEEN IDOLS

Teen idols are the best boys on the block. They wear new Adidas and date
infrequently, being more interested in us. For fun they swing on monkey
bars and smile into Nikons. Always romantic, they sign their photos "I think
of you and you're beautiful" and then "love always" and then their first
names. They know how to please us, to keep us hanging on.

There are magazines to present them endlessly, in love and lonely, to hand
us tours of their houses. We meet their brothers (like Xeroxes of them, but
not bad). The boys lounge suggestively each moment of their lives. Pictures
prove that. In some ways these photos are the idols, not the boys behind
them, not their 45s. Shaun Cassidy's not here to make BEGGAR'S
BANQUET. He's here to glow. His records, just his side of the conver-
sation.

These boys may o.d. in a Hollywood nightclub on Friday night but by
Monday they're cuter than boyfriends again. We don't want to know their
secret vices. We do want to know what they'd like from us. This appears
to be money and our warm eyes gazing up at them in audience, lives blown
like a wheat field by their beauty, our wild applause — their jackpot.

Forgetting bitter parents, pissed off boyfriends and even poems that won't
jerk into the cosmos, we reach for a TEEN BEAT, flip its pages to Shaun
(the All American Boy) or Leif (angelic surfer) or Lance (cute class clown)
or Scott (dark and mysterious). We wet our lips and feel our favorite moving
nearby. In a simpler time our idols seduce us, their cocks semi-hard, our
lumps in our throats.

DAVID CASSIDY THEN

David Cassidy picks me on *The Dating Game*.
I walk around the partition
and there he is. A quick kiss,
then Jim Lange gives us the good news.

"David, we'll be flying you and your date
to . . . Rio de Janerio! You'll be
staying at the luxurious Rio Hilton
and attend a party in your honor!"

At the Hilton we knock the chaperone
out with a lamp, then we jive
around, smoke a little Colombian.
David says something to let me
know he's willing, and I get
to chew his clothes off.

He dances Swan Lake naked
and I sprawl out on the bed.
He saunters over scolding me in French,
and covers my face with his modest rear.

He gives me a few minutes
then he's up, blow-drying the drool
from his legs. He slips on a white jumpsuit,
runs a thumb across his teeth, and
turns to where I sit, still dreamy on the bed.

"Come on," he says, full of breath.
Never so proud, I bring my hands up,
rub his stink into my face like a lotion.
I will wear it to the party!

As the lobby doors open
reporters start the sea of lights.
The cameras take us kissing, dancing.
They angle to get David's sheathed body.
Girls watch his ass like a television screen
of men stepping onto the moon.

Little do they know what really lies there,
that this is no tan. "This is David,"
I say, smelling my face like a flower,
and pull him close, stoned out of my gourd.

·

FROM SOME ADVENTURES OF JOHN KENNEDY JR.

In School

When the professor tells his class
their homework is to write poems,
young John brings down his fist.
"But tonight the Knicks are playing Boston!"
He'll have to give his front rows away.

Instead he slogs through poets,
hates them all until William Carlos Williams.
"You mean this is poetry?" He leaps
on his notebook. "I can write this stuff
by the ton." And so he does, a twenty pager.

It's about his own brief life,
praise for the sports stars, shit for the press,
close shots at his deep dark family.
The next day he's graded on his reading;
John's poem is "I'm Going Nowhere":

"I never thought anyone died,
especially not me,
then my father and uncle got it from maniacs
and Ari kicked the bucket the hard way,
and I've started thinking of my own death,
when will it come and how,
by some madman out to end the Kennedys?
I hope so, and that it happens
before I have a chance to show my mediocrity.
I know that's clumsy rhythm
but what have I got to lose, man? . . ."

When John gets to these last words
tears shake his sullen reading.

Amazed, the professor looks straight
through John's tough punk texture,
and then an A+ flies John's way
like a fastball, or a perfect pass.

•

10 DEAD FRIENDS
FOR ISHMAEL HOUSTON-JONES

Cass Romanski, 23, and his fiancée made dinner at his family home in Arcadia. After his parents went to bed, they argued over the date of their forthcoming marriage. He became hysterical, walked into the next room, locked the door, and shot himself in the head.

Eric Brown, 16, was riding a motorcycle near his home in Glendale. He went over a bump, lost control of his bike, and was thrown across the handlebars into some rocks.

Mervyn Fox, 56, spent the night in the pool house at his estranged wife's home in Altadena. He'd looked ill for several weeks. He read part of Aldous Huxley's *The Devils*, swallowed a bottle of sleeping pills, and lay down on the bed.

Bunker Spreckles, 28, was at a party. He'd shot heroin for the first time earlier that evening. Excusing himself from his friends, he walked out to his car and shot up twice as much.

Robert Benton, 43, was having trouble with his lover, John Koenig. They argued and Koenig left. Benton's oldest friend, Annetta Fox, came by and tried to comfort him. They drank a bottle of champagne, then she went home. Soon after she left, he shot himself in the chest. Annetta said that at that moment her car jerked sharply to the left.

John Wells, 25, was loading his surfboard into his van alongside Pacific Coast Highway in Huntington Beach. It was a clear spring day. A speeding car struck him, throwing him thirty feet in the air.

Michael Thompson, 28, drove his black Cadillac up Laurel Canyon Boulevard to Mulholland Drive. He pulled off the road at a remote spot, left the motor running, and lay down across the backseat, sucking a hose that he'd attached to the tailpipe.

Annetta Fox, 55, entered the hospital for bronchitis. It was discovered she had lung cancer. They removed one lung. A month later at home, she stood up from a chair to go to the bathroom and her legs gave out. She was rushed to the hospital, where it was discovered the cancer had spread throughout her body.

John Flanigan, 26, was confined to a wheelchair. Year by year he grew frailer and finally stayed in his bed. On the night before his 27th birthday, worn out from excitement over the next day's party, he lapsed into a coma.

David Sellers, 17, met an older man at a bar and went home with him. They had sex. The man gave him some money. Afterwards he walked to a nearby phone booth and called his roommate to ask for a ride. Midway through the conversation, a blood vessel in his brain burst.

·

POEM FOR GEORGE MILES

When I first sharpened a
pencil in purpling language
and drew my first poem
from its raveling depths,
it "poured my heart out"
as thoroughly as I would,
make that could, at nineteen:
"His eyes are the color
of silk just inside a mink
jacket, always lukewarm
like his hand as it rests
on the nape of my neck till
my shorter hairs bristle."
That was ten years ago.
My eyes were black pinpricks
in sharp, tensor light
which my indistinct moods
were explored with, pried
open like tenement doors
on their shadowy hideout
while homework, porn books,
and rough drafts piled up
beneath with a pedestal's
sense of illuminating that
which was most elaborate.
The poem is now cleaned
out of power, as bed is
once sunlight has entered.
I see its mathematics: lines
built as an ornate frame
around a skeletal feeling
that's faded from sight.
Who knows what I meant?
With time, I can guess
that I thought and worked

hard, watched my words,
made them bright as they'd
beam, until I could say
to myself, This is full.

.

DREAMT UP

I'm not looking at you, though it might seem that I am. I'm looking back through my life, and my friend's death is what's important to me. It changed me, gave me this slightly defensive expression which only a few people see through. If you hold the pages of my journal up to the light you'll see contrasting, interrelating images dealing with him. If you hold this one up you'll find my head is full of the words of another writer. I'll say anything, I suppose, that keeps me out of the jail of my own heart, where I might run into my thoughts about him, like the white lies I told nurses so I could stand by his deathbed for ten seconds way back when. I learned my lesson. I just can't see him as dead. All I can see is what's great about him, though that's all caked up in artifice now, and cloaked in recent history's scariest light. His eyes were circled, deep brown, neither friendly nor wary of anyone. Mine are bright blue and possibly evil in their search through the recesses of friends' private parts while they sleep forever.

ALFRED CORN

·

TO HERMES

Lord Quicksilver, god of erections, come down
in your winged Nikes, your hard hat brilliant
as an oiled mirror, and lend some assistance.
I have a young partner, handsome and eager,
whose love I want, whose pleasure pleases me.
When a smile as mischievous as his seems to ask
for a second round or a third, naturally
every spurred nerve aches to pump up the tempo,
like a dark horse the last heat of the day,
sweatsoaked and burning to win. My age, though,
men are long past the satyrs we once were,
flesh quickens or not after its own will or whim.
Now, I have no use for clever devices; so take
your wand (its twin snakes intertwined like vines),
touch my equipment, and work your famous magic.
If you do this, I will free two doves in your name
to fly beside you on your early morning errands.
Divine messenger boy, send me like a letter,
a fox to its burrow, a hand in its silk-lined glove.
Let me keep unwavering purpose—to embody feeling
till all the senses answer, blazing the path to our own
Olympus, no medal like the light in each other's eye.

·

KIMCHEE IN WORCESTER (MASS.)

Raw cabbage marinated in vinegar with chilies:
it's what Koreans use instead of Worcester sauce.
We'd said we'd marathon it as far as Maine tonight,
but the American brown bear rarely skips dinner;
and, if break we must, it might as well be here,
in the big sleepy burg where Frank O'Hara grew up.

Who would have predicted finding the R*O*S*E G*A*R*D*E*N*
restaurant, though, or being seated opposite
a video featuring Korean MTV
and karaoke (Japanese word that *sounds* Hawaiian)
for songs like "The Great Pretender" and "Love Me Tender."

Glossy Korean teens in miniskirts and jeans
wander through the streets and parks of Seoul
as sound-track imitations of vintage r&b
try to add pep to lust or love that looks rehearsed.

Across the street is Worcester's 1905 cathedral,
a huge Romano-Byzantine palazzo in marble.
Out front, in gilded stucco robes, the BVM

blesses her flock (the little black sheep too? I wonder).
We all start somewhere, Frank, but most don't have the smarts

to split. You did. Oh, waiter! What's "check" in Korean?

·

A MARRIAGE IN THE NINETIES

They've said the art of poetry resembles,
on one hand, song, with poet as the rara
avis that makes his birdcage play in tune;
it's also been compared to hard labor.

Scrubbing our kitchen tiles today, on all
fours, and humming something like the blues,
I thought of Yeats's line from "Adam's Curse,"
Better go down upon your marrow bones,

and so forth. How much did a man with servants
know about it? As the decals say,
"I'd rather be writing." But Manhattanites
like us don't keep a car, so where to stick it?

Don't answer that. (Polish, polish, polish.)
It's not that you don't do your share, Chris;

you're a good "husband," women's lib won't help.
Wages of poetry got us at least this far:

we've all of three small rooms to keep in shape.
Just maybe two of these sixth-floor apartments
are decent-sized, and only one tenant straight—
a youngish, ash-blond broker from Belgium,

who that first spring after arriving took
the measure of his present situation
and planted redwood terrace-garden boxes
with pansies by the hundreds, nothing but pansies!

I watched him crouch over small purple-and-yellow
Pekinese faces and waved when he looked up.
Life in the Village. He and a series of girlfriends
haven't seemed flustered at all, they've been nice neighbors.

A marriage in the Nineties. New York City,
if we sign papers, will consider us
"domestic partners." Somehow, though, it feels
more romantic not to. Getting older

pushes mavericks always further toward
the middle class, so why speed up the process?
Insurance offers safety but soaks up feeling—
which brings in risk. Remember Portugal,

the anger we routinely felt for whatever
addict or refugee it was that nicked
our luggage from the car? Those Avis decals
tipped them off, most likely. Property

is theft, granted, but theft of property
also felt like theft. My diary gone,
snapshots we'd taken, worthless to *them*, as well
as other items of "sentimental value."

Both sets of house keys, too, which meant having
a locksmith break into our own apartment
(Russian, moonlighting, his real profession
reproducing Baroque violins).

He scratched his beard and squinted like a watch
repairman at locks he then hauled off and smashed.
At least we got a smile and compassionate handshake,
plus new keys and a bill for two hundred bucks.

Disaster? No, nothing like what happened
to Christophe (our Belgian) the same star-crossed,
snowbound day we returned, his bedroom flooded
by a heating pipe that froze, then cracked, then spewed.

Or to our next-door neighbor Steve, just out
of intensive care for a bout with Pneumocystis
during his vacation in Key West,
two balmy weeks with an IV in his arm. . . .

We're very lucky. No microbes have broken
in and made off with our lives or health.
Nor are we homeless like Devane, the guy
who sits all day outside our building, hailing

strangers or neighbors like us who halfway know him.
Time and again I've said, "Devane, a man
as smart as you has no business on the street."
He agrees, yeah-yeah, and blames cocaine and booze,

which he plans to kick someday. Today?
Well, no, it helps him stand the cold and damp,
but one great morning . . . ! He also tells me he's
bisexual, but that one I let pass.

As a schoolboy in, say, Brussels, Christophe —
funny, it just occurs to me that you
and he have the same name — may well have read
Pascal's *Pensées*, as I did back in college.

He'd probably recognize the one that says,
"The more intelligence one has the more
people one finds original. Commonplace
people see no difference between men."

Devane, for instance, calculating each
potential donor's quirks and soft spots so
he can "articulate sweet sounds together,"
magic words to make it rain down gold

or silver, any tribute but the pennies
he loathes but must of course pretend to want.
Or Steve next door, who says he prayed to survive
once more because he hadn't yet determined

his true identity and what he's here for.
Or us, sweetheart, this February 14th,
which I didn't think of in time to find
a present. Middle age's curse, defective

memory—as good an excuse as any
"for getting it all down." That, and a chance
to image feeling with exactitude,
love for an irreplaceable hunk, whatever.

From Lisbon to Beijing to Brussels, song
breaks forth to say inclinations have changed:
"The life devoid of sentiment is not
worth living," a news flash ricocheted off Telstar,

dense wavelength webwork of the global village
where we make a present of ourselves
to stranger and neighbor, hoping it's the thought
that counts. Come this June, I'll write mine out

and see if Christopher wants to anthologize
one more *pensée* with those in his terrace boxes.
To you, Chris, hearts and flowers of the day,
and kitchen tiles that will just have to do.

•

LONG-DISTANCE CALL TO GREGG, WHO LIVED WITH AIDS AS LONG AS HE COULD

Because we hooked up most days courtesy
of Ma Bell, only now and then arranging
to meet for lunch or coffee, it's your graveled,
ambling voice I miss, the live connection
"no longer in service," as the tape-loop says.

Remember that haiku I jotted down
on a café napkin several years back?
How cities, even with their gridlock, noise

and pollution, also sheltered gardens? Your eyes
crinkled with pleasure: *Those cool, green inward places—*.

The one you've moved to may not yet be wired
for cellular, but here's my morning call,
dialed by habit or a "burning desire"
to speak. And how much does it matter if
the message and the channel are the same?

Though Asian verse forms seldom clicked for me,
they hung the moon for *you*, so here's a haiku
six-pack for the picnic, sent in hopes
of making you smile. This time they do me, too,
as any image would that brought you back.

                         *

*Red oak leaves floating
On clear water and, below,
Speckled rainbow trout.*

                         *

*Stripped by cold or blight,
Bare elm trees. On a high branch,
Clumps of mistletoe.*

                         *

*March snow falls and falls.
Droplets bead down my window.
Cloud, light, one substance.*

                         *

*A single reindeer
Moves north across the frostwhite tundra.
Fog. The rising sun.*

                         *

*Spring winds. Mourning dove,
Perched on the telephone line,
Is it warm up there?*

                         *

*July 4th. Blue eyes,
Glancing up from a full plate,
Smile so hard they close.*

—< ✣ >—

MARK DOTY

·

MY TATTOO

I thought I wanted to wear
the Sacred Heart, to represent
education through suffering,

how we're pierced to flame.
But when I cruised
the inkshop's dragons,

cobalt tigers and eagles
in billowy smokes,
my allegiance wavered.

Butch lexicon,
anchors and arrows,
a sailor's iconic charms—

tempting, but none
of them me. What noun
would you want

spoken on your skin
your whole life through?
I tried to picture what

I'd never want erased,
and saw a fire-ring corona
of spiked rays,

flaring tongues
surrounding—an emptiness,
an open space?

I made my mind up.
I sat in the waiting room chair.
Then something (my nerve?

faith in the guy
with biker boots
and indigo hands?)

wavered. It wasn't fear;
nothing hurts like grief,
and I'm used to that.

His dreaming needle
was beside the point;
don't I already bear

the etched and flaring marks
of an inky trade?
What once was skin

has turned to something
made; written and revised
beneath these sleeves:

hearts and banners,
daggers and flowers and names.
I fled. Then I came back again;

isn't there always
a little more room
on the skin? It's too late

to be unwritten,
and I'm much too scrawled
to ever be erased.

Go ahead: prick and stipple
and ink me in:
I'll never be naked again.

From here on out,
I wear the sun,
albeit blue.

·

HOMO WILL NOT INHERIT

Downtown anywhere and between the roil
of bathhouse steam—up there the linens of joy
and shame must be laundered again and again,

all night—downtown anywhere
and between the column of feathering steam
unknotting itself thirty feet above the avenue's

shimmered azaleas of gasoline,
between the steam and the ruin
of the Cinema Paree (marquee advertising

its own milky vacancy, broken showcases sealed,
ticketbooth a hostage wrapped in tape
and black plastic, captive in this zone

of blackfronted bars and bookstores
where there's nothing to read
but longing's repetitive texts,

where desire's unpoliced, or nearly so)
someone's posted a Xeroxed headshot
of Jesus: permed, blond, blurred at the edges

as though photographed through a greasy lens,
and inked beside him, in marker strokes:
HOMO WILL NOT INHERIT. *Repent & be saved.*

I'll tell you what I'll inherit: the margins
which have always been mine, downtown after hours
when there's nothing left to buy,

the dreaming shops turned in on themselves,
seamless, intent on the perfection of display,
the bodegas and offices lined up, impenetrable:

edges no one wants, no one's watching. Though
the borders of this shadow-zone (mirror and dream
of the shattered streets around it) are chartered

by the police, and they are required,
some nights, to redefine them. But not now, at twilight,
permission's descending hour, early winter darkness

pillared by smoldering plumes. The public city's
ledgered and locked, but the secret city's boundless;
from which do these tumbling towers arise?

I'll tell you what I'll inherit: steam,
and the blinding symmetry of some towering man,
fifteen minutes of forgetfulness incarnate.

I've seen flame flicker around the edges of the body,
pentecostal, evidence of inhabitation.
And I have been possessed of the god myself,

I have been the temporary apparition
salving another, I have been his visitation, I say it
without arrogance, I have been an angel

for minutes at a time, and I have for hours
believed—without judgment, without condemnation—
that in each body, however obscured or recast,

is the divine body—common, habitable—
the way in a field of sunflowers
you can see every bloom's

the multiple expression
of a single shining idea,
which is the face hammered into joy.

I'll tell you what I'll inherit:
stupidity, erasure, exile
inside the chalked lines of the police,

who must resemble what they punish,
the exile you require of me,
you who's posted this invitation

to a heaven nobody wants.
You who must be patrolled,
who adore constraint, I'll tell you

what I'll inherit, not your pallid temple
but a real palace, the anticipated
and actual memory, the moment flooded

by skin and the knowledge of it,
the gesture and its description
—do I need to say it?—

the flesh *and* the word. And I'll tell you,
you who can't wait to abandon your body,
what you want me to, maybe something

like you've imagined, a dirty story:
Years ago, in the baths,
a man walked into the steam,

the gorgeous deep indigo of him gleaming,
solid tight flanks, the intricately ridged abdomen—
and after he invited me to his room,

nudging his key toward me,
as if perhaps I spoke another tongue
and required the plainest of gestures,

after we'd been, you understand,
worshipping a while in his church,
he said to me, *I'm going to punish your mouth.*

I can't tell you what that did to me.
My shame was redeemed then;
I won't need to burn in the afterlife.

It wasn't that he hurt me,
more than that: the spirit's transactions
are enacted now, here—no one needs

your eternity. This failing city's
radiant as any we'll ever know,
paved with oily rainbow, charred gates

jeweled with tags, swoops of letters
over letters, indecipherable as anything
written by desire. I'm not ashamed

to love Babylon's scrawl. How could I be?
It's written on my face as much as on
these walls. This city's inescapable,

gorgeous, and on fire. I have my kingdom.

.

LILACS IN NYC

Monday evening, E. 22nd
          in front of Jimmy and Vincent's,
a leafing maple, and it's as if

Manhattan existed in order
          to point to these
leaves, the urbane marvel

of them. Tuesday A.M.
          at the Korean market,
cut, bundled lilacs, in clear

or silvered cellophane—
          mist & inebriation,
cyclonic flames in tubs

of galvanized aluminum
          all along Third Avenue,
as if from the hardy rootstocks

of these shops sprouted
          every leaf-shine and shade
of panicle: smoke, plum, lavender

like the sky over the Hudson,
          some spring evenings, held
in that intoxicating window

the horizontal avenues provide.
          Numbered avenues,
dumb beautiful ministers . . . Later,

a whole row of white crabapples
        shivering in the wind
of a passing train; later,

a magnolia flaring
        in a scatter
of its own fallen petals,

towering out of a field
        of itself. Is that what
we do? I've felt like that,

straddling my lover,
        as if I rose
out of something

which resembled me,
        joined at the trunk
as if I come flaming

up out of what I am,
        the live foam muscling
beneath me . . .

Strong bole thrust up
        into the billow,
into the frills and the insistences

and elaborations,
        the self flying open!
They're flowers, they know

to fall if they bloom;
        blessed relief of it,
not just myself this little while.

You enter me and we are strangers
        to ourselves but not
to each other, I enter you

(strange verb but what else
        to call it—to penetrate
to fuck to be inside of—

none of the accounts of the body
        were ever really useful were they
tell the truth none of them),

I enter you (strange verb,
        as if we were each an enclosure
a shelter, imagine actually

considering yourself a *temple*)
        and violet the crush of shadows
that warm wrist that deep-hollowed

collar socket those salt-lustered
        lilacy shoulderblades,
in all odd shadings of green and dusk . . .

blooming in the field
        of our shatter. You enter me
and it's Macy's,

some available version of infinity,
        I enter you and I'm the grass,
covered with your shock

of petals out of which you rise
        Mr. April Mr. Splendor
climbing up with me

inside this rocking, lilac boat.
        My candlelight master,
who trembles me into smoke-violet,

as April does to lilacwood.

·

FROM ATLANTIS

3. Michael's Dream

Michael writes to tell me his dream:
I was helping Randy out of bed,
supporting him on one side
with another friend on the other,

and as we stood him up, he stepped out
of the body I was holding and became
a shining body, brilliant light
held in the form I first knew him in.

This is what I imagine will happen,
the spirit's release. Michael,
when we support our friends,
one of us on either side, our arms

under the man or woman's arms,
what is it we're holding? Vessel,
shadow, hurrying light? All those years
I made love to a man without thinking

how little his body had to do with me;
now, diminished, he's never been so plainly
himself—remote and unguarded,
an otherness I can't know

the first thing about. I said,
You need to drink more water
or you're going to turn into
an old dry leaf. And he said,

Maybe I want to be an old leaf.
In the dream Randy's leaping into
the future, and still here; Michael's holding him
and releasing at once. Just as Steve's

holding Jerry, though he's already gone,
Marie holding John, gone, Maggie holding
her John, gone, Carlos and Darren
holding another Michael, gone,

and I'm holding Wally, who's going.
Where isn't the question,
though we think it is;
we don't even know where the living are,

in this raddled and unraveling "here."
What is the body? Rain on a window,
a clear movement over whose gaze?
Husk, leaf, little boat of paper

and wood to mark the speed of the stream?
Randy and Jerry, Michael and Wally
and John: lucky we don't have to know
what something is in order to hold it.

6. New Dog

Jimi and Tony
can't keep Dino,
their cocker spaniel;
Tony's too sick,
the daily walks
more pressure
than pleasure,
one more obligation
that can't be met.

And though we already
have a dog, Wally
wants to adopt,
wants something small
and golden to sleep
next to him and
lick his face.
He's paralyzed now
from the waist down,

whatever's ruining him
moving upward, and
we don't know
how much longer
he'll be able to pet
a dog. How many men
want another attachment,
just as they're
leaving the world?

Wally sits up nights
and says, *I'd like
some lizards, a talking bird,
some fish. A little rat.*
So after I drive
to Jimi and Tony's
in the Village and they

meet me at the door and say,
We can't go through with it,

we can't give up our dog.
I drive to the shelter
—just to look—and there
is Beau: bounding and
practically boundless,
one brass concatenation
of tongue and tail,
unmediated energy,
too big, wild,

perfect. He not only
licks Wally's face
but bathes every
irreplaceable inch
of his head, and though
Wally can no longer
feed himself he can lift
his hand, and bring it
to rest on the rough gilt

flanks when they are,
for a moment, still.
I have never seen a touch
so deliberate.
It isn't about grasping:
the hand itself seems
almost blurred now,
softened, though
tentative only

because so much will
must be summoned,
such attention brought
to the work—which is all
he is now, this gesture
toward the restless splendor,
the unruly, the golden,
the animal, the new.

—<✵>—

BEATRIX GATES

·

TRIPTYCH

FOR RON KING, LYNNSEY CARROLL, AND TRACY SAMPSON

I. RON

Charlie said he wanted to die
and Dell and I were the ones,
of course, who were going to
help him do it. You know Dell—
Charlie's ex, most recent
ex. Well, the exes were
elected, me and Dell.
No one in the family
was going to do it, and Charlie said
he was ready this time. You know last
summer he almost died, we had
bedside vigils, the whole bit, then he
felt better and went to Florida
for the winter. Stayed in the trailer park
with his brother, Dirk. Yeah, that's right,
same time that I broke my leg,
six foot four inch faggot in a cast
and Charlie was feeling okay then
so he rode me all around the fucking
trailer park on that giant
tricycle. What a picture.
Anyway, Charlie was ready to die,
so we did all the preparation,
read the book by what's-his-name—
Humphries—got the pills.
Everyone knew, the family
was supportive. None of them
wanted to *be there*, but they were ready
because Charlie was ready. They all
came and said their goodbyes, so Dell and I
go over to Charlie's house on Saturday night
with all the stuff expecting to wake up
with Charlie dead. All three of us—

Dell, Charlie and me—had read the instructions
five or six times each, of course, but we
were nervous as shit. The pills are supposed to
work better with alcohol, so I had
some Scotch ready. He wouldn't take it.
He was adamant, he wouldn't touch the
stuff, said it had been hard enough
to get sober and stay sober. He insisted
on water, even though I begged
him. I told him it didn't make any
difference. He wanted to go out
sober though. So I gave him the pills—
with water. He had stopped eating—was just
taking fluids, so swallowing the pills
wasn't easy. He took every
one of those suckers, ten of them,
drank them down one at a time, thanked me
and lay down. We waited, set beside him
for two hours, then went in the other
room. Dell lay down and I set the clock,
just in case, but I couldn't sleep at all,
of course. Got up at 2, went and checked
on him, he was still breathing,
the fucker, so I went back
and told Dell, who was wide awake,
that he was still alive.

I got up again at a little after 3, looked
in and his chest wasn't moving. I was sure
this was it. I woke
Dell up, told him Charlie had
stopped breathing. I'd promised
to call Charlie's brother, Dirk,
yeah, the straight one, the one closest
to him, and there was Sue, a really close
woman friend from the program. She
said she wanted to know when he died. So I called
Dirk's and got his machine. Couldn't deal
with that so I hung up. I got
Sue and she thanked me. I sat down and had
a cigarette when Dell came back in the room,
and said he had closed Charlie's eyes.
I shrieked, "You what? His eyes weren't
open when I was in there." We ran

back and took his pulse. It was
going. The fucker was still alive
and I swear he wasn't breathing when I was
in there. We didn't know what to do, felt
guilty as hell that we'd failed him,
went in the kitchen to talk and have more
cigarettes. We found a garbage bag
in there and decided to try
and smother him. So there's Dell and me,
scared to death, creeping up either side
of the bed, ready to pull this bag
over his head and hold him down if he
struggles. What a picture we must've made.
We're just ready to slip the bag
over his head and his eyes pop open.
We just couldn't do it: pull a bag over a man's
head with him staring at us. We left
the room and talked and talked,
harangued over not doing
our job, about failing him,
and finally, thank God, we realized we'd done
enough, that it wasn't our job to do
anymore. It was his job and he'd have to
do it himself if he wanted to die.
I had to call Sue back
and tell her Charlie was not dead.

I am exhausted waiting
for Charlie to die. I feel this
incredible weight but I just can't
do anything more about it. This week
I realized the fucker repeated
the same thing that happened
over and over in our relationship. I'd get
all the information, try to do it
all for him, and he wouldn't be ready.
Then when I'd just about given up, he'd go
do it himself. Well, this is something
I can't do for him. I love him
but he's just going to have to die himself.

II. CATHY

Well, since I became a lesbian . . .
You mean last week, Lynnsey
interrupts laughing. We all
laugh, glad to, after Charlie's
funeral, laughing at how much is
possible after all. Cathy
leaps ahead headlong, Yeah, well,
it's been three weeks, actually.
I'll tell you my life has really
changed. Being HIV Positive
is nothing compared to this.
Course I can't stop talking
about it and you know, not
everyone wants to hear about it either.
This gets a big laugh from back and front
seat. And you people, well my God,
I've got four dykes
right here in one car.
I have to hear all
about how you met, you know,
how you got together.
I don't know what I'm doing.
I've been talking
about it in my meetings
but they think they've heard enough,
what with me being HIV Positive
and all, they don't want to hear
about my being a lesbian too.
They've been through Harry,
my ex-lover dying from AIDS, two
years now it's been, and my ex-
husband and his being positive
now too. You just don't know.
Now my ex-husband, he's
great about my being a lesbian. He's not
threatened or anything. And my support
group in Bangor, they're good,
and of course, the gay/lesbian meeting, but
I need to talk about this a lot
and my regular AA home group
in Bangor, well, one of them,
I thought she was my friend, she says

to me, Cathy it's too much. We're just
here to talk about problems of alcoholism.
We heard all about Harry's IV drug use
and your HIV, but this is too much.
They think it's a tragedy. She doesn't
understand that I'm happier
than I've ever been in my whole entire
life. After thirty-two years, I am finally
in the right place at the right time.
I'm fine. I don't want to drink. Another thing,
a lot of straight people, they think
if I've said it out loud
once, I should be done.
They don't understand this being
a lesbian changes everything in my life.
Everything. I barely know
what to say anymore, I want
to tell everyone of course, my family
and my old friends from school but I can
see from the reaction at meetings
that I'm going to have to be more
selective, pick and choose who
I talk to because I don't need
any shit about this — like I said,
this is the best thing that ever
happened to me. And it *is* related
to my sobriety, goddammit. If I wasn't
sober, I wouldn't know how to think
over anything. I was hiding
all the time, drowning in booze.
Now I'm making some real
choices and I'm pleased as punch
about it. I listen to everyone
else tell about their relationships —
wives, weddings, bosses, you name it.
I don't complain. I get something
out of it. Well, they should
be able to, too. It's crazy.
They haven't heard near
enough from me. Why
shouldn't I be able to talk
about being lesbian?
It's good for 'em
to see there are other ways

of loving. My ex-husband,
he understands—no problem.
He's one of my best friends. He
called in the middle of the night, the other
night. He was freaking out—
not about me—about being Positive
now too—and he couldn't think of anyone
else to call. What guy can he call?
Guys don't talk to guys, at least not straight
ones. He doesn't have any supports yet, it's so new.
He kept apologizing for calling
but he really didn't know
who else to call. So I talked with him
for a while, calmed him down
some, told him it was a big
adjustment and he didn't have to
do it alone, that there were
all kinds of supports now—thanks
to you Lynnsey and you Tracy.
I told him how 2 lesbians started
Down East AIDS Network and got the guys,
the political ones, working too,
and how you worked with the state
agencies and got grants, how you
started it all in your own home,
had the office on the stairs
and how D.E.A.N. had a big office now
and two paid positions, all because
you just fucking did it, organized
it right here in downeast Maine.
I told him how it was for lovers
and family members, for straight
people too. I gave him
the whole nine yards. I told him he can go
to the support group like I did—
get mad, talk about it,
let it out, and eventually he'd
maybe get to where he could accept
it and get on with his
life. You know it makes you
think. I didn't paint too rosy
a picture for him. The anger, grief,
and pain all come back, after all
we're only human. But he can

find people, good ones
he can trust, then
get on with it, the way
I have. Anyway, he said he felt
a lot better and thanked me
and said "God bless 'em" about
you Lynnsey and you Tracy.
He'll be all right. I know
he will. But I got to meet
some women. I need to hear
all I can to get ready.
Now Lynnsey and Tracy, you met here in Maine,
right? So there's hope for me.
I need to hear all
about it, everything. Then
we can move on to you Bea
and you Roz. You're from another
country. I'd like to hear about that.
Hell, maybe I should come down
to New York and meet some women.

III. HOMELESS

Morning sun outside D'Agostino's, a young man bends,
crooked towards a parked car, heavy brown
raincoat, denim jeans and white shirt.
Smooth face, dark brown beard, hair shiny
in gentle curls away from his face.
His skin: translucent, taut across the bones
in his face, pink cheeks. His brow: a dome
over liquid brown eyes, deep-set under dark
eyebrows, long lashes. In one hand, he clasps
a sheaf of papers, his fingers curled.
He holds the papers up, shield at shoulder-height.
"Excuse me, I need help."
I walk towards him, he's not
threatening. I see his physical
weakness. "I was in a hotel," he says. "I was robbed,
they beat me up." I see the bruise on the side of his face
and look again into his eyes. I stop,
rest my bags at my feet. "It's dangerous
now," he continues, "it's no good anymore. They ruined it.
The addicts. They steal everything. They stole
my money, my medicine, my AZT. They sell it on the street."

His eyes start to brim. "I get my check this week, see,"
he holds the papers towards me, "see, here's my ID,
here're my papers. See, it's me." The tiny square
snapshot shows a large head, shorn.
I tell him to hold on to his
papers. I don't need to see
them. I ask if he's been to GMHC. "Yeah,
they got me a place, at the AIDS hospice,"
he gestures down the street towards Christopher.
"GMHC only takes people under $5000, my checks put me over,
but they got me a referral to the hospice." He stops,
eyes brimming again, "I'm sorry," he looks down, shifts
his weight, stumbles in the space between the car
and the curb, touches my arm inadvertently, draws back
fast, "I didn't mean to touch you, I'm
sorry." "It's OK," I steady his elbow. "I'm so tired,"
he leans against the brown coupe outside the French restaurant.
"What do you need?" "I'm so ashamed, I hate asking
for anything. I ate out of a garbage can this morning.
I never did that before. I ate someone's leftover McDonald's."
"It's OK, you were hungry, you got some food."
He begins to cry, then stops, "I'm gay, my father,"
he's Italian, he's homophobic. He won't help me,
he disowned me, my father. He's so sick,
he doesn't understand, he's so sick, my father."
"What's your name?" I ask. "What do you need?"
"I'm so ashamed for asking like this,
I just have to. I got to get to the McBurney Y,
they have a room for one night they said,
if I get up there. I need to rest. I have lesions,
on my legs," he pats his blue-jeaned thighs,
"they get infected, I got to clean them out, get
some peroxide." I know I have money
in my pocket, thirty dollars in the bank.
I reach in my pocket, pull out a ten-
dollar bill, direct him, "Go out to Hudson, you know
the park . . ." "I need to sit down," he interrupts, "I'm so tired . . ."
"You know the benches, you can sit down and rest
on one of the benches down the street by the laundromat.
When you're ready, get a cab
on 8th Avenue. It'll take you right up
to the Y." I have never given anyone
a ten-dollar bill on the street before. "I can get your address

and pay you back, I get my check next week." "Forget it,
go sit down, go to the Y, sleep, rest." "I can't thank
you enough. Bless you, thank you." He crosses Greenwich
towards Hudson. I turn, my hands barely able to grasp
the two bags of groceries, lift the weight,
carry them around the corner.
I turn, see the back of his
raincoat, the beautiful chestnut curls
over his collar.

Next week, I am headed to the bank
to deposit a check. I am celebrating
inside, Thank God! Down to my last two dollars. Right outside
the bank, I see him at the corner of 8th
and West 12th in his raincoat talking
with a young woman clearly on her way to work.
She is gesturing, "Go to the Center, the Gay/Lesbian
Center on West 13th St.," she is overpronouncing
her words. He is repeating, "the Center, the Center,"
as if he has never heard of it. I pass them
quickly, fury carrying me into the bank.
Lying son of a bitch, goddam faggot, draining off women's
energy, lesbian energy like no one
ever dies from anything besides AIDS. Community,
my ass. How many faggots are nursing women
with breast cancer or anything else for that matter?
All he had to do was get to the fucking
YMCA. It didn't happen, goddam liar.
I make out my deposit slip, fill in
the date, bank account #, the deposit for $357,
sign my name. I decide to confront him
when I'm done, if he's still out there. *Remember me*
I'll say, *What happened to my*
ten dollars, you son of a bitch?
I pad quickly over to the express
deposit, put in my bank card,
check my balance: −$10.50. Shit, what happened?
I seal the envelope, pop it
in the slot, punch in the envelope number
and it drops safely in.
Get the deposit slip, $2 till tomorrow—$1
for milk, 65¢ for a cup in the morning, 35¢
for NEWSDAY, and by 3 the check will be clear.

Minus $10.50, what happened?
Christ, who knows. At least I got
paid, I'll be OK.

Outside, the corner is empty, swept clear, a short
line to the ATM. *Remember me . . .*
Maybe he wouldn't remember, maybe
he couldn't remember . . .
Why didn't he know the Center?
I begin to choke on my own breath
as I realize he may not remember.
AIDS in the last stages.
Is he lying or not remembering?
Is he dying or running a scam
or both? Does he know the difference? Do I?
Do I need or deserve to know
because I gave him $10, because
I'm a lesbian who has seen too
much of this disease?
Anything could have happened.
We live in New York City.
I wanted it to be simple: cross
the street, go sit down, rest,
get the cab uptown, then sleep.
In the morning breakfast,
take a cab to the AIDS
hospice. Here he enters the place where
he will die. I want to know
I have finished. But he has not
arrived anywhere. I bumped into him,
the motion of his life down the street.
He showed me that it was the world,
not he himself alone who held
his body in his hands.

＜☼＞

ELENA GEORGIOU

·

A WEEK IN THE LIFE OF THE ETHNICALLY INDETERMINATE

Monday
Sitting in McDonald's on 103rd & 3rd
I notice a couple staring at me
and hear them say *Indian*
they walk towards me
the woman has white skin
blonde hair, blue eyes
the man has ebony skin
black hair, brown eyes
excuse me, says the woman
we were wondering
where you were from
yeah, says the man
because you look like
our people
I look at the whiteness
and the blackness
wondering who their people are
we're Puerto Rican, they say
and walk away

Tuesday
Walking to the store
in Crown Heights I see
an African-American man
sitting behind a table
selling incense and oils
he calls out sister, hey sister
baby and then makes a noise
like he's calling a cat
I don't respond
on the way back
from the store
he calls out *mira, mira,*

hey baby,
in any language,
English, Feline or Spanish
I don't respond

Wednesday
I am buying lunch
at the falafel stand
on 68th & Lex
and the man serving me asks,
you from Morocco?
no, I say, Cyprus
where's Cyprus, he asks
above Egypt
to the left of Israel
and below Turkey
oh, he says looking blank
how much for the falafel, I ask
for you three dollars
for Americans three fifty
I go to pay and another man
stares hard into my face
and says, are you a Jewish chick
no, I say, just leave me alone
I know who you are, he screams
I know who you are
you're just a nigger from Harlem
passing for white
with a phony accent
nigger, he repeats
as I walk away

Thursday
My boss calls me up
I have a funny question
to ask you, he says
when you fill out forms
what do you write for ethnicity
I check *other*, I say
well, I have to fill out this form
and it doesn't have *other*
we look really bad on paper
all the positions of power are white

and all the support staff are black
could you be Asian?

Friday
I am with my Indian immigration lawyer
do you mind if I ask you
a personal question, he says
go ahead, I say, thinking
he is going to ask me
how I've reached my mid thirties
and have never been married
but instead he says
I know you're a Cypriot
from London
but do you have
any Indian blood in you
there are so many
mixed marriages these days
and you look like the offspring

Saturday
I am at a conference
and a European-American woman
looks at me excitedly
as though she's just won a prize
oh, I know where your from, she says
my daughter-in-law is an Indian
with a British accent too
I'm not Indian, I say
continuing to not see me
she concentrates on
hiding her anger
for not winning the trophy
in her self-imposed
guess the ethnicity competition
and then she walks away

Sunday
I go to lunch at the home of a friend
whose family are Africans of the diaspora
they don't ask me where I'm from
later my friend tells me
they've decided you are
a biracial Jamaican

Later, Sunday evening
I'm at a poetry reading
and an African-American woman
crosses the room
to ask me this question,
are you the colonized
or the colonizer?
what do you think, I ask
you could be both, she responds
and walks away

.

THE SPACE BETWEEN

Stuck in an unnamed place
halfway between love and in love,
you call me late at night and ask if
I'm sleeping. I tell you, I'm writing.
You ask about what: Love, I say.

When I write about us, I stop myself
from saying *we make love* or *we have sex*.
I search for a euphemism that won't bind me,
won't define us. I arrive at the phrase
move together. And only now, in writing
this poem, do I see how fitting it is.

The way we moved together vertically
is what made me want to move with you
horizontally. Music joined us,
but even in this joining, I didn't know
how to behave, how much or how little
to say, how to choose to be me.

An old friend told me if I feel
smaller than myself with a lover
this is the wrong lover for me.

Yes, I make myself smaller; I shrink
my politics, my conversation. I shrink
in mind, but I grow in body.

And don't think I don't know
when the movements are fluid
we look for ways to draw each other
nearer, name each other soulmates.

I have been a two-time witness
to how easily the soul-thread can be
cut, leaving the so-called soulmate
dangling in an empty world of one.

The same old friend comes back
to say a lover should love
in me what I love in myself.

Trouble is, we don't know what we love
in each other. We exchange tapes of songs
to hint at the possibility of a feeling,
admitting nothing, partially exposed
in lyrics so, if pushed, we can deny
we meant the words that way.

We skirt around edges hoping
the space between will stop closeness
because close is where we are
fighting ourselves not to be.

I preach distance to you. I inflict it
on myself. I invent barriers like age gaps
and bad timing. But only now, in writing
this poem, do I learn how the word
distance can magnetize lovers.

You obey my demands. You don't
call. We don't speak. But you find
a strand of my hair in your freezer
and I still write with the taste of
you in my mouth.

·

TALKIN' TRASH

I want the phone to ring.

I want the sound of your voice
to smack my body as waves hit rock,
grinding down mountains, opening up
secrets hidden between my shoulder blades.

I want you to beg me to let you come
over to wash my hair with rose-water.
When I refuse, I want you to hang up.

I want you to call back when I'm doing my laundry
and whine until I agree to let you be with me,
the next time it's washday,
so you can fold it.

I want you to ask me if I miss you.
And when I say: *Yes, I think about you
night and day*, I want you to know
I'm lying.

I want you to tell me you'd buy three bridges,
cross two oceans in a thunderstorm
to make my lie of missing you a reality.

I want to tell you that for a small
part of the Caribbean Sea I'd turn into
a hungry anemone that sucks you closer.

I want you to ask me if this is all I want.
I want to tell you, no.

I want you to be my boy, my girl.
I want to paint your toenails gold,
massage your fingers with homemade oil
named after the smell of your neck.

I want to dust my mattress with baby powder,
lie on satin, tie ivory shells around my hips
and prepare myself for your coming.

I want you to call one last time,
ask me to unlock my door,
lie on my bed and wait.

I want to hear your bag drop to the floor,
the drag of your feet move to my bed.

I want to feel the weight of your body
sink the mattress two inches lower.

I want your arms
to come from behind and hold
my breasts in an open prayer.

I want to hear you call on God
and give her credit for making me.

I want to watch you plead: *Lord
have mercy*, as you slide your mouth
from my navel to the back of my knee.

I want you to make me speak in tongues.
I want you to make me reach for things
you swear to me aren't there.

I want you to flip me, hold me
with one arm around my waist,
press your stomach to my spine,
fall and rise with me,
slide into night with me.

And when morning offers the hush of sleep,
I want you to open your tired eyes,
wrap my hair around your fingers,
pull me closer and murmur: *Yes, baby,
I promise I will be your toy.*

INTIMATE MIXTURE

I have electricity in me.
If lightning strikes me, I can die.
If I don't pick up my feet as
I cross a carpet, I make sparks fly.

I think about this as my electricity starts
to jump over the synapses of my dendrites.
And my body goes *bam!* and I say, Good God!
Lightning strike me dead, right here.
Now I've seen you
there's nothing more to live for.

But, lightning doesn't strike.
And I remain standing as my endorphins
kick it to my adrenal hormones.
And my parasympathetic system
overpowers my sympathetic system.
And my heart starts speeding.
and my blood increases flow to muscles
I use for big time physical attraction,
and instead of dropping dead and dying
I look at you and say, Hello.

We dance. We talk. We dance some more.
I take you home. I hand you the record.
You wipe away the dust. And as your arm
makes circles on vinyl, our attraction builds.
Smokey sings. Our clothes stick together.

You touch me. I smell the mist
around your neck. You take off your shirt
with one hand, pull me closer with the other.
We're opposite. We attract. We undress.

With oil, I sweeten your wrist, you perfume
my breasts. You put your mouth to my hipbone,
I burst into the flashing light of a firefly.
I put my mouth to your thigh, you grow wings
that spread into the song of a humming bird.

We kiss until our lip-prints are so familiar
we could track each other down next time
either one of us commits a love crime.

We rock until we make heart-shaped sweat.
We burn candles. We burn fuses.
There is so much fire between us I hear NASA
counting down 5 4 3 2 1. And damn,
I swear, we definitely have lift off.

.

FROM WHERE I STAND

Monet tires of painting lilies.

He drops before me to paint
a pubic prayer—a V of tender
black strokes.

He holds his palette
in one hand, brushes in the other,
the smaller ones clenched between his teeth.

From where I stand I notice
the top of his head, his hair is thinning.

I snatch a brush from his mouth
to color his crown. I paint in his hair
with long strokes as he paints in mine.

We are the gods of hair.
We let this power go to our heads.

We paint short strands in unexpected places—
on all sides of the Eiffel Tower.

We turn this landmark into a bearded rod,
erect, reaching to disturb a cloud.

But wait.
We do not want to go crazy.

What makes hair special is how it comes
in small ways, small places: the pit under our arms;
the arcs over our eyes; the expanse across our shins;
the circles that cover our heads; the half moons that recede
and eventually abandon.

I feel another artist inside me.
                              Yes,
I feel his brush strokes swirling.

He is painting the walls of my womb
with stars and a turbulent sky.

He is singing: *To make blue you need yellow and orange*
Monet recognizes this voice. He tells me
van Gogh has crawled in my uterus to paint.

Van Gogh dives into delirium.

He paints an olive tree on my ribcage.
I lean on the tree while he slaps on more blue.
The wildness of his strokes knocks me off balance.

I lie on my bed. His painting swells my stomach.
Van Gogh's head presses against my cervix.

I feel myself widen. My contractions produce sky.
My labor pains make stars. After a day of pushing,
I give birth to a *Starry Night*.

I look down at the canvas of my skin.
Monet has finished. He has painted
thirteen silver crescent moons hiding
in the curls of my triangular night sky.

I part his thinning strands to kiss his head.
He stands and kisses each of my cheeks.

As the tip of his mustache brushes my lip,
I think about my own hair and how
it brushes my own lips, how it curves
to hold my folds in its crook. It's gentle—

a dainty army that shuffles towards
this cloister of flesh between my legs.
The hairs cry into this sanctum: Create.

Monet is captivated.

⤝✵⤞

ROBERT GLÜCK

·

INVADERS FROM MARS

Every family has a genius
who sits at the head & when
there's an argument
father must be sent away.

Who puts his shoes outside
his door to get polished
by the mom, he smiles ruefully
& says: service with a smile.

And no one can understand
how he turned so
wooden & misfit, his
father's favorite, more precious
than a daughter, so that he
mortgaged his house to send him
to the best,
now he wears ho-chi-minh
face hair & drinks. Now
he's a loner, builds bombs
in Livermore. Now he can't
relate. Now he hates us.

In the film *Invaders from Mars*
the Martian is mankind advanced to
the highest level. He's a silver head
inside a crystal globe, his body is
flippers or undersea plants waving
uselessly.
With the slightest flex of his face
he commands his crew — their narrow
shoulders & big hands & feet & hips.
They carry him around
& do his dirty work.

Since he doesn't have a body he's
free from nature & by extension free
from limitations (death) & by extension free
from morality. (Morality? You better talk
to your mother about that one, son
she's the boss in that department.)

Like *Donovan's Brain*, another movie,
the Brain suspends in glucose becoming
malicious & invulnerable.
Like so many movies that we watched
in nuclear radiance, movies about
heads cut loose & the radiance lighting
our dream screens.

How grotesque the Beats looked, living
with their bodies.
Dear Abby was always printing letters
by unfortunate citizens with beatnik
neighbors who *walked around naked!*
ugg! Pull down your
shades, said Ann Landers. Pull them
down Abby chimed in.

Not forgetting the expression "he's a
brain" in order to dismiss him & wasn't
he relieved? Dark & Gregorian he studied
the stars while some went pink
& black eating two old-fashioned glazed
& a coke, & others read through lyrical tears
about Quasimodo's broken pitcher
of a body, dumb love.
Still others were glamorous
loved evil & thought on suicide &
Bye-Bye Land, said
"each breath is a mistake,
it would be a mistake to breathe"
& went on to lash themselves
with spiders of a foreign tongue.

There is the beauty of regularity in
balanced environments like the salmon &
the wolf & the beauty of extravagance
we share with animals that live in

extremity like deep-sea fish of glowing
jaws & the desert toad with its
flags of skin.

So his parents wear the mixed feelings of
pride & hysteria when they regard him,
like the parents in Diane Arbus's photo
"The Jewish Giant." He's so far above
them & beyond them.

Meanwhile someone comes across the lawn
whose name he can't remember. They talk. Then
the person finally stops talking & goes away.

He's on a knoll & looks up, there's a big pink
cloud relating by contrast to the steel gray sky.
He says to himself, "just look at that pink cloud,
just look at that pink cloud, just look at that
pink cloud," to summon more & more of himself
but it's no use—he & the pink aren't equals
& everything, even the pleasure, especially the
pleasure, is against him & in spite of him.

.

PASOLINI

1

2 crows walk down the road.
One says, "Brother, when the state
is truly communist & out of
the jeweled grasp of church & capital
where even the weeds are looking for a better cemetery,
brother, then we will see—"
Every haystack trembles for the body.
These birds talk good sense. Later they are eaten &
their bones deliciously picked clean.

2

2 crows: politics: to believe and believe.
They experiment, one lies & the other believes,
obvious lies & obvious faith.
What's left stands on one scaly foot,

its head under its wing
and a wink of complicity from the state.

3
2 crows, 2 crows walk down a road
that was shattered by economics.
One crow says, "Brother,
I don't know how to make a living.
When I wake up in the morning
tears already stand in my eyes
ready to flow. Brother,
to live in the world,
to change the world."

4
2 crows walk & talk on the desolate
theme of early death.
"Yet lest we may be too one-sided, brother,
notice with what beauty & justice
the sun rises, colors
reflect off their objects, muscles flex,
breath is accepted & enjoyed."

•

BURROUGHS

fleshes his dirty rotten hunka tin   I am right   strapped into head elec-
trodes   he sticks a gun in teen age drug   Harry S Truman decided to drop
first   I am right   sequence   repeat   dim jerky far away smoke   cop rat
bares his yellow teet   kicks in the door   I am right   survivors burned   time
and place   he throws atom bomb   knocks man to floor   you are wrong
you are wrong   he was looking for are wrong   Breaks through door I'm
poli   outside bar   Hiroshima   has strayed into Dillinger's right   is mak-
ing a difficult decision   right   survivors burned   mixed you child I am
he kicks him into 1914 movie   if you are gay I am right   wrong   execu-
tioner   officer   I am cop   right enough you are I am right   right   wrong
Pentagon   dim jerky far away smoke.

I cut up his cut-ups, allegory of an allegory of an allegory of an allegory of
a waterfall of mental curlicues whose new meaning is no meaning in
extremity. Is a Burroughs to eat? I am timid, abstract, complete, light fever,
timid. Barefoot, yells Hey Pop, got any more Dick Tracys? Burroughs am

paying one wrecked penny for the pleasure he's wreaking on some "boy"; shooting quarts of toxins, skin a welcome mat, body heroically disjunct Picasso (two profiles, left front thigh . . .). The stapled urge for self-protection that . . . Danger is a refuge from more danger. Don't even know what a Burroughs is.

Manhattan Project, first atom bomb test, New Mexico 1945: Oppenheimer and *his* boys think the planet could go critical. Oppenheimer refigures, the probability remains, "What the hell." So-and-so many blasts: radioactive sex causes untold genetic mutations. A carnival of giants, vile luminosity sheeting off their scales and exoskeletons, march out of that desert looking for something to eat. I don't want to die but witness APPETITE and MURDER tread the vile luminous sand: ant spider Gila monster rattler wasp rat locust lizard grasshopper rabbit praying mantis crow ant spider wasp. . . . The entire town of Soda Bluff stampedes down narrow canyons scattering funeral lights beneath their trembling feet. The destruction of today. Last men, mercenaries on the last patrol, eat rations with dog mouths, then fool around in caustic green dusk; they wear Mylar capes and copper-studded jockstraps. Bud's withheld a basket musta weigh two pounds of fresh peaches. Bud squirms down with a deep sigh, odor of penetration, he says "I want to be so *embraced.*" The last ant cold mandibles his thigh, a howl and spasms from Bud's lifted body mean death. I send my own spear into the enormous insect eye shattering a thousand selves — point touches pinpoint brain, blue sparks, burning isolation, burning rubber, ant collapses, cold heap of old parts. The reason Bud dies, so that his orgasm stays beyond. I don't wonder *who* I am, I wonder *where* I am — still, nothing to do now but kick back and wait for orders.

•

FROM THE VISIT

2

Odd to close my eyes during the day and open them at night, but any separation gives a form to longing.

You promise what you will never give — I say to trick the distance. If I accept fate it's a strategy of last resorts. That's why I like pine tar. John Dee. The poem as industrial ruin. Melted window glass. The ornate splendor of stopped time. The end of the world in history. The error of lyricism. A helicopter's ability to hover ramifies in my chest a pleading tremolo. Mirrors make me dizzy because I *fall* into the aging.

I'm frightened — I've grown worse in your absence than the present can cure. Thought demands less of itself. Light passes in distractions — Venetian blind, glass on the sill. One term doesn't lead to the next, it brings its contrary in unions of faint commitment to scatter again like dice.

10

A famous monk dropped to his knees before a giant image and cried, "I am nothing before you, before you I am nobody." He gazed at the effacement he had yet to attain. Shapeless, he differed from the resolved ovals and extreme repose, and from the pines and the sky. A scholar was so moved he also fell and cried, "I am an unread book, nothing." He closed his eyes like the hollow embodiment. "Let the light that reflects off my body forget its captivity." The highest judgment is the court of pines and sky, but he felt his name would decline if he began to learn again. I'm so moved by their rapture I fall to my knees. The image deprives us of our depth without allowing us to be shallow. The scholar turns to the monk and says, "Look who thinks he's nobody."

11

This image is alive with my longing for you. When I close my eyes I see you in lewd positions which are units of longing as tenderly programmatic as Sunday for the boaters and children. I am often bitter, lazy, candid, and sharp-eyed. Stasis dressed as Time, a prince in disguise, gives me the present like a glittering trinket draped on an orchid in a backstage comedy. Night shines inside like reaching music. I am grateful for the present. Problems remain unsolved but they subside in the photo—temporal, the slanted sunlight falls on the big pine for a few hours of oration. Odor of hemp and grilled hot dogs. I wish but can't interpret. I miss you though you are with me. That is, each person and thing is aroused and lonely because we consent to time. For a few hours the mood holds, we call to each other from the boats, get a little drunk, make barking sounds. When I drink it's like a crowd surrounds me.

MELINDA GOODMAN

·

COBWEBS

I walked around in my mother's high heels
I put her stockings over my head
ran my fingers over the black shiny beads
on her evening bag before she went out

I loved going through my mother's wooden bureau
top drawer was shallow with partitions
purses, gloves, hankies, and a gold cigarette lighter
with a built-in watch
the second drawer to the right   was deeper
underpants and bras
scented with smooth round bars of pale soap
a rubber disc inside a round box of bath powder
looked like a tiny trampoline or a yarmulke
I thought it was there to keep the powder   fresh

from the Fuller Brush man
there was an ivory colored oval hand mirror
it was so heavy I had to use both fists
to hold it up

In the second drawer to the left were slips and nighties
perfume blue and barely pink
I plunged my arms up to my elbows
in soft folded petals of my mother
I fingered the tiny rosebud
that floated on her necklines
summer nighties blizzarded with flowers
slippery thin straps   I liked best
the ones that were most worn   when she wore them
she looked like she was dressed in sheets of rain
I watched her blurry through the sliding glass
door in the shower   blindly washing her hair

When it was time for a bath
she squeezed ivory liquid under the tap

and put two or three of us   naked
into the tub
rising suds   our beards and mustaches

she threw in her stockings

we played till our fingers shriveled
we played till our lips turned blue.

.

FEBRUARY ICE YEARS

Walking south down Broadway
she wiped her nose
and smelled a woman still
on her knuckles
stiff from the cold
reminding her of eighth grade February ice-
years back. That
big woman on top of her
smelling like spit, cum, sweat,
and Nivea lotion
that narcotic blue
jar filled with white cream
so peaked
she was afraid to touch it
so wide and wet
she could hear it speak
Easy to see a baby's head ready to crown
watch its gum cut a tooth
Easy to lose a hand
inside the soft large butter
rum thighs

There was the smell of paint,
dope, incense, and sandwiches
there was the scent
of the Electrophonic eight-track stereo
glowing quadraphonic blue
like low flames under pots
on the chipped enamel stove

It was warm in that stolen king-sized bed
blinds down and bath towel hung
like moss on the iron tall
four-foot-high radiator
standing guard against
the steam-heat pipe-banging night
it was dark under that woman
whose reefer tongue moved inside her mouth
like it was her own
whose weight held her fast
to the sheet
whose hand pulled her hand down
to musky soft liquid
yolk between legs
then back to lips

Head buried between that woman's breasts
she didn't have to think
just bite
the gold
charm of her necklace
just suck
those nipples like the child she was—
knowing soon she would switch
to something more grown
like fucking
that woman
with most of her fist
'cause two or three fingers
were lost
children in the wilderness
pennies in the drum

With her face pushed in the pulsing wetness
she could not hear
Marvin on the radio
or the wind blowing the sign on the check-cashing place
back and forth on rusted hinges
yelping like a puppy with a broken foot
Just those thighs like shells
clapped over her ears
Just the ocean inside her head
Just in the morning that woman's voice
telling her

get up, sugar
it's time
for school.

.

LULLABYE FOR A BUTCH

Saturday night November 1980
I am 23 driving a '72 Delta east on 4
to the George Washington Bridge
jockeying with other drivers
coming off routes 80 and 47
for a clear veer to the lane my lover
works: the 3 to 11 post-Thanksgiving shift

She grabs my hand as I fly
money-green flags
in her direction
laughing over the moan of diesel brakes
her wool gloved fingers pry then tangle
in my naked palm
Ignoring the blaring horns outside the booth,
our mutual radios pump the club
version of Grace's "Warm Leatherette"
as she steps out on exhausted concrete
to place an orange cone
between my bumper and the
bumper behind mine

I like her uniform:
fresh polyester dark blue
and bright white collar
topped with overcoat,
scarf and ski cap for the blizzard on the way.
If it snows, the Port Authority
puts her up at a motel—otherwise
she stays at my place but has to be back
by dawn or be counted AWOL
So she's up before five
folding her flowered pajamas
into the bottom drawer
of my colonial chest

with handles like rings
through a bull's snout

"You got my nose"
moaned the only teenaged woman
who ever loved me
and my tollbooth honey
reminds me of her
as I chain the door behind her
hearing footsteps down five flights
to the street, the Bridge,
and the gunmetal morning

I always loved
gentlemanly attentive butches
even those who won't fuck
for the first five dates
'cause they "want to get to know you"
til you beg
and by that time
you're married
They want to make sure
all those free concerts
fish dinners
and stories about home
won't get thrown back
in their teeth
after all . . .
butches are vulnerable
it's the femmes that are fierce
with their long legs
and tight jeans
making you watch them
Butches are the sweet ones
with their clean shine shoes
and socks
and underwear
smelling of baby powder
and Camay
I loved
the way she wrote her name
in purple script
all over the top sheet

on my coloring pad
when supper was done and dishes stacked

I wish I could kiss her now
slide my tongue through her teeth
erase the years I fell
for women as distant as Queens
is from the Bronx
Just hold this butch in my arms
make her know
it's not the 2 condominiums
she bought with rare pennies
collected on her job
but *her*
strong back
and big hips
and corny sparkling eyes
when she walks around
to open the door
on my side of the car
in front of the skinny eyes
of the fat boy dealers
strutting in and out
of their customized vans
and the heads rolling in
from Jersey
She doesn't even see
the tooth sucking teens
as she walks back around
in her ten gallon brim
to slide behind the wheel
Doesn't tell me where we're
going til we're parked and walking
out of the lot
up the block
arms linked
to see Patti LaBelle
LIVE at the Savoy
and I'm on my heels
all night screaming
through til the last song
running my fingers up the back of her neck
til the walls come down, tables break in half,
everybody's glass explodes

ice cubes hailing the city for miles
as Patti rains on—

warriors
turning rainbows
upside down
in a
lulla-
bye.

•

NEW COMERS

Saturday:

Nobody trusts CD cause she
plays like she's in love
when all she wants
is to fuck.

She gives me a big juicy hug
when I walk in the meeting.
Rubbing her breasts all on mine. I can barely see her
through my shades that are too dark but go
with the outfit. Kissing me on the mouth, she grrrs
in the back of her throat like some imitation
tiger woman.
I smile
and get away from her.

Monday:

Here I am at another meeting.
CD's there on a bench.
Nothing but men here today.
I feel like leaving.
Then CD spots me . . . motions . . . come sit next to her.
I go over. Feel the heat of her arm
pushing against the side of mine.
We're supposed to be listening
to what these guys are talking about
but all I know is CD's thigh

against the side of *my* thigh.
Then she says in a low voice,
"Come."

We go to the crumbling
church basement bathroom.
I feel her belt buckle that says "CD" in brass
as she pushes me through the stall door
kisses my back
unsnaps my jeans
rubs hard through the seams of my Wranglers
going in layered stages
like I can stop her anytime
teasing my clit
like a diamond earlobe
tightening my nipples.
I lick her lips
unbuckle her belt
she spins me toward the stall wall
pulls down my pants and plunges
up to my eyeballs
with nicotine fingers.

Bending my knees to take her deeper
I reach back to feel her bigger
hips pushing against me
cheekbones rub
graffitied metal
fingers
stiffening inside
as I come
quiet
resting
against her
catching my breath.

She pulls out
warm wet
fingers steaming in the cold air
put to my lips
to be sucked clean
fucking my mouth
til I can't taste me anymore.

I pull up my jeans
tuck in my blouse
she unlatches the door
whispers some bullshit
about what a hot mama I am
then we leave.

She can't wait to tell her friends
she got me
I don't care
she was
on my list.

•

OPEN POEM

This is an open poem
for the lesbian community
with its tired-ass softball leagues
who want only "serious" players
and its pretentious poetry readings
with abstract verse about the moon going down into vaginal flora
boring confessional "pieces" about
first times with that counselor at
Camp Minn-ee-ha-ha

This is an open poem
for the lesbian community
destroyed by our fathers until we've become just like them
equally unable to be close to a single other being
let alone woman
though you don't find out
til she's got you by your own raped ovaries
and she's sailing down the block
with another politically-righteous-
emotional-time-bomb-
used-to-be-friend-of-yours
trailing your fallopian tubes behind them
like pink velvet ribbons from the fist
of a lesbian pride wedding bouquet

This is an open poem
to the lesbian community

with its folding chair resources
to help in your recovery from
alcoholism, sex, drugs, food, smoking,
starving, vomiting, gambling, and love
but nothing for recovery from *it*
as it drags itself like a tired dog
nipples scraping the broken glass and phlegm
of "alternative" facsimiles
of the same old heterosexual
betrayals and empty promises
the same old bleeding
you were always so good at
the same old dishes hitting
the same old love-stained walls

This is an open poem
to the lesbian community with its bitterness like a poisoned thumb
that never cuts its nails no matter
how many nights it scores
who never calls when you've stopped being funny
and your skin's turned to oatmeal
from allergic reactions to anti-
depressants and all your friends
are confusing you with other lesbians
of the same race and ethnic origin

This is an open poem
to the lesbian community
in hopes that we will one day
stop lying to each other
learn to be out
not only for ourselves
that the real work
is being able to go the distance
that loving a woman
can sometimes mean
knowing when not to fuck her
that what is truly erotic
is the power we each have
to stop
this
pain inflicted
harder than any dick
because it comes from the ones

who knew us
and loved us
and could stick it to us
best.

MARILYN HACKER

·

GOING BACK TO THE RIVER
FOR K. J.

Dusk, iridescent gasoline floats on the
rain puddles, peacock feathers on macadam.
   Schoolgirl beneath an awning pulls her
   collar up, here comes her bus. She's gone now.

Nine-thirty, and there's light behind thunderheads.
Storm over, in an hour it will rain again.
   Meal done, across the street a neighbor
   shakes out her tablecloth from the window.

I have a reading lamp and an open book.
Last glass of wine, last morsel of Saint-André
   prolong my dinner and my chapter
   into the ten o'clock Haydn program.

What will I say to you when I write to you?
(What would I say to someone who isn't you?)
   I'm home, I've cleaned the kitchen, taken
   charge of my solitude, taken long baths.

What do I tell myself when I open and
write in the notebook keeping me company?
   Don't stay indoors tomorrow morning.
   Do the week's shopping at Sunday market.

Go to the river, take what it offers you.
When you were young, it guarded and promised you
   that you would follow other rivers
   oceans away from a landlocked childhood.

Yes, I indulge myself in hyperbole
since I'm not going out for a walk in this
   wet weather, though I'd walk from someone
   else's place, stop on the bridge, look over.

Seine, Thames and Hudson (sounds like a publisher):
one river floats down into another one.
    Where did I sit and read alone, who
    walked with me which afternoon, which evening?

There was a river when I was leaving you.
That morning, with our *café con leche*, we
    slouched on a bench above the Hudson,
    washed in the wind of a near departure.

Not rupture: each one went where she had to go.
Still, I'd be hours and borders away from you.
    We bluffed like adolescent soldiers
    at the significant bridge or crossroad.

"Your father," you said, "would have been proud of you."
"My mother never would have imagined it."
    Poor Jews in an antagonistic
    city, they pulled in their walls around them.

One city would have looked like another one:
hard work, a clean house, food without seasoning.
    Scrub Europe from a neutral palate,
    blend and assimilate, mistrust strangers,

know in an instant which are the *lanzmänner*.
No Yiddish pet names, gossip or baby talk.
    Brownshirts outside the door would pass on
    innocent, bland Mid-Atlantic Standard.

Is any accent that safely nondescript?
Their child, I bruise my brain on two languages
    (neither the one they lost) four decades
    after they earned me this freedom, passing

as what they weren't: rooted American.
Their daughter, I come home to two continents,
    live with my roots tied up in parcels,
    still impecunious, maybe foolish.

Another child of children of immigrants
(Russian, Italian), you've chosen languages
    written in symbols meant to have no
    country of origin, color, gender

(though every symbol's chiseled with history).
There, you are learning, chemical formulae:
   meals on the run, a book you started
   months ago under the bed, abandoned.

Life's not forever, love is precarious.
Wherever I live, let me come home to you
   as you are, I as I am, where you
   meet me and walk with me to the river.

•

THE BOY

Is it the boy in me who's looking out
the window, while someone across the street
mends a pillowcase, clouds shift, the gutterspout
pours rain, someone else lights a cigarette?

(Because he flinched, because he didn't whirl
around, face them, because he didn't hurl
the challenge back—*"Fascists"*—not *"Faggots"*—*"Swine!"*
he briefly wonders—if he were a girl . . .)
He writes a line. He crosses out a line.

I'll never be a man, but there's a boy
crossing out words: the rain, the linen-mender,
are all the homework he will do today.
The absence and the privilege of gender

confound in him, soprano, clumsy, frail.
Not neuter—neutral human, and unmarked,
the younger brother in the fairy tale
except, boys shouted *"Jew!"* across the park

at him when he was coming home from school.
The book that he just read, about the war,
the partisans, is less a terrible
and thrilling story, more a warning, more

a code, and he must puzzle out the code.
He has short hair, a red sweatshirt. They know
something about him—that he should be proud
of? That's shameful if shows?

That got you killed in 1942.
In his story, do the partisans
have sons? Have grandparents? Is he a Jew
more than he is a boy, who'll be a man

someday? Someone who'll never be a man
looks out the window at the rain he thought
might stop. He reads the sentence he began.
He writes down something that he crosses out.

•

INVOCATION

This is for Elsa, also known as Liz,
an ample-bodied gospel singer, five
discrete malignancies in one full breast.
This is for auburn Jacqueline, who is
celebrating fifty years alive,
one since she finished chemotherapy,
with fireworks on the fifteenth of July.
This is for June, whose words are lean and mean
as she is, elucidating our protest.
This is for Lucille, who shines a wide
beam for us with her dark cadences.
This is for long-limbed Maxine, astride
a horse like conscience. This is for Aline,
who taught her lover to caress the scar.
This is for Eve, who thought of AZT
as hopeful poisons pumped into a vein.
This is for Nanette in the Midwest.
This is for Alicia, shaking back dark hair,
dancing one-breasted with the Sabbath bride.
This is for Judy on a mountainside,
plunging her gloved hands in a glistening hive.
Hilda, Patricia, Gaylord, Emilienne,
Tania, Eunice: this is for everyone
who marks the distance on a calendar
from what's less likely each year to "recur."
Our saved-for-now lives are life sentences
—which we prefer to the alternative.

YEAR'S END

FOR AUDRE LORDE AND SONNY WAINWRIGHT

Twice in my quickly disappearing forties
someone called while someone I loved and I were
making love to tell me another woman
had died of cancer.

Seven years apart, and two different lovers:
underneath the numbers, how lives are braided,
how those women's deaths and lives, lived and died, were
interleaved also.

Does lip touch on lip a *memento mori*?
Does the blood-thrust nipple against its eager
mate recall, through lust, a breast's transformations
sometimes are lethal?

Now or later, what's the enormous difference?
If one day is good, is a day sufficient?
Is it fear of death with which I'm so eager
to live my life out

now and in its possible permutations
with the one I love? (Only four days later,
she was on a plane headed west across the
Atlantic, work-bound.)

Men and women, mortally wounded where we
love and nourish, dying at thirty, forty,
fifty, not on barricades, but in beds of
unfulfilled promise:

tell me, senators, what do you call abnormal?
Each day's obits read as if there's a war on.
Fifty-eight-year-old poet dead of cancer:
warrior woman

laid down with the other warrior women.
Both times when the telephone rang, I answered
wanting not to, knowing I had to answer,
go from two bodies'

infinite approach to a crest of pleasure
through the disembodied voice from a distance
saying one loved body was clay, one wave of
mind burst and broken.

Each time we went back to each other's hands and
mouths as to a requiem where the chorus
sings death with irrelevant and amazing
bodily music.

·

SQUARES AND COURTYARDS

Across the Place du Marché Ste-Catherine,
the light which frames a building that I see
daily, walking home from the bakery,
white voile in open windows, sudden green
and scarlet window-box geraniums
backlit in cloud-encouraged clarity
against the century-patinaed gray,
is such a gift of the quotidian,
a benefice of sight and consciousness,
I sometimes stop, confused with gratitude,
not knowing what to thank or whom to bless,
break off an end of seven-grain baguette
as if my orchestrated senses could
confirm the day. It's fragrant. I eat it.

Confirm the day's fragrance: I eat, bit
by bit, the buttery *pain aux raisins*
shell-coiled beside my steaming afternoon
tea. It's the hour for a schoolchild's treat,
munched down, warm in waxed paper, on the street,
or picked at on chipped earthenware (like mine)
beside books marked with homework to be done
while the street's sunlit, dusk-lit, lamplit.
She sucks her pencil, window-framed. I sip
nostalgia for a childhood not my own
Bronx kitchen table, with a fire escape
in the alley shaded by sumac trees
which filtered out the other languages
I heard the airshaft's cross-currents intone.

I heard the airshaft's cross-currents intone
below the minyan davening morning offices.
A childish rasp that slurred and sputtered was
the Polish janitor's red-knuckled son
helping his father empty garbage cans.
His voice was why I thought him rough (as is
English when uttered by its novices)
—a voice I never heard speaking its own
language. His name was Joseph. He was six.
Other syllables connected news
from gutted Europe to the dusty motes
of Sabbath morning. Ash settled on bricks,
spun up the shaft with voices of old Jews,
was drawn down garrulous chain-smokers' throats.

Drawn up from garrulous chain-smokers' throats
at square tin tables on wet cobblestones
just hosed down by a green-clad African
street-cleaner: strikes, prices, who still votes
Left, sex, a sick child. Hands unbutton coats
halfway. The wind's mild, but it looks like rain
above the Place du Marché Ste-Catherine
where charcoal-bellied clouds converge like boats
in the mutable blue harbor sky.
Another coffee, another *blanc sec* —
as if events were ours to rearrange
with words, as if dailiness forestalled change,
as if we didn't grow old (or not) and die
as long as someone answered when we spoke.

As long as someone answered when I spoke
—especially someone walking a dog—
I'd launch into juvenile monologue:
Greek myths, canine behavior—and could I stroke
the Lab or spaniel? Speech and touch evoked
my grandmother, the bookkeeper from Prague
who died as I emerged out of the fog
of infancy, while lives dispersed in smoke
above the camps (and Dresden, and Japan)
and with them, someone else I might have been
if memory braided with history.
I pressed my face into the dog's warm fur
whose heat and smell I learned by heart, while she
receded into words I found for her.

Receding into words I found for her
delight, someone was dispossessed of her own
story (she thought) by mine.
                                        Receding in-
to words, the frail and early-rising neighbor
who died during my cancer-treatment year
is not summed up by "centenarian."
Her century requires a lexicon.
I wrote a girl on paper when I bore
a child, whose photocopied life became
letters tattooed across a watermark,
a woman's in the world, who shares her name.
And Gísela, who took me to the park,
for whom I pieced together sentences
— it's all the words she said to me I miss.

It's all the words she said to me I miss,
down to unechoed accents. Did she speak
Yiddish to me? With whom did she speak Czech?
German was what my father spoke till his
sixth year, first grade (when did he tell me this?)
— his parents' common tongue. And did they make
love in their second language? The air's thick
with cognates, questions and parentheses
she'll scribble down once she's back in her room,
chewing her braid, tracing our labyrinthine
fragments. She zips her anorak
and shifts the heavy satchel on her back
waching low clouds gather as she walks home
across the Place du Marché Ste-Catherine.

Not knowing what to thank or whom to bless,
the schoolgirl at the window, whom I'm not,
hums cadences it soothes her to repeat
which open into other languages
in which she'll piece together sentences
while I imagine her across the street
as late light shifts, sunlit, dusk-lit, lamplit.
Is there a yellow star sewed to her dress
as she exults, confused with gratitude:
her century requires a lexicon

of memory braided with history
she'll have reflective decades to write down?
Not thinking: she'll get old (or not) and die;
thinking: she can, if anybody could.

E L O I S E   K L E I N   H E A L Y

·

C H A N G I N G   W H A T   W E   M E A N

Turning your back, you button your blouse. That's new.
You redirect the conversation. A man
has entered it. Your therapist has given you
permission to discuss this with me, the word
you've been looking for in desire.
You can now say "heterosexual" with me. We mean

different things when we say it. I mean
the life I left behind forever. For you, it's a new
beginning, a stab at being normal again, a desire
to enter the world with a man
instead of a woman, and of course, there's the word
you won't claim for yourself anymore, you

who have children to think of, you
who have put me in line behind them and mean
to keep the order clear. It's really my word
against yours anymore in this new
language, in this battle over how a man
is about to enter this closed room of desire

we've gingerly exchanged keys to, and desire
isn't what's at issue anyway, you
say to me. Instead I learn a man
can protect you in a way a woman only means
to but never can, and this world is too new
when there's life out there, word

after word for how normal looks, each word
cutting like scissors a profile of desire —
a man facing a woman, nothing particularly new
or interesting to me. I've wanted only to face you
and the world simultaneously, say what I mean
with my body, my choice to not be a man,

to be a woman with you, forget the man's
part or how his body is the word
for what touch can contain, what love means.
If this were only about desire,
you say, I'd still desire you.
But it isn't passion we're defining, new

consequences emerge when a man and desire
are part of the words we hurl, you
changing how you mean loving — this terrible, final news.

·

CHANGING THE OIL

I get her up on the curb, two wheels off the street
and dive under with my tools — my favorite blue-handled
wrench and a drop-forged hammer with a no-slip grip.

Her, her, her — always the female car. And now I'm under,
lying on the news of the day before yesterday, slowly turning
the warm nut. She's above me like a womb or heaven
about to rain. I'm slowly turning my way into her
black blood, slipping on the wet bolt, diving into
the underworld we women crawl into with our new pride
fresh from the parts store. Turning the beautiful
implements over in my hands, tenderly
the oil spurts free — and I have done it.

·

LOUGANIS

If Praxiteles had been an animator, this form
is the one he would have set in motion —
a spinning diver hurtling down
toward the surface of a pool,
its smooth skin raised to ripples
by an automatic wind machine.

He'd sculpt Louganis like a beautiful machine
poised against the cloudless sky, then charge his form
with action — the rippling
muscles of the torso tensing with explosive motion

as the diver vaults, kicks out and plunges into the pool
where cameras follow him down,

a sheath of bubbles wrapping him, down
where applause is a watery blur, the machine
of celebrity waiting above him, the press pool
of reporters eager to surround, touch his form —
a boy-god, perfect in stasis or motion,
an athlete who could ignite any crowd, send ripples

of excitement through an arena, ripples
of awe around the globe, even after he stepped down
from competition. I saw him once, pure motion
in a dog show ring, his Great Dane puppy not yet machined
into perfection. Greg was the one all form,
perfectly balanced on his toes, emerging from a pool

of dog handlers as the star. Outside a swimming pool,
nobody recognized him at first, but ripples
of applause picked up, formed
a little cup of sound, then settled down
again as he was one of us, no machine
of glory, just a guy and his dog in motion.

That was before rumors of HIV set chaos in motion
and sports shows ran films of his infected blood coloring the pool.
Predictably, the story fed into the tabloid machine,
and the customary scornful ripple
of reaction to anybody gay threatened to drive his name down
from Olympus, but no bigotry could change the form

of his achievement, no machine of hate or ripple
of fear for his life could alter the timeless motion into a pool
of a beautiful boy falling down from heaven into perfect form.

WHAT IT WAS LIKE THE NIGHT
CARY GRANT DIED

Cary Grant was dying all that time
we took to talk about romance
and what little chance there is
to see on screen even the evening we spent,
talk and turn of events, how everything went
this way for the dyke singer and that
for the queer star, and what a funny
type we are, so normal in our taste
for bliss, but then there's the way
we kiss, unseemly on the screen
to see so much between two women,
the queen card played upon the queen.

And Cary Grant was dying until dawn
the night we carried on and on
about romance, the chances in a glance,
the votes we cast for whom we've asked
into our hearts' open beds. What was it
Dietrich said? No more talkative alive
than dead, that one, and who's to blame
for her closed case, the gorgeous face
that couldn't change its straight facade.
It would have been too odd to see
a woman in a pair of pants begin
her dapper dandy dance. An audience
would have died from it—the fragile pair,
the dalliance, the slicked-back hair.

The King of Romance drifted off from Iowa
and Hollywood the night he was to say
what it was like for him. The night he died,
that night we came away from talking until dawn
about the scenes and sounds that don't go on
the screen in living color of what's between
a woman lover and her lover.

·

FROM LOS ANGELES LOOKING SOUTH

Orderly traffic, a normal day
and 350,000 Salvadorians are in hiding
in Los Angeles.
Four women sit on the patio of El Rescate,
dirt packed hard from use.

Lydia's the weaver of this story
and two local women translate the Spanish,
pull the threads straight for me.

She has given this testimony for others
besides me. She's slight, simply dressed,
a former philosophy student, a suspect.

Her husband dead, her baby, living perhaps
with an aunt under another name.
Guernica again
hangs before us in the air
as the translators nod and check out
the current slang or a new word
from the war.

The sun is full strength
as I walk out onto Pico.
I take Lydia's testimony home,
stand out on my deck
and look south.

Down the hill, the banana trees
fan each other and two black dogs circle
in a fenced yard.
There are no people on the street
and cars pass like flashes of sun
through the pastel afternoon.

Not here, but somewhere else,
an incident in a field or at a gate
hatches the Guardia like flies.
The interrogation team changes tactics
to machine guns and disappearances.

Not somewhere else, but here,
the poem I am writing
already wonders about its worth.
I won't be shot for what issues
from the small house of my mouth
in this country of the tomb of language.

This poem will never need to lay a finger
to the lips of the person writing it
or head north
wrapped inside a bundle of my clothes.

MELANIE HOPE

·

SIXTH GRADE

I knew the dick size of every boy in my class,
my measure being how it filled my fist
when I squeezed it through their jeans. In return
I let them feel my tits,
among the biggest in the grade.
Some girls hadn't graduated to bras, but even they
were squeezing dicks. I, muscled tall and thick,
was known for being rough: boys feared me and hoped
I would be the one to conquer their dicks.

Our teacher had a pregnant wife. I would try
to imagine his dick, turning away whenever
my gaze locked with his ambiguous
blue eyes. I remember squeezing dicks
and flaunting tits, thinking
I must be learning something about love.

·

BARE FLOORS

The first time
I was on my back
On the stale basement floor
I didn't care that the foam mat
Had been rotting for months
The blood colored cloth draping it
Was home to pubic lice eggs
I just wanted his dick in me
To end this game
Be able to line up
With my friends again
Compare it to putting a tampon in
I didn't care when he left to pee
From all the beer we had shared
I waited with my pants

Bunched around my knees until
He came back proudly
Fingering his twenty-one-year-old boner
Ready now to stick it in
Steadily
Moaning my name
In a way I had never heard
In all the years
Through childhood we had played
I pretended not to care
When I slid from the foam
My coccyx bone scraping
The damp cold cement
I assured him it felt good
Everything
Trying to think of
Words to use on Monday
When I told my friends

ONLY DAYS

Of course only days after I meet you I am imagining
      ways we will make love
Of course we will sit opposite each other in staff meetings
      so no one will suspect anything resembling
      sexual tension has wedged between us
Of course you are married to some degree and have no intention
      of messing around
Of course for a while work will not matter
      we will come and go easily in our crushed-out bliss
Of course we will have days when we are sure
      everyone in the office knows what's going on
Of course I will try to like the things you tell me of your lover
      in an attempt to be open
Of course one day we will both call in sick
      and meet at a hotel near the airport to make love
Of course we will pay for the room in cash
      and leave separately fearing someone is watching
Of course no one is watching
      and we use this hotel every time we make love
Of course we will have lunch together every day
      and leave together at the end of the day

Of course I get jealous if you do anything
    with anyone else in the office
Of course people start expecting to see us together
Of course we will visit each other's desks
    to flirt as often as we can
Of course we will want to tackle and fuck
    right there on the gray coffee-stained carpet
Of course one day your lover comes to pick you up at work
    and I am forced to meet her
Of course I pretend I barely know you
    and avoid her eyes
Of course I notice how well she knows your movements
Of course she doesn't notice anything
    distinguishing me from the rest
Of course you try to call me that night
    while she's in the shower
Of course I don't pick up the phone
    and you don't leave a message
Of course you know I am there
Of course I know it is you who has just called
Of course it is Friday so I have two days to be without you
    and no plans
Of course you are without me too
Of course we don't talk about it on Monday
Of course I skip lunch together that day
    because I want to punish you
Of course I will try to fill my thoughts with someone else
    try to imagine a different body when I jerk off that night
Of course we will be naked together again
    but not as often as before
Of course you take this time of distance as a way back
    to your lover
Of course you want to get away from the lying and guilt
    hovering over everything we do
Of course I will help open the door
    that will free you
Of course I don't want to risk rejection
    by asking for more
Of course we won't ask for anything else
Of course you think things are better than ever
    with you and your lover
Of course weeks later we will flirt again and wonder if
    the other is thinking about making love
Of course we both are

•

I N R I *

This morning while waiting for you to wake
Wondering what you say to yourself
Inside your hollow sleep
I placed a pebble in each palm
Lay down on a plank of wood
My arms stretched out to my sides
My face to a relentless gray sky

I thought how each breath I took
Was bringing me closer to my final death
I thought of you and Jesus
Sharing a cigarette

You have me now so fascinated
By Jesus, blood, death
The fire you have walked through
I thought of this

I suppose by the time he died
He was hypnotized by the
Rhythm of his blood leaving
In droplets from his flesh

There was nothing holding my feet
So I continued to walk through
Thoughts, desires ruled by you
For a while wanting to be Jesus
But only because he intrigues you so
Maybe then you would tell me more of
The volcano that birthed you
The meaning you seek in death

As it is all I can do is plot a way
To sneak up on you
Tear your mouth wide open
Rescue words crouched inside

*Christian: Jesus of Nazareth, King of the Jews.
Pagan: She or he who has walked through fire.

I want them all
The ten-dollar ones
The forgotten ones
And of course the lonely desperate ones
That are so like you and me.

•

SACRIFICE

there was rain this morning
a mist sprinkling over our world
a slick coat like
a lizard's belly skin
that glistened iridescent
over oil patches
in the street

I thought of the morning you
I'd left in bed
weary atrophied
locked stiff in today's dream

at the bus stop I flinched
watching children dart between cars
crossing the street
and remembered how fearless
we too had been
leaving campus
on a mission to annihilate
sinister black-face jockey statuettes
relieve them from their
permanent position of servitude
smashing their skulls and right arm
we succeeded in conquering three
a sacred number we agreed

that was during the time
you'd only eat apples
which I thought was some sort of
overidentification with Eve
you said our next mission
would be planting trees

nine years have passed
and you still love apples
but the rabble-rouser in you is gone

knowing alone is more frightening
I cannot leave you
even when you don't allow me to touch you
and your eyes must struggle to see me
I deny anything
is really that wrong
because as reckless women
we fell in love
and as women we are taught sacrifice

I recall headless one-armed jockeys
we left on those Ohio lawns
what a comical trinity they would be
suitable only at an altar
in this grand circus whose tent
we can never escape
as it eats us from inside
insistent as a nematode
devouring ripe pieces of fruit

—◄ ✳ ►—

MICHAEL KLEIN

·

THE RANGE OF IT

I want to love my real father so he can see me.
I'm hiding from him in these trees that will bloom up on
Riverside Drive.

I've been hiding from my father into every summer
that I am born again and sometimes he calls from Germany
to sing happy birthday to (me) over the sea.
I actually love him more than my stepfather
(at least in the little show I wrote about them).

In the little show, the worst thing my father does
is marry again in a country he has to switch languages for.
But I can never find my father fully. He leaves so many
false clues like bread crumbs into Düsseldorf or converted money
falling from a bag.
The way he loves me is like the way you remember money—owing
it to someone.

This morning he called to say he wants America again—teach high school
maybe in New England. And the way he says it it's like someone owes it
to him—someone owes taking him back into his dream
back into American trees, American afternoons.

There was an afternoon made of my father once
when I stayed with a football in the shadow
of the American tree and wouldn't play
because it was boyish and loud without music—an afternoon
a gender couldn't contain a tow-headed boy. And my father
recognized me not as the product of love
but the range of it. And turned away.

·

THE TIDES

The motel pool wasn't flat as safety.
It gleamed like a twisted muscle
under an operating room light
in Oyster Bay. 1966. I'm fourteen.
From my room I hear a machine buzz at night
through the smell of chlorine.
I don't know what it does.
I lie in bed imagining it forces the gravity
into the water to keep it from flying
over the fence into the miniature golf course next door.
I'm with my parents.
It's the first summer I want sex.

I hate my father's sunburned lips
on his Camel cigarette, stuck there
until he gets mad and starts cursing, and I come
out of the sun-drenched daydream of men done in
by suntan lotion, sliding off their lounge chairs
like otters. They have to flex every muscle
just to stay put.
They make me think of the goldfish
sunlit without minds, in the dizzy water
of my great-aunt's old pond.
We're here to see her, but we don't much.
It would mean my parents couldn't fight.
At least in the motel room they have the freedom
to move through fragments of their private life
or stage their anger with alcohol or Librium. I don't care.
I want sex. I am no longer their child. I am in
my non-child body and I want the pool guard
to come to me through the buzz of the machine
in the dark, after my mother's last pill
has been swallowed, after the smoke
from my father's rage of mouth is gone,
after the abbreviated apologies
because it is too late to explain what brought
them together in this life.

Sometimes the pool guard winks at me
the way you'd wink at someone too blond from life
against the light that falls on a landing, and you have

to wink by mistake, just to see.
And every day, sliding off my chair,
I notice his cock like a goldfish trapped
in latex, as if it were separate from his life.
He can't imagine that I can know
passion or feel safe in the sinewy strength
of his swimmer's arm
wrapped like a golden ring around me, pulling me
to land, water falling from the non-child body
into the saving life.

.

LETTERS FROM THE FRONT

Because we are doing better
than I am doing, these letters East and North
invent a God I can pray to.

I am sending the part of my life that burns
through the parentheses you left me in.

Dear X, one letter begins,
the ocean is an upheaval of green we saw it once
turn over during Vietnam. The clouds tonight are black
as oil spills. That's the difference between the two wars:
a way to talk about clouds.

Or: Dear X, I miss breaking the fast with bread
we both touched. P.S. The ghost you left can't dance
so I went to a meeting of people who want to be loved.

Love comes to us, it seems, after our rage at
not being God leaks out.

Dear X, have we insisted yet on that, for more
than being lowered into life like two angels working
on the steeple? two angels who still smoke?

Someone said what was hard
about two men together was the ramming. Don't laugh.

We are goats pumping iron, lost in a fire of bells.
Then we are men working in studios and labs on a new world order.

One letter begins: Dear X, I am working on a new world order.
It goes backwards to just before we ever saw into
the blossom of fission of Japan. With you,
it is hard to fully suffer the atrocious.

Did you know it cost 74 cents to mail a rock?

I wrote in white paint across one: my heart
is strong enough to go through this. And this is no different

than writing on paper. Sometimes these letters have to speak
to something cold.

One letter ends: you came to me in a dream and said:
"after we pray . . ." And I said: "we teach."

.

GUARDIAN LIFE
FOR BRIGID CLARK

Mostly, we try to keep it from happening
with a simple line or circle of ourselves
a ring of healing.
Or at the highway crashes
the sobering procession of cars;
cops who walk the tightrope
of a bridge to keep a suicide
from taking whirlpooling light
down into water: part our habitual vigilance
over the unthinkable, part the need to guard life.

And I suppose experience anchors one
to form. But it is form anchoring me
to experience today:
an insurance sign in the sky
spells GUARDIAN LIFE
and underneath it a crowd
has loosely converged at the escalator
at Grand Central Station
where a boy has managed to lose a boot
in the space where the step disappears.

God, how those faces
at public accidents become suspended
as though between worlds,
as though having human faces
is the outcome of witnessing
what could be lost
to an undertow of human essence
we never see, a kind of under-spell
that suddens the human form, by leaving it.

I think if it is us,
we keep each other alive
by being attentive, knowing how the stories
we carry sometimes open wide enough
for anyone to fall through.
And despite the spaces that can take us
we live
more human around the circle
we leave open
even if it's as ghosts already
who take a breath in this world
and let it out in the next.

·

SCENES FOR AN ELEGY

I haven't learned to live abandonedly yet, Mother,
  and wonder, when I dream of you, if I'm meant to,
and if there's such a thing as light going on
  without us — or if we die into what I think
we do: something finished
  that we're just adding *us* to.

On the morning of your addition, the moon set
  behind a beaded curtain in an after-hours bar
and my hands were on the shoulders of a stranger as
  you were choking on a glass of milk that threw
your body into my sister's settled arms. My body
  was spending life like borrowed money, thrown
on a bed, and what made me queer — apart from sex —
  was the in-spite of booze that made Berryman a poet.

13 years away from that have given me
  intermittent dreams and in the one where
I float in the point of view, you are walking
  in a summer dress down 11th Street, asking me what I love,
or if it matters, or if I *am* loved. And I am, Mother,
  loved as much as the spread-fan quality
of how it is given, when the threads of friendship take
  precedence sometimes over *what* I love — when passion
for a thing changes with a kind of lazy strike,
  outside of passion, into someone else.

How strange it always seems
  knowing these two scenes are
merged on an axis: your death, my life that morning
  countersunk into the morning you were lowered
in a coffin strangers had to buy — when my imagination
  put you in a grand piano and shook
the awful coffin-light into shivers of grace
  then made you dead again — shoved,
like a doll my sister outgrew, into a box.

When is sex anonymous? When is death?

⊰✿⊱

WAYNE KOESTENBAUM

·

TEA DANCE

"Young men always expose themselves to me on Amtrak.
 Am I so plain that they think I can't refuse?
Fire Island is a shadow of its former self.
 The days I miss, when men jacked off on stoops
Along Christopher Street: I didn't have to get dressed
 Or leave my building to find a trick." Thus spake
My hairdresser. After I dreamt that Darjeeling tea
 Was synonymous with genius, I tasted
The word *tea* for days, mystified. Then I remembered
 Tea dances: the dance I stared at a swarthy
Mesopotamian stele of a man and felt
 His member in the bathroom. These are the fleet
Radiances I return to when I swim in the lane
 Made tempestuous by the thrashing freestyle
Of a man whose laps I time with mine so that we meet,
 As if by accident, at the side, and stare
At each other through blue goggles. Will I behold him
 Languidly soaping his ass in the shower
As if I'm not watching? I always watch. I don't wrap
 My towel around my loins, but parade between
Sink and toilet with abandon: the stalls have no doors,
 So I observe in the mirror, while combing
My hair, a Professor Emeritus. How I love
 The sight of genius striving to defecate!
In the Japanese tea ceremony, the seating
 Mirrors the cosmos: my tea ceremony
Takes place in memory—my mother's Constant Comment,
 My silent father shunning tea for Sanka.
Threat of hysterectomy hung over my childhood
 Like a cloud of locusts—wasn't my mother
Always on the verge of one? Why does sapless mint tea
 Bring me back to my father's vasectomy?
Am I morbid to return in imagination
 To the place where I began—the ligaments
And chambers of my father's reproducing genius,
 His genitals a kind of feudal guild hall,

Good pewter on the table? On Boston's underground—
    The T—a young man who asked me for the time
Pressed his leg against mine between Government Center
    And Copley stations—a recuperative
Idyll. Like a shady priest, or mesmerist, he drew
    A holiness from me, without saying his name.
Krafft-Ebing grotesques are now my domesticities,
    What I see in the mirror. My hairdresser:
"In the smoking car, a cute boy—scandalously young,
    Maybe thirteen—played footsie with me, and when
Lights flickered and went out at New Haven, he flashed me
    And played with himself. I tried to look kindly.
I didn't want to discourage his professional
    Ambitions, so early in the boy's career."
As a boy, I stayed after school to discuss revolt
    In the colonies—the Boston Tea Party—
With my history teacher: I hoped he'd seduce me.
    I wore jeans that rode low, a shirt that rode high,
To trick him into forgetting morals. But I lived
    By the light of this theology: the hands
That caress Mozart's limpid phrases cannot also
    Touch cock. Did my father—shy in his boxers,
His urinating a remote rill in a far room
    I was barred from—encourage this chaste belief?
Do I think that the tea leaves would have told differently
    If my father had invited me to watch
His toilette, if he had taken me into his bath?
    I once vowed that if I grew into a full
Adult male I would spend my days before a mirror
    Marveling that I had passed over Jordan,
And had not been left, a eunuch, on the other shore.
    My body has become the body I thought
Was a distant, desired star, but this has brought no change.
    My best friend from high school is still my best friend:
Then, our favorite joke was the man in Emergency
    With a carrot broken off in his rectum.
It's been years since I saw my friend nude in the boys' gym
    We now admit to each other was a place
In which we willed our members down by thinking of death.
    How much more gripping our lunches might have been
If, over bologna, I had said to my soul's twin:
    "Did you notice that Coach Wasserman's penis
Seems waterlogged, inhumanly long, like a dildo
    Or the kind of apparatus a sex-change

Patient dreams of acquiring? Did you notice how red
    And juvenile Craig's prick looks? Like a crayon
With its paper wrapper, a foreskin, worried away.
    And Robert's is like a cougar's lolling tongue!
He beat off in his clubhouse to the tune of his dad's
    Jazz singles and porno playing cards that showed
Cotton candy pubic hair." I gave my best friend bites
    Of my sandwich every day: my mother piled
Meat generously, his mother gave only one slice.
    Would it have ruined the universe's plans
If we had touched each other, or discussed at leisure
    The parts of friends, or if I'd said: "My father's
Is not so enormous. I am not frightened by it.
    It has the guilelessness of the animals
God loves the best. What is your father's like? Will you grow
    To match it? It's nice having something to live
In anticipation of, like a cadence that haunts
    The first movement, though it happens in the third.
If we were to touch, what would be our first position?
    I certainly couldn't put yours in my mouth
Unless you washed it first. And what about geometry,
    The proofs we were assigned? I'll prove that the point
Of prayer is exactly this, though your youth group leader
    Would disagree: this longing is the reason
Ancient Greece is justly famous, and why the vases
    Possessed me in the museum — not the jade
We were required to study, but the huge erections
    Of the gods — oddly uninviting, like spears,
Or the toothpicks with which one seizes cocktail hotdogs.
    Brave Bull — the bowling alley — might be a good
First place to try: brave men have drilled peepholes in the walls
    Between toilet stalls, and if you're shy you can
Watch the kaleidoscopic panorama of men
    Passing your window, even if you don't
Scrawl your intentions on a square of toilet paper
    With a Bic pen and pass it to your partner —
Like square dancing, or bridge, a ritual you can learn.
    I love being hypnotized. Am I a good seer?
I am trying to be a clear medium through which you
    Can hear the past speaking as it wished to speak.
May the trance never end. This is how I feel when tea,
    Mystical Darjeeling, rinses out my sight
So I can see the heartache in the center. Is this
    Truly the past? It's not as dark as you said —

Not as gloomy. Are you sure I'm not in the present?
    Look down at my body to reckon if time
Has altered it. Did you see Kevin's penis standing
    At half-mast? What turned him on? The wrestling match?
I think I will grow up to be an expert on flesh,
    I gaze at it so. My penis has blossomed
To the size of a small doughnut because I played it
    For too many thrills last night, watching Popeye
When my parents were gone. It's not that I thought Popeye
    Was erotic, but I had to watch something,
I had to fill my mind with images. Images
    That plague me now will turn to paradise
In twenty years. I must have patience. The stalking men
    Will rise from comic strips, like dead from their graves,
And plant my mouth with kisses. I am not alone here:
    Listen to the water. This is a trance,
But when I wake I will know everything that has passed,
    And what I am dreaming now I will turn
Into daily life—and though in this childhood I can't
    Talk out of turn, I will never stop talking
In that future where it is eternally my turn."

·

FROM EROTIC COLLECTIBLES

1977

This is how I learned
arts of suction, how stars
and comets of ancient sway
fumbled for preeminence

in my still adolescent body:
at the library
I interrupted *Paradise Lost*
to use the lavatory.

Hole between the stalls afforded
a view of my first man:
the archetypal divinity
student. We walked

through unearthly foliage
to his neo-Bauhaus
fascist-era dorm.
Down went our pants.

He had only one ball.
What happened to the other,
ghost ball? I stayed
until dawn, came home with guy taste

in my mouth, wondered
if my straight bunkbed mate
would sense my new
uncomely fellatio aura.

Was I aglow?
Was I visibly fallen?
This night had been
necessity, not pastime.

Burning, I revisited the trick
one numinous evening.
"I've got spring fever," I said,
justifying perversion

with the comforting old saw.
I wore Lee overalls.
Swashbuckler, he undid them.
"Enfold me, Satan," I thought.

By day I snubbed him;
only at night could I admit
I wanted to lie
naked and hoovered in his bed.

He had no extra flesh;
I remember his Irish
spareness. Now
you may be dead, my ethereal

initiator, you who led me
through foliage.
Each gesture was an accident.
No mythic embroidery

surrounded us, only
the story I am telling now:
the last time I saw you
I was drifting in cowboy boots

through the immense white
mystery of Garden Street,
my Bartók score
within a gloved hand,

sun against the already
fallen snow so unnaturally bright
I thought I was walking
toward catharsis —

my trio rehearsal at the block's end.

1980

Sedans cruised past our bench,
overrun with vines,
as if this were the backyard
scene of *Sunset Boulevard,*

checkered by mishap and design:
absolute darkness
and brightness, a Manichean night.
He was pre-med, I

was pre-nothing: empty,
I sought the stars
in any street tramp's eyes.
The flatterer glozed,

"You look like Sal Mineo."
He meant waif;
he meant the stoics.
He was lying, or drunk,

and I became his disciple.
Yet when this innocuous
boy in a blood-red bomber jacket
wanted, for one night only,

my body, wanted my companionship
or my semen, wanted me
to want to stroke his
particulars, I decided VD

was a good alibi.
I took the name of disease
in vain. I lied: "I think I have VD."
If I woke the next morning

to sores and strange discharges,
would it have served me right?
Through his jeans I sensed
size: glimmering fish-sway.

My recently cut hair
had borrowed a Roman seriousness.
"Who are you?" he said
to my marble head,

heavy on my shoulders.
Unattainable, shorn, I was
Antinoüs, the morally
compromised boy, the fiasco,

the miscalculation.
So far I'd slept with twenty men.
I wanted to reach fifty
by spring. I doubt

I ever made it to fifty,
unless you count brief, silent
trysts in which the passionate
parties don't speak or touch—

interstellar episodes,
unsigned, pagan;
for example, the mimed
romance that began

when, at a revival theater,
I absently traced
my index finger—semaphore—
along my cracked lips,

applying imaginary Max Factor.
It was January 1980 —
the world was stealthily
moving into epidemic,

and I was innocently
writing about the separation
between "word" and "emotion"
in the early poetry

of Ezra Pound, a thesis due the Ides of March.

1992

One man's dick had the quaint
malleability of Gumby —
and a Cheops eminence.
It was a private

theatrical. I smiled
at the melodramatically
self-exposing man and he
smiled back — intimacy

via mirrors in the men's room!
I'd made a friend
amid the dream's bulrushes!
There was no temporality,

no progression, no drama:
only teeming, succulent sight.
The proffered dick
in question was, naturally,

my childhood friend's: Dougie's.
It had the same hotdog quiescence,
the same look of threat.
Meat-colored, it stiffened —

a revolutionary
Gorgon or papyrus, veined
and brought out of pants
with a sensation of surprise

attack and anticlimax.
So one acknowledged
the penis but also said goodbye
to it, ignored it, nourished

no reverence. These men
were postcards; they wore
an arty stillness.
My chest's short wiry hairs

never converged
to form a general picture.
My terse pectorals
had a breast look. In the hollow

between the mounds
a saint's medallion hung,
to ward off injury.
You understand that in the dream

I was a timorous youth,
no nimbleness informed
my sexual conduct.
Outside, time's cataract cascaded,

and the weird tiled eternity
of the basement, the dive,
continued, a travelogue
I can't transfigure.

This was my vision.
These were the exposures
that lit up my night.
I saw the naked men,

I was one of the troupe,
and now I am telling you
about their tendrils, anatomies, smiles.
My never-to-be-fathomed men come here

to unzip their pants
and show me their message,
their lullaby,
their ghost story—

whose haunted ending never shifts.

—≺✲≻—

JOAN LARKIN

·

HOUSEWORK
FOR M. W.

Through this window, thin rivers
glaze a steep roof. Rain: a church of rain,
a sky—opaque pearl,
branches gemmed with rain,
houses made of rain.

I am in the kitchen
killing flies against the cabinets
with a rolled-up magazine,
no Buddhist—
I live by insisting on my hatreds.

I hate these flies.
With a restless wounding buzz
they settle on the fruit,
the wall—again, again
invading my house of rain.

Their feelers, like hard black hairs,
test the air, or my gaze.
I find I am praying
Stand still for me.
I'll devil the life out of you.

The human swarm comes in
with wet leaves on their sticky boots.
They settle on me with their needs; I am not nice.
Outside, headlights of dark cars are winding the street.
The mirror over the sink will do me in.

At five o'clock, rain done with, in darkness
the houses gather. In the livingrooms
Batman bluely flickers; the children all shut up,
all but an angry baby or a husband.
The suburb is wreathed in wet leaves.

I forget what I wanted. Was it old music
laying gold-leaf on the evening?
lamplight sweetening the carpet
like honey from Crete? a dream of/door to Egypt?
Something to do with the life force.

December turns the sky to metal,
the leaves to gutter-paper.
Leak stopped, the bedroom ceiling starts to dry.
Its skin of paint is split and curling downward.
There is a fly in this house that will not die.

.

ORIGINS

It was a party; I had on my party dress.
There was something wrong in Grandpa's friend's throat.
I kept him waiting outside the bathroom
while I read *Mother West Wind "When" Stories.*
When Mama yelled at me to *Make it fast,*
I wiped. I flushed. I came out on the landing
holding the blue book behind my back.
His lighted cigar was the red eye of an animal.
He reached a hand up—big, spotted like an animal—
under the short skirt of my party dress.
I felt pleasure, and I felt afraid of the hand.
Nice girl, he was smiling,
and the red eye shook and smelled like a cigar.
This was at the top of some stairs—
what house was it?
Were there stairs on Westminster Avenue?
How little was I? I remember. Little.
I said, *Mama, the man touched me.*
No, she said. She was worried
about the party; she was serving
a tray of green things and pink things.
She explained the facts to me quickly.
No, she said.
The man is a nice old man.

BEATINGS

They beat me different ways.
My mother was standing
in her light summer suit and hat.
She was late; it was my fault.
She was almost sobbing. A cord
was twisted around her breath,
an animal trying to escape
from her throat. Her knuckles landed
hard on my shoulders, in my ribs and guts.
Her face was close. She was yelling,
yanking me by the hair, and I saw my brother
standing near us in the hall, watching.
Standing and forgetting why he was there
watching and what he liked about it.

I was younger. I think we were all there,
four or five in the kitchen, father home
for supper between shifts. He lifted me
over his knees to hit me. Belt,
brush, or his large hand came down
open and steady on both buttocks, burning
and stinging through thin underpants,
big voice in control, saying *This
is for your own good. This
hurts us, This is because we love you.*
I cannot remember my crime, only my face
against his knees. His hands, his strong
voice telling me I was loved.

When the man beat me later
in the bed in Brooklyn, the kind man
with big lips and hands, the man
who loved me and beat me
with the same voice, when years later
in the same bed, the thin woman with tattooed
wrists told me I couldn't receive
love, thrusting the dildo till I was
sore and crying *Stop*, she laughing,
shouting I couldn't love her—
it wasn't true. I loved the rising
of their voices—his dark, steady one,

sure, in control, and her demented one
rising like my dead mother's wild voice.

·

GOOD-BYE

You are saying good-bye to your last
drink. There is no lover
like her: bourbon, big gem
in your palm and steep
fiery blade in your throat,
deadeye down. None like her
but her sister, first
gin, like your first
seaswim, first woman
whose brine took to your tongue,
who could change the seasons of your cells
like nothing else.
Unless it was wine, finally
your only companion, winking
across the table, hinting
in her rubies, her first-class labels,
of her peasant blood
and the coarse way she would open you.

Good-bye, beauties. You don't want to say it.
You try to remember
the night you fell out of the car
and crawled to the curb, the night
two of you stood
screaming over your daughter's crib.
You remember deaths
by gin, by easy capsules—
the friend who fell in silence
and the friend who quoted *Antony* in his suicide note.
All this helps for a moment, till your heart
blooms and stiffens with desire.

INVENTORY

One who lifted his arms with joy, first time across the
      finish line at the New York marathon, six months
      later a skeleton falling from threshold to
      threshold, shit streaming from his diaper,
one who walked with a stick, wore a well-cut suit to the
      opera, to poetry readings, to mass, who wrote the
      best long poem of his life at Roosevelt Hospital
      and read it on television,
one who went to 35 funerals in 12 months,
one who said *I'm sick of all you AIDS widows,*
one who lost both her sisters,
one who said *I'm not sure that what he and I do is safe, but*
      we're young, I don't think we'll get sick,
one who dying said *They came for me in their boat, they want*
      me on it, and I told them Not tonight, I'm
      staying here with James,
one who went to Mexico for Laetrile,
one who went to California for Compound Q,
one who went to Germany for extract of Venus' flytrap,
one who went to France for humane treatment,
one who chanted, holding hands in a circle,
one who ate vegetables, who looked in a mirror and said *I*
      forgive you,
one who refused to see his mother,
one who refused to speak to his brother,
one who refused to let a priest enter his room,
one who did the best paintings of his life and went home from
      his opening in a taxi with twenty kinds of flowers,
one who moved to San Francisco and lived two more years,
one who married his lover and died next day,
one who said *I'm entirely filled with anger,*
one who said *I don't have AIDS, I have something else,*
one with night sweats, nausea, fever, who worked as a nurse,
one who kept on studying to be a priest,
one who kept on photographing famous women,
one who kept on writing vicious reviews,
one who kept going to AA meetings till he couldn't walk,
one whose son came just once to the hospital,
one whose mother said *This is God's judgment,*
one whose father held him when he was frightened,

one whose minister said *Beth and her lover of twelve years
were devoted as Ruth and Naomi,*
one whose clothes were thrown in the street, beautiful shirts
and ties a neighbor picked from the garbage and
handed out at a party,
one who said *This room is a fucking prison,*
one who said *They're so nice to me here,*
one who cut my hair and said *My legs bother me,*
one who couldn't stand, who said *I like those earrings,*
one with a tube in his chest, who asked *What are you eating?*
one who said *How's your writing? Are you moving to the
mountains?* who said *I hope you get rich.*
One who said *Death is transition,*
one who was doing new work, entirely filled with anger,
one who wanted to live till his birthday, and did.

·

MY BODY

Throat puckered like crepe,
right hand throbbing with arthritis,
right hip permanently higher than left, right leg shorter
after years of books slung from one shoulder.
One breast smaller, both sagging like Grandma's,
shriveled around the nipples,
upper arms lumpy, veins in legs varicose,
back freckled from sunburn when I passed out on the beach
in 1964,
face creasing, still breaking out, hairs bristling from bumps
I didn't start out with,
nose pitted, burst capillaries on nostrils,
two extra holes pierced in the left ear so I'll never forget
those months with Sido — thank God I refused the tattoo,
two vaccination scars,
shoulder stiff from fracture in 1986 when I fell on a stone
floor at Cummington,
skin dotted with — what? moles? age spots? melanoma that
killed my father?
sagging belly, testament to fear, dieting, birth, abortion,
miscarriage,
years of fighting booze and overeating still written in my flesh,
small cysts around labia, sparse pubes — not yet like my head

full of gray that first appeared the year I had two jobs and pneumonia.
Eyes needing bifocals now, no good for driving at night,
still blue and intense, tired but my best feature —
or maybe it's my hands, strong, blunt, with prominent veins.
Lungs still wheezing after years of asthma and smoking,
all of me still full of groans, sighs, tears,
still responsive to the slightest touch,
grief and desire still with me
though I hardly ever have reason to close the curtains,
naked fool for passion —
and wonder if I'll live alone the rest of my time in this body,
my old friend now,
healed and healed again,
still walking and breathing,
scars faded as thin silver signatures.

•

LEGACY

When my mother finally left her body
it was mine to keep
along with her ring,
some blackened silver,
a box of Jewish books.
At first I though it would be a difficult fit
but here a tuck and there a seam let out
and you'd swear it was made for me.
My freckled throat,
creased stomach,
soft, white hips —
even my thoughts at 3:00 a.m. are hers.
I'm lying here in her body!
She doesn't miss it,
she likes the way I look in it,
winks when I feed it her favorites.
Sunday I'll walk down the aisle at my daughter's wedding
and the thin breasts in gray silk
will be my mother's. Veins in sticky hose,
bunioned feet in shoes that match the dress —
more and more will be hers.
I'll walk past the narrow eyes of those who doubt me
safe in my mother's armor —
faux-pearl choker and stiff, glittering clasp —

as their whispers weave around me
my face wearing her little smile,
her scared eyes shining in triumph.

·

COLD RIVER

My mother disappeared in a shoddy
pine coffin in the rain
while my brother complained of its cheapness
and one aunt whispered
as I took my turn shoveling
in black clothes and shame.
Before that, she disappeared
in a useless body we fed,
lifted, tortured, four months.
Suddenly the house was full
of thin, rose-painted china.
The valuable ring she'd kept
where they couldn't steal it
felt loose on my middle finger.
The day I phoned from Shelburne,
the nurse whispered to me,
Now her legs are weeping.
I was resting from her long dying.
Mother, I said. I'm in the cabin.
I can hear you — twice
she dragged words to the surface.
I can't forget that voice.
It was my first. The bitter
edge I hated as I grew wild
was the only weapon of the woman
who called me *Daughter.*
Now it's a current in me
like the cold river
I take grief swimming in.

⋅❈⊱

MICHAEL LASSELL

·

KISSING RAMÓN
FOR RAMÓN HODEL

One kisses Ramón goodnight on Bank Street in the Village.

At the corner, the bank is expanding into the bookstore, and Ramón tells you about the poet laureate of the Philippines, who lives right down the street, on Greenwich.

Sometimes the kisses are long and deep, and there are passersby.

Sometimes one grows hard almost instantly.

"Shut off your fucking engine," the policewoman bellows through her bullhorn.

Bullets.

Sirens.

Sometimes his ear is ice on one's flushed cheek.

A fat man in a tight jacket turns the lights of his van on from a block away.

Masculine Principle No. 1 (Urban)
All men must own a car. All cars must have alarm systems. All alarm systems must make intrusive electronic noises whenever activated or deactivated, no matter how obnoxious this may be to one who is trying to cheat the dark of its tariff (insomnia) by falling asleep before midnight realizes what's happened.

Masculine Principle No. 1 (Rural)
Insert the words "pick-up truck" for the word "car" above.

Masculine Principle No. 2
One kisses Ramón and wonders about the moisture that lingers on one's lips and in one's mustache, despite all published evidence that kissing, even

deep wet sloppy kissing, is relatively safe. But what is safety in this day and age?

One wipes away the saliva, feels guilty, brushes one's teeth, feels guilty, masturbates, feels unfulfilled, falls to sleep, is wakened by:

Men's voices: angry shouting.
Women's voices: hurt, weeping.
Intrusive electronic noises.

Mice running in the walls; rats warring in the walls.

Screaming in feminine French.
Screaming in masculine Spanish.

"Shut off your fucking engine," the policewoman bellows through her bullhorn.

You think you'd like to swallow bullets: soft, sweet, deadly.

Sometimes one touches Ramón's ass just for luck, like Buddha's belly.

Masculine Principle No. 3
Ramón buys baklava at a deli on Ninth Avenue. One waits with Ramón in the cold for the Abingdon Square bus. One mentions the death of a mutual friend. Ramón explains his life on Planet Positive, his fear of death, his anger and denial. Speechless with grief and without experience, one still feels a need to respond.

Sometimes one feels Ramón's cheek and it's soft as sifted flour.

Kisses.

Bullets.

Sirens.

•

HOW TO WATCH YOUR BROTHER DIE
FOR CARL MORSE

When the call comes, be calm.
Say to your wife, "My brother is dying. I have to fly
to California."
Try not to be shocked that he already looks like
a cadaver.
Say to the young man sitting by your brother's side,
"I'm his brother."
Try not to be shocked when the young man says,
"I'm his lover. Thanks for coming."

Listen to the doctor with a steel face on.
Sign the necessary forms.
Tell the doctor you will take care of everything.
Wonder why doctors are so remote.

Watch the lover's eyes as they stare into
your brother's eyes as they stare into
space.
Wonder what they see there.
Remember the time he was jealous and
opened your eyebrow with a sharp stick.
Forgive him out loud
even if he can't
understand you.
Realize the scar will be
all that's left of him.

Over coffee in the hospital cafeteria
say to the lover, "You're an extremely good-looking
young man."
Hear him say,
"I never thought I was good enough looking to
deserve your brother."

Watch the tears well up in his eyes. Say,
"I'm sorry. I don't know what it means to be
the lover of another man."
Hear him say,
"It's just like a wife, only the commitment is

deeper because the odds against you are so much
greater."
Say nothing, but
take his hand like a brother's.

Drive to Mexico for unproved drugs that might
help him live longer.
Explain what they are to the border guard.
Fill with rage when he informs you,
"You can't bring those across."

Begin to grow loud.
Feel the lover's hand on your arm
restraining you. See in the guard's eye
how much a man can hate another man.
Say to the lover, "How can you stand it?"
Hear him say, "You get used to it."
Think of one of your children getting used to
another man's hatred.

Call your wife on the telephone. Tell her,
"He hasn't much time.
I'll be home soon." Before you hang up say,
"How could anyone's commitment be deeper than
a husband and wife?" Hear her say,
"Please. I don't want to know all the details."

When he slips into an irrevocable coma,
hold his lover in your arms while he sobs,
no longer strong. Wonder how much longer
you will be able to be strong.
Feel how it feels to hold a man in your arms
whose arms are used to holding men.
Offer God anything to bring your brother back.
Know you have nothing God could possibly want.
Curse God, but do not
abandon Him.

Stare at the face of the funeral director
when he tells you he will not
embalm the body for fear of
contamination. Let him see in your eyes
how much a man can hate another man.

Stand beside a casket covered in flowers,
white flowers. Say,
"Thank you for coming," to each of several
hundred men
who file past in tears, some of them
holding hands. Know that your brother's life
was not what you imagined. Overhear two
mourners say, "I wonder who'll be next?" and
"I don't care anymore,
as long as it isn't you."

Arrange to take an early flight home.
His lover will drive you to the airport.
When your flight is announced say,
awkwardly, "If I can do anything, please
let me know." Do not flinch when he says,
"Forgive yourself for not wanting to know him
after he told you. He did."
Stop and let it soak in. Say,
"He forgave me, or he knew himself?"
"Both," the lover will say, not knowing what else
to do. Hold him like a brother while he
kisses you on the cheek. Think that
you haven't been kissed by a man since
your father died. Think,
"This is no moment not to be strong."

Fly first class and drink Scotch. Stroke
your split eyebrow with a finger and
think of your brother alive. Smile
at the memory and think
how your children will feel in your arms,
warm and friendly and without challenge.

•

BRADY STREET, SAN FRANCISCO
FOR ROBERTO MUÑOZ

The apartment
is still standing, still about to fall.
It's circled now in Technicolors of
competing graffiti
more artful than we were to

stay in love.
Our names in cement are long gone.
It's my first time back since the news.

From the street
nothing seems to have changed.
My mind, too, has trapped the action in mid-flight:
how I hid in the closet (naked) the
first morning your family descended unannounced
and told your father we'd had
balls for breakfast when my Spanish slipped on
eggs. You shot your
one-note nasal laugh and spun on your heel,
but I'd cracked the shell of tension.
Your mother sat on the couch —
a miniature goddess of plenty, her feet
not touching the floor — and adopted me
in her knowing smile.

Here's a junk drawer more of memories:
an orange cat that lived through an air-shaft fall;
the Twin Peaks fog from our bedroom window bay;
snacking on Stevie Wonder and your skin;
the double mattress we had to carry home
from the Mission on our backs because
it cost every cent we'd saved.

After the first fight over nothing, you
slammed into the street. I screamed
from the third floor into the dark I'd
die if
you didn't love me; you cried and
crept back up the stairs creak by
indolent creak.
We stayed together.
That time.
And when the loving was over —
three years, two apartments,
and a continent later —
no one died. Not
altogether. At least not
right away.

We left behind the odor of queers in the carpet,
the grease from our last
cooked meal,
a hole I punched in the plaster with my anger
and covered with the *Desiderata* so
the landlord wouldn't howl.

You see, it only takes a score of years
to make the bitter memories sweet,
like lemons in a sugar glaze.
I'd eat an orchard of them for you now
if you could be alive again to see me try.

·

SUNSET STRIPPING:
VISITING L.A.
FOR SWEET WILLIAM HILL

I'm sitting by the pool at the Mondrian
Hotel with Elton John's backup band.
The pigeons are making metallic click-
clicking noises on the aluminum ladder
into the deep end of the aqua dogleg.
The sun is swollen, like a cotton ball
at the back of a night-table drawer.

Barnet's directing two new sitcoms (one
for each of last year's Emmys), but he
starts to cry over his cantaloupe because
his brother-in-law, age 26, died of AIDS
over Labor Day weekend. His wife has
taken her grief indoors, devotes herself to
childrearing and interior decoration. We
decide the mantel is inches short but
quite wide enough for the dining room.

Betty and Terry throw a party and everyone
shows up—
except for Michael, whose lover died on
Sunday;
Bill's a day out of UCLA, where he's on a
new drug study;
Barry's doing a film on AIDS for Columbia;

HBO killed Gerry's.
Paul was nominated for a National Book Award
but he's got KS now, so
Winston wants a tattoo but is worried about
Jewish burial.
And everyone loves the would-be mayor—
who woos
the crowd with his smile—and eats caviar
and cassoulet.

Richard thinks I need to take charge of
my life. Oy! He's on disability, so sees
me at home, a tight-assed white condo in
West Hollywood. The advice is all right.
His lips are pale, like Connie Stevens's
on 77 *Sunset Strip*. It's a color I've
seen before, as if AZT were a glass of
milk one drank instead of Scotch. If I
move back, and if he lives, he'll see me
again, fees to be donated to the AIDS
support group of my choice.

Rocco and Heidi fly out for the opening
at the Taper, a play about AIDS and angels.
In the dressing room, Joe is exhausted,
wants to wear a sweater, to walk in New York
fall. It's the same dressing room Franklyn
used for that Orton play before he moved
back to Brooklyn and died. The full moon
is swollen, like the Eucharist dissolving
in a plate of indigo wine, or a drop of
grease dissolving in a cold cup of Bold.

My new tattoo itches. But it's a wing,
of sorts, so I assume it just wants me
to fly—and I am in such desperate need
of flying. Of flying and of flight.

•

THREE POEMS

1. *For Anthony*

The Hudson is angry, white-capped, splashing
on the rocks by the garbage dock. Under
its surface, the river is calm, moving
with the certainty of centuries — as
when Hudson sailed his *Half Moon* into the
full mouth of the unknown waters and sank
into legend: Thunder? The crew at ten
pins. The river was born before the land
I live on was a swamp the lost natives
hunted for food, and will live as long as
it's immune to the human virus. At
one, the phone rings, the moment Anthony's
funeral begins at the Algonquin.
Gray today. There's thunder, but no lightning.

2. *Photo*
FOR J. CLARK HENLEY

Here, at the bottom of a box at the
back of a drawer: a photo of Clark in
a graveyard standing by a stone. It bears
his family's name, as does the style of
shirt he's wearing. Was he sick already
when this was taken? I forget. His wry
eyes look out over the bushy mustache
that left wet traces on my lips. Here, on
the wall near a small kitchen: a Palm Springs
photo of Clark in a frame I bought in
the Catskills. Remember how he kept his
vast collection of children's books in the
upper cabinets in lieu of food? I
remember, Clark. Eight years. I remember.

3. *Ramón*

Regie tells me he *thinks* Ramón is dead.
In fact, he knows, but sidles into the
news to soften the blow. "Yes, I believe

he passed away," he says on the phone—passed—
in August (when Terry died and Steven,
who looked so ashy pale and thin the last
time I held him, his hair a hint of the
thick curls I'd lusted for). So there is no
more kissing Ramón, who slipped from my life
into hospitals and family, a
nephew opening in the Manila
Miss Saigon, the book I lent him a gift,
as it turns out, tendered with guilt and a
longing they've seen before at St. Vincent's.

·

GOING TO EUROPE
FOR MY FATHER

I'm going to England. And France.
I'm going to England and France tomorrow with
my father, who is 80 years old—
for two weeks on a bus. Don't ask why.

We've both been to England before. And France.
We've each been to places the other will never go
and we've both been to other places in common—
to Berlin, for example:

I was there before the Wall was torn down;
he before it went up—an open city.
When my father was in Berlin he sold black market watches
he brought back from Paris under the Brandenburg Gate.

I was cruising men in the park and was threatened with arrest
by the East German guards at the Brandenburg Gate
and brought back crabs to Paris.
(It was a different kind of concerto.)

When my father was in England, he was the same age
I was when I lived there—more or less. Five years.
My father went to England to make the world safe
for democracy; I went to get away from him. And her.

When my father was in England, he was waiting to see
if he would get home alive; I was learning to be who I am—

gracelessly. When my father was in France, he was learning
how to get off Omaha Beach without being killed;

I was missing Clark at the Musée d'Orsay
and trying to get Luc to fall in love.
My father was successful.

We both have vivid memories of Normandy
(beaches strewn with bodies). We both remember
bunkers sunk in the sand bluffs.

In my father's day, they were wet with German blood.
My mother's parents were German. They died the same year
my father was in England. And Germany. And France.

Next week, we'll both be back in Normandy,
my father and I—where I fell for Luc as he played piano
and sang in the foyer of a Norman-esque hotel.

A thousand years ago, some Normans left this coast
and went to conquer England. Some of them eventually
became the ancestors who eventually became us,

a father and a son both named for a Jewish émigré from England—
and for the angel of Mont St. Michel. Soon, we'll sleep in its shadow
in a second-class tourist motel. In the aftermath of dawn,

we'll climb the medieval mount—slowly, breathing heavily
in concert—as the golden angel who gave us our names
starts gleaming through a fog (as thick as Whistler's pigment)
from his perch atop the abbey spire, flying close to the sun.

We'll sleep in the same room . . .
Tomorrow, in London, we'll sleep in the same room alone
for the first time in our lives. I will be alone with my father
for a full day and night—fourteen times.

The first time we were alone all day we went to see
Ben-Hur at Radio City Music Hall. It was 1959. I was 12.
I was in love with him. The next time was in Palm Springs.
It was in the '70s or '80s. I forget.

By then, he was a bit in love with me—or in awe.
When I was a child, he used to beat me.

I used to think it was because he hated me.
He used to think it was because I was misbehaving.

We were both partly right. We're not close. We have nothing
"in common"—but he's my *father*: The need to be a Good
Son hasn't died just because he was angry when he was young,
swollen then on the same rage that runs and ruins me now.

So we're going to England together—and to France—
and we're both looking forward to it. I don't know why.
Maybe now that we're both old, we can love each other
for two full weeks without hating each other at all.

TIMOTHY LIU

·

VOX ANGELICA

I sing to a breeze that runs through the rafters.
A woman skins a snake. She turns
but not enough for me to see her face.
In the sink, the peelings have begun to pile up
in a mound the color of dirt.
She hears the oil hissing on its own
and thinks of throwing something in —
ginger, garlic, chopped rings of green onion —
but doesn't, lets the oil brown
until the smoke rises
and fills the dark corners of the kitchen.
The birds tonight are louder than ever
perched beside a river of flying fish.

*

The sweat on her feverish face
dissipates, flying upward
to God as she clings to the shoulders
of death, her feet touching
neither heaven nor earth.
They say death has a nobility of its own
but all she could hear was weeping —
not entirely a human sound
but a sound as if made by a machine
that played again and again
like a tape she could not erase.
She tried to explain the sadness,
the leaves changing to a color
she could no longer describe.

*

The hour of the Bible is dead.
Neither dirt nor flowers
can keep her body warm enough.
Driving from the service,
I keep my hands on the wheel

as if steadying myself
the way silence holds each word in place.
I imagine lying down next to her
as earth is sprinkled over our eyes,
our mouths filling with dirt.

*

The angels are singing
in the shadows of the house,
night a black cat sitting on my chest,
claws extended toward my face,
the scar on my body
a witness to that place where the world
had once been opened, muscle
and blood. How a vision
pinned me down until my scream
reached two worlds
on both sides of the glass.
Everything happened twice
in the cat's eyes,
the slow engine of happiness
seducing me back to sleep.

*

The words I speak I cannot revise.
All art is an afterthought,
an attempt to interpret a dream
that by its nature is perfected,
the bed unmade, and me almost late
to my next appointment where more of me
must get cut out. The horror
of getting beyond the skin,
the small white aberration that I dreamed
would not grow back, not enlarge
to fill my entire conscious body.
I think of how the mystics read
by the light of their own bodies.
What a world of darkness that must have been
to read by the flaming hearts
that turn into heaps of ash on the altar,
how everything in the end is made
equal by the wind.

•

MAMA

If I had known this burden on my tongue,
would I have refused the first syllable
she taught me in the garden? *Ma. Ma.*
It would take me years to make any new
distinctions: *milk, truck, book, clock,*
facets to a glass house I was trapped
inside, until one day, that great stone
of marriage fell from my mother's hand.
Such freedom gave me grief to visit
her poorly lit efficiency across town,
the streets I had to name in order
to get there: *Dogwood, Cherry, Orchard Creek.*
It grew more difficult. She moved twice
in a week before the county moved her
behind buzzered doors and wired glass
where a sign still hangs: *Closed Community.*
Good Sam hospital was too new for maps.
A voice on the other end of the line,
impersonal as God, helped me get there
before explaining how an unnamed man
went down from Jerusalem to Jericho
and fell among thieves who wounded him,
leaving him half-dead, how a priest and Levite
spat on him while a certain Samaritan
dressed the open wounds with oil and wine,
gave up his own beast and left two pence
for the host at the inn. I marveled
at such buildings named after the nameless,
how as a college freshman, I sat in Franz Hall,
understood at last what Mother said to me,
her *poverty of content,* a kind of *word salad:*
I dreamed he had folded six times. Jesus
said the sheep he called would make one fold.
I thought at the time the Latin for six
is sex, that the number of the beast is 666.
Is sex then beastly? All people have eyes.
These blind people are led about by a boy.
One can hear too much. It took me years to turn
from Adler, Skinner and Freud back to the Good
Samaritan's words: *whatsoever thou spendest*
more, when I come again, I will repay thee.

Mama, the debt incurred from just one word.
Locked up for twenty years, only syllables now
for what we left unspoken: *rage, shame, guilt,*
everything you taught me from the start.

·

THE SIZE OF IT

I knew the length of an average penis
            was five to seven inches, a fact
I learned upstairs in the stacks marked 610
            or HQ, not down in the basement
where I knelt behind a toilet stall, waiting
            for eight-and-a-half inches or more
to fill my mouth with a deeper truth. The heart
            grows smaller, like a cut rose drying
in the sun. Back then I was only fourteen,
            with four-and-three-quarters inches
at full erection. I began equating
            Asian with inadequate, unable
to compete with others in the locker room
            after an icy swim (a shriveled
bud between my fingers as I tried to shake
            some semblance of life back into it).
Three times a day, I jacked off faithfully, yet
            nothing would enlarge my future, not
ads for vacuum pumps, nor ancient herbs. Other
            men had to compensate, one billion
Chinese measured against what? Some said my cock
            had a classical shape, and I longed
for the ruins of Greece. Others took it up
            the ass, reassuring in their way,
yet nothing helped me much on my knees at night
            praying one more inch would make me whole.

READING WHITMAN IN A TOILET STALL

A security-man who stood, arms crossed, outside
the men's room (making sure that no one lingered)
met my eyes with the same dispassionate gaze as
a woman inside, kneeling to clean the toilets.

The faintly buzzing flicker of fluorescent light
erased the contours of a place where strangers
openly parade their sex. Efficient, silent,
all ammonia and rubber gloves, she was in and

out of there in minutes, taking no notice
of the pocket Whitman that I leafed my way through
before the others arrived. *In paths untrodden, /
In the growth by margins of pond-waters, / Escaped*

from the light that exhibits itself—how those words
came flooding back to me while men began to take
their seats, glory holes the size of silver dollars
in the farthest stall where no adolescent went

unnoticed. O daguerreotyped Walt, your collar
unbuttoned, hat lopsided, hand on hip, your sex
never evading our view! how we are confined
by steel partitions, dates and initials carved

into the latest coat of paint, an old car key
the implement of our secret desires. *Wanted:
uncut men with lots of cheese. No fats. No femmes.
Under twenty a real plus.* How each of us must

learn to decipher the erotic hieroglyphs
of our age, prayers on squares of one-ply paper
flushed daily down the john where women have knelt
in silence, where men with folded arms stand guard

while we go about our task, our tongues made holy
by licking each other's asshole clean, shock of sperm
warm in our mouths, white against the clothes we wear
as we walk out of our secrets into the world.

STRANGE FRUIT

Spray-painted across a garage door.
No names to attach to the crime.

No cause for alarm—some lesbians
returning home to find their cats

still hanging from a coat rack
in the entry hall—Holiday's muted

voice echoing through the house
on that CD player left on repeat.

JAIME MANRIQUE

·

TARZAN

When I was thirteen
there was in my hometown
a man we called Tarzan
because of his build.
An outcast in Barranquilla
infamous for preying on youths
Tarzan wore T-shirts
that bandaged his torso;
he swaggered down the street
like a Pied Piper who could
lure boys like me
and ruin us.

Late in the afternoons,
when the *amapolas* gashed
dusk with their scarlet
and the honeysuckle
infused the hour
with its sweet languor
Tarzan appeared
on my street
announced by the catcalls
of the neighbors
hiding behind their blinds,
calling him names,
which he shook off
like a macaw, after preening,
shakes off its down.

Every afternoon I read
in a rocking chair
waiting for that moment
when he'd appear,
my heart beating so fast
I'd place an open palm on my mouth
as he strutted

a defiant animal
singing the song of perdition.
Not once did he ever look
in my direction
though he must have known I was there
because I felt the heat
of his ways —
a tongue of fire singeing me.

I was repelled by Tarzan
by his daring,
his cat eyes that bored
into my soul —
as a bird with a burning beak
spears the heart of a flower.
I was afraid Tarzan would expose me
for what I was —
someone like him, someone
who craved the touch of men.

Thirty years have passed
since that time.
I'm writing in a cabin in the woods
on top of a white hill.
It's been snowing all day
and I look out my window
through gleaming icicles.
Though Tarzan does not appear
on my ghostly street
the longing I felt then grips me
reminding me of the pull of the flesh
bringing back memories
that still brand me
after all these years.

·

MY NIGHT WITH FEDERICO GARCÍA LORCA
(AS TOLD BY EDOUARD RODITI)

It happened in Paris.
Pepé asked me over to dinner
to meet a guy named Federico

who was on his way to New York.
I was nineteen years old.
Federico was eleven years older
and had just finished
a relationship in Spain
with a sculptor
who had been rotten to him.
Federico only had two lovers —
he hated promiscuous queens.

We were both Gemini.
Since astrology
was very important to him,
Federico took an interest in me.
We spoke in Spanish.
I had learned it
from my grandmother, a Sephardic
Jew, who had taught me
sixteenth-century expressions.
Federico was amused by all this.

We drank a lot of
wine that night.
In the morning, when I woke up,
his head lay across my nipples.
Hundreds of people
have asked me for details:
Was Federico fabulous in bed?
I always give them my standard answer:
Federico was emotional
and vulnerable: for him,
the most important thing wasn't sex
but tenderness.

I never saw him again.
The following day he left for England
then New York and Cuba.
Later, the second love
of his life was murdered
defending the Republic.

All this happened in Paris
almost sixty years ago.

It was just a night of love
but it has lasted all my life.

.

BAUDELAIRE'S SPLEEN

All this fall
traveling on the Metro-North
along the Eastern shore
from Vermont to D.C.—
the leaves
have been turning for months;
soon the trees
will be bare,
their flushed leaves
covering the welcoming earth.

Today the train
passes by bronzed cornfields
and the rushing world
is a glowing canvas
that does not warm me.
An unshaved young man
sitting next to me
and writing in his notebook
awakens my curiosity.
He's like a matinee idol
of another era—
a young Leslie Howard.
When he's absorbed
contemplating the fiery landscape
I glance at his notes:
"Finish reading the Baudelaire poem?"
he's written.
Which Baudelaire poem,
I wonder, and why the question mark?
Underneath this line he's added:
"Radio Shack—fractals."

My love,
since September
after a cold, pluvial summer
my days and nights

have filled
with nostalgia for our future.
Neither you nor I
is like this youth
whose life is just commencing.
He has whole realms
to discover:
poems by Baudelaire
that will make him wonder
more than all the mysteries
of Physics.
And he'll love—
if he hasn't loved yet—
and he'll suffer;
and if Fortune's kind to him,
he'll ride this train
on many occasions
until one day,
just as I do, at the end
of this autumn
of glad melancholia,
he, too, will travel
toward his loved one,
toward arms and lips
that are an earthly home,
toward his future,
a continuum of shared lives,
until one day
he'll arrive
at an unknown—but familiar—place
like one of those Baudelaire poems
to which we return
years, lives
after having visited it
for the first time
when the future seemed limitless
and we could hold all our past
in a cupped hand.

To this youth
I say:
all this will pass
someday.
This autumn

our love
this city I travel to
this yearning for knowledge
and truth
these lines
will pass;
you and I
will pass
as the train passes
over these tracks
across these fields
of fallen leaves
and these blue skies
that remind me of your eyes
and all the icy-blue stars
that bloom at night;
and all my thoughts
great and small
and my dreams
and his and yours
they, too, will pass
until no onc remembers them
except the memoryless earth
that feeds and replenishes
and prevails
after youth and love
and history
—and even Baudelaire's poems—
are no more.

·

BARCELONA DAYS

Soon it will be twenty years,
and like the tango says, that's nothing.
And the burden of memories we've
accumulated since then—
that's nothing either;
what's heavy, too heavy,
is disordered flesh,
the wrinkles of the spirit
no surgery can remove.
Maybe your monuments

have grown old. But the patina of their surfaces
is nothing compared
to the collapse of my illusions.
Today I live just to live,
and what's left of yesterday's illusions
is in poems, blurred memories,
letters that pierce us like knives.
Recently, walking the streets,
I've recognized in passersby
the faces of my dear dead:
Andrés, Mike, Douglas, Luis Roberto,
reincarnated in a gesture, a lock of hair,
a Chabrolesque frame.
The man I was yesterday,
and soon it will be twenty years,
I can't remember.
I see him, the other Manrique,
a hero in a postwar novel,
a classic, a myth
forever repeating itself.
Today I am a foreigner
writing lines filled with nostalgia
for times when I didn't love either,
wasn't happy, wasn't even myself.
Sometimes, recently, when I ride
the subway,
it's as if I were traveling
through the circles of hell.
And I know that though I live
I am dead, that only in death,
perhaps, Barcelona, I'll walk
your boulevards again,
looking for him, with his eternal moaning,
trying in vain to fill in the squares of a crossword puzzle
that grows large
and larger
and more uncertain.

—translated by Edith Grossman

J. D. McCLATCHY

·

MY MAMMOGRAM

I.
In the shower, at the shaving mirror or beach,
For years I'd led . . . the unexamined life?
When all along and so easily within reach
(Closer even than the nonexistent wife)

Lay the trouble—naturally enough
Lurking in a useless, overlooked
Mass of fat and old newspaper stuff
About matters I regularly mistook

As a horror story for the opposite sex,
Nothing to do with what at my downtown gym
Are furtively ogled as The Guy's Pecs.

But one side is swollen, the too tender skin
Discolored. So the doctor orders an X-
Ray, and nervously frowns at my nervous grin.

II.
Mammography's on the basement floor.
The nurse has an executioner's gentle eyes.
I start to unbutton my shirt. She shuts the door.
Fifty, male, already embarrassed by the size

Of my "breasts," I'm told to put the left one
Up on a smudged, cold, Plexiglas shelf,
Part of a robot half menacing, half glum,
Like a three-dimensional model of the Freudian self.

Angles are calculated. The computer beeps.
Saucers close on a flatness further compressed.
There's an ache near the heart neither dull nor sharp.

The room gets lethal. Casually the nurse retreats
Behind her shield. Anxiety as blithely suggests
I joke about a snapshot for my Christmas card.

III.
"No sign of cancer," the radiologist swans
In to say—with just a hint in his tone
That he's done me a personal favor—whereupon
His look darkens. "But what these pictures show . . .

Here, look, you'll notice the gland on the left's
Enlarged. See?" I see an aerial shot
Of Iraq, and nod. "We'll need further tests,
Of course, but I'd bet that what *you've* got

Is a liver problem. Trouble with your estrogen
Levels. It's time, my friend, to take stock.
It happens more often than you'd think to men."

Reeling from its millionth scotch on the rocks,
In other words, my liver's sensed the end.
Why does it come as something less than a shock?

IV.
The end of life as I've known it, that is to say—
Testosterone sported like a power tie,
The matching set of drives and dreads that may
Now soon be plumped to whatever new designs

My apparently resentful, androgynous
Inner life has on me. Blind seer?
The Bearded Lady in some provincial circus?
Something that others both desire and fear.

Still, doesn't everyone *long* to be changed,
Transformed to, no matter, a higher or lower state,
To know the leathery D-Day hero's strange

Detachment, the queen bee's dreamy loll?
Yes, but the future each of us blankly awaits
Was long ago written on the genetic wall.

V.
So suppose the breasts fill out until I look
Like my own mother . . . ready to nurse a son,
A version of myself, the infant understood
In the end as the way my own death had come.

Or will I in a decade be back here again,
The diagnosis this time not freakish but fatal?
The changes in one's later years all tend,
Until the last one, toward the farcical,

Each of us slowly turned into something that hurts,
Someone we no longer recognize.
If soul is the final shape I shall assume,

(—A *knock at the door. Time to button my shirt*
And head back out into the waiting room.)
Which of my bodies will have been the best disguise?

·

LATE NIGHT ODE
Horace, IV.i

It's over, love. Look at me pushing fifty now,
    Hair like grave-grass growing in both ears,
The piles and boggy prostate, the crooked penis,
    The sour taste of each day's first lie,

And that recurrent dream of years ago pulling
    A swaying bead-chain of moonlight,
Of slipping between the cool sheets of dark
    Along a body like my own, but blameless.

What good's my cut-glass conversation now,
    Now I'm so effortlessly vulgar and sad?
You get from life what you can shake from it?
    For me, it's g and t's all day and CNN.

Try the blond boychick lawyer, entry level
    At eighty grand, who pouts about the overtime,
Keeps Evian and a beeper in his locker at the gym,
    And hash in tinfoil under the office fern.

There's your hound from heaven, with buccaneer
    Curls and perfumed war-paint on his nipples.
His answering machine always has room for one more
    Slurred, embarrassed call from you-know-who.

Some nights I've laughed so hard the tears
    Won't stop. Look at me now. Why *now*?
I long ago gave up pretending to believe
    Anyone's memory will give as good as it gets.

So why these stubborn tears? And why do I dream
    Almost every night of holding you again,
Or at least of diving after you, my long-gone,
    Through the bruised unbalanced waves?

•

FIRST STEPS

1. 1946, 1957
How to put this exactly? I mean without
Hurting those who've known me long enough—
From long before the start, let's say—

To think what's called "hurt" is confined
To episodes at hand and waved aside,
The sky darker, more like itself again,

After the tracer's hairsbreadth giveaway.
And at the same time, without forgetting
What was left in the dark, entrenched,

The cold sweat of others' knowing rubbed
Off like earliest memories. Theirs,
I'm told, are of my refusing to take a step,

Backing across a roomful of women (my father
Was away at war), then crawling, crabwise,
Toward, or against, the half-foot drop

Onto the porch where they'd wait, the women,
The Member of the Wedding downturned
On my mother's knee while she clapped.

That is their memory. Mine is from the next year.
My birth had given my father the "points" to send him
Over the top, demobilized from sea to the shining
Jersey shore, to the women in my grandmother's house,
And me, the firstborn at last. One ear gone deaf
In enemy fire, his head would have been cocked
For his new comrade-in-arms' syllabic babble.
He liked to carry me shoulder-high, my legs locked
Around his head, hands in his hair. The infant Judith
Might have been so portrayed, pilasters instead of pier,
Her gaze intent on the future. Simple-minded revenge,
Like betrayal, at the heart is calm as a broadsword.
And I was screaming. *That* is my memory. It was when
He walked into the surf, as into a tent at night,
His head dipping, pretending to spill me, laughing.
The bladebright breaker. The loosening grip.
It's then I remember screaming. Both of us knew,
Or thought later, it wasn't the water. Years later
He said, "You *never* trusted me." That cannot have been
True, because it still is not, old general idea.
Your hold is playfully tight to this day. No,
It must have been the water after all, its sharp
Command and penitent sucking, the mocking foam.

This country's wars come in decades. One later,
After a summer in camp, flagpole to fireside,
I'd fallen for my counselor. His name was Red.
He slept during naptime and could be watched—
The namesake stubble, the sweatband, the upstart
Nipple, a dream's drool on his chin. That he seemed
Not to care for me at all, lined up beside me
For letters, mine from my mother, his from a girl
(Her snapshot was taped to the shelf over his bunk),
Became the secret I'd whisper to myself. The first
I'd kept. Or not that, but lying on a log, under
The cabin as under a shelf. The lake shone.
Then glittered with frog-spit.
                              I kept that too
From Father Ayd during open-air confessional,
And learned to live in sin, though not in embarrassment.
What I kept to myself was one thing. What others
Could see for themselves, another. Sheepishly
I'd take communion. But I stuck it to the roof
Of my mouth, like a stamp from the Vatican, then wet

And unpeeled it into a shell I kept in my footlocker.
It was a time bomb. My grandfather, who had died
In the arms of a memory of himself, a captain
At the Meuse, had replaced the detonator with a clock.
I kept it hidden, wound, ticking against the time
I was forgiven—what? The fight against the self?

August was home again. The sins told over and over
In the dark, I wrote them down, transfigured
Into a self-knowing tone, letter-perfect to Red—
Then in lines of his own as a freshman at UVA.
They told tales on the camp cook, made up new endings
To stories he'd read at bedtime, and told my own,
Of "*boring* people" on the beach, of the impetigo
Scare, the drowned lifeguard. I never mentioned
My parents, that I had any, anyone else but whom
I'd cast out for his amusement, embarrassed by them,
As by this thin wafer, this thick wave, between *us*.
I'd given up hope to his long silence when one day
Two letters arrived for me. His "Hi, kid!" was one,
Under three Greek letters. "Gee, it was great
To hear from you, and all those funny stories.
Well, back to the grind." Lines, I thought, loaded
With feeling, to be read between tomorrow, not now.
The other was from the Ukrainian cook, more of the same
Warm misspelled gush she'd served up at camp.
My parents had "sampled" that on Parents Weekend,
So it was read aloud, to sniggers at precociousness.

And Red's? Red's was casually rushed to the beach
And buried, on a line with the pier and lifeguard shack,
So I could overturn the hourglass sand anytime
I cared. A day passed to show I didn't.
Pleasure postponed is redoubled in eternity,
The nuns had taught. Each imaginary grain—
Running, prickling, that much further, now
Closer—was. Each sentence, committed to memory,
Given a new gesture of gratitude at being dug out.
If sleep came, it came like three fraternity brothers
To say I'd been chosen too. Red. Hazing. It was dawn
When I woke. The tides had changed guard.

Love is up and about on tiptoe, the back steps,
Boardwalk, beach. Shells, empty-hearted homes,
Had washed up on maps of seaweed. I made for my X.

I look back on myself, as from my father's window,
Digging through a panic. How could I not
Have put it exactly? Each square circled twice,

Who'd put his trust in secrets kneeling there,
Fistfuls of sand thrown away on nothing,
Myself thrown down, away on the water.

2. 1871

Chasing on the margins of pond-waters, the sun
Then dips the sweet flag's quill into his mouth.
Glume and gloss, concentric drawls of whitebeard
Unspool around the stalk, its lazy hours widening
On a leaf, now shoreward drawn, and drawn up
By the boy there, the new contract, this America.

"Intense and loving comradeship, the personal
And passionate attachment of man to man —
Which, hard to define, underlies the lessons
And ideals of the profound saviors of every land
And age, which promises, when recognized
In manners and literature, the most substantial
Hope and safety of the future of these States . . ."
America, then, as the place for this idea,
Closest because last discovered to the original,
The slip of fate. If we are angels unable
To fall, who move among tragedies unmoved,
We are Nature's first democracy. That estate
Precludes the claims of property, the thicket
Brambled with caprice, prick of father's blood-right,
Family's subsoil of exclusion, the accomplishing
Tribe, its branches and departments of hollowness
At heart, the organization of desire
And its hoopsnake political mythologies.
What have Americans to do with these?
Fitly born and bred apart to make
Their acquaintance with sky, air, water,
The quibble of dew on history's low relief.

Original relations. That is the democracy,
Sublimity in repose, slow cloud, hard clay.

The eye's devotions, the pond face to face
With the cloud's wet cargo in the hold
Of spirit, open to itself and to what passes
On it, unfinished as our idea has been.
So the eye of each man is on himself,
As once on the vast inland sea un-islanded
By others. The first desire is this silent
Communing. If we blink, or put off
A quiet providence, the cloud becomes a pillar,
A quaver, the mill and helpmeet, the law
Of the land. Conventions are what we make
Of them, the brood and license of example.
The past is a parent's myth, that pyramid
Built on capital, monopoly, and fear
To the ruling point that stares from a dollar,
The hungry child's eye. Myth sets
Rivals on, its dominion over time by division
Of space, men and women driven by death
Toward crisis or idolatry. Now the future
Is unloosed from that stage, those masks,
From the usual pleasures of those who do not
Believe in men. Income of its own accord,
Authority in itself, our democracy
Entrusts us to you, and him, and her,
Each ready to hand. And what is our care?
The breath gone into us. The air's caress.
Democracy is a sexual system, a secret
Society, the underground in each self,
All outcroppage cut back to eye and root
That stay, equal with the earth, to start
Again the idea of ourselves in this place.

Let us say the idea is where it belongs.
If still tentative, then gripped by purpose.
If humiliated, then buried deep in a ground
That does not sicken, in the sour peat-damp.
Let us say it is the wound under a compress,
A bullet-hole torn through the lung.
In the division hospital, a rank of young braves,
Mutilated boys, and our shy animal, a farmer's
Son, his frame naked, a coolness alert

In his limbs. By the pallet, a man takes down
A letter home, holds his hand, tousles his hair,
Sings the homemade music of friends passing over.
Flesh made word, the great poem of death is being
Written, underlying life, leaping time
That had wrecked them both together. O metaphysics!
What proves the democracy but soul and solitude?
The mind builds them to itself, then imagines
A nation of orbs in the free paths of heaven.
That touches a man closest. He will not let go
The boy's hand, even to put it at rest.

From the cat-eyed upper story windows
The Capitol's dome seemed to brood on
An old baffled romance. He's turned back in.
Somewhere the sun makes a western settlement,
Heat-thunder giving stamp to the prairie,
To the bronzed pond tilting toward the boy,
Armor out of the old books, advancing,
To a score of straw-colored psyches circling
Some everlasting there. A horse blanket up
Around his knees, and the lamplight speculating
In its own oil, he's bent to the last leaf.
"I can conceive such a community. . . ."

3. 1971
"What do *you* think?" The question my head
Had hit against for weeks. Where, I wanted
To know, was *it* at? The Health Service's
Ten Free Sessions, as if help were a home-trial
Vacuum, was the first question—along with Will,
The interne I was assigned to, a turtlenecked
California blond, young enough—a kid!—to trust
And condescend to at once. Rehearsed, reticent,
Those first fifty-minute hours soon gave way
To long-distance calls that seemed to reach
An answering machine, its taped instructions
Androgynous, parental, the buzz both static
And signal for a message to be left.
                                        What?
"What do *you* think they want?" But wasn't
The point what *I* wanted? Wanted to say?
The welling point, shipwrecked on the verge
Of eyes fixed on Will, was made in sputtered

Remorse code: DON'T LET ME . . . DON'T LET ME GO.
That did the trick. That was what I'd wanted,
To be thought a special case, better than Lowell,
A real life study, feelings not just historical
But intractably unnatural. (I was in the slough
Of a dissertation on the confessional poets
Whose hearts, those instruments of experience,
Were made blunt in verse. Or at my typewriter.)
Will agreed. Supervisors were consulted, action
Recommended, the visits extended. A pipe
Appeared. This would "take some work."
It did. I found his car in the lot, his address
In the hospital directory, glared at the backseat
Baby-bucket, and parked outside his complex.
Years before, I'd persuaded my parents to build
A swimming pool so I could change with my desires.
I was used to waiting, breath held off the deep
End, the uplit bodies diving over me. Will
Came home later, paler, his wife once flapped
Out a sheet, my car stalled. The sessions, too.

Getting the story out was hard, but at last
He opened up. His father the crossroads tyrant,
His younger brother the actor (later to play
Luke Skywalker), the time a new baby takes . . .
I drew out each grief, each grievance,
The understudy disaffection a patient ear
Makes the leading man. I hated myself
For doing it, fascinated by the curl another's
Story, like pipe smoke, takes around currents
Of sympathy, how anyone's secrets open the window
An inch. Had he ever . . . ? He *had*? Oh yes,
California. Do you want . . . ? We made a date.
He'd phone next week. The transference was complete.

By which I mean—the call soon came—I was
Transferred to another doctor, a graybeard
I couldn't afford. I called my father to cover
The fees, on trust, breezing through the reason.
(A year later, coming out to a pre-echo of "we know,"
I was told this doctor had telephoned, to cover
His fee, and told why. That silent wave my father
Had carried himself through—how long? Dear man.)
We sat for our face-off, the reason less clearly

Discernible beneath the shade of diplomas over him.
His nickname was mine, his surname what I wanted
To be—*Schreiber*. That desire up front, we plunged
Back, back to . . . a happy childhood.
How I hate to disappoint, and zero in on anything
To accuse. The time I screamed at my grandmother
Not to watch me change. The turd in the linen
Closet—will that do? An account of Red—*yes?*
No. Silence is a chapfallen look, a writer's
Imperative. The more I tried to please, the more
I grew convinced it wasn't a choice—like pleasing—
But a discovery. And his, not mine who'd always
Known what I wanted, and wondered now at earlier
Choices. They all seemed right, if unforeseen.
At prep school, the Jesuits had offered one:
Science or Classics, as if a syllabus for life.
At sixteen, there was no hesitating between
The knife and the verbwheel, its tombola spin
Of voices, declensions, conjugations, exceptions
To the rule of its own momentum. Through its little
Thumbed cardboard window I could see the future
I imagined was an iron cot behind a Chinese screen,
An Oxford text propped on the scraped oak table.
There was everything to recommend it but a body.
I was told to recite Homer aloud, between spoonfuls
Of applesauce, in the basement—what was that
Meant to hide? Not a taste of sealife, but the fact
That metaphor enlivens loneliness. The body is literal.
Wasn't that what Achilles came to know, came to grief
Upon? I slumped in my chair.
                                        And on my barstool perch
Of eager nonchalance, boredom paired with bashfulness,
To pick out, those nights, beneath the revolving disco
Balls of facets, trick spots and flanks of stop-and-go,
A possible evening star who'd highlight by daybreak,
So help me, an end to fast and loose routines
Stunningly echoed underfoot by the thud—or therapy—
Of mindless concentration, the contact high of someone
Else's Rush, the umpteenth blast of jungle drums
Or "Smarty Pants," the sinking feeling of having been
Here—was it called Plato's or Circe's Cave?—too often.
The floor was full of them, bodies, the cavaliers
In designer jeans, busy at their job of being new
By flaunting it, stuffed into the glamour of types,

Dropout honcho, wasted dopehead, a guardsman
With advanced degrees, each partnered by the trance
He'd turned himself on to. Into that corral (*Whistle*
Siren   Wail) a black magic voice is luring
So much beef on the hoof, their flickering, slow-motion
Flail of dream-sex, fist and heel, heads thrown back
To the promise of more. ". . . What you've been waiting for."

More what? What did *I* think? The waiting
Seemed interminable. All that small talk
While a fantasy hurriedly undressed was getting
Nowhere. I told him so. He wasn't choosy.
"Rejection especially tells us what we want,
Now doesn't it?" What I wanted was a body,
My body, not the versions of it here or there,
Neither the fear, as if under water too long,
The last breath wrung bubbled to break
On the arching image, nor the trembling
Under a sheet, but a body that feels itself
In the world of men, a weight that bears.
My draft on Lowell was done. The bar as well
Had been raided. Heart racing, I walked out
Of the office into a sudden heat. The news
Was being delivered up and down the street.

4.
The spirit sets about its task, but slowly,
Preoccupied with theories of itself:
Escaping trace element, the doll-mother
Propped on the god's knee, the careworn case
All the samples are in. Take this first one.

A baptismal dress, laid out now on the couch,
Its bobbined, spreading family tree of lace,
The stains of storage and ceremony the same
Color as the weak tea served after I,
My father and grandfather before me too,
Had worn it. What of that first water
Of belief? A golden-rule chrism is poured
On it, and candles lit to make such
A light no evil can see its way into.
"Infantile sexual researches," could
They begin there, once the senses are cured
In soul? The pediatrician had warned

My mother, the analyst later reminded me,
Of what are called hydraulic pressures,
The up-and-down of desires satisfied
At the cost of long-drawn-out helplessness—
As if there were some amniotic preference
To hug the shore than chance the open sea,
To watch the waves undone to a ruffle of froth
Around my feet. My feet . . . I was past three
Before I learned to walk. Dandled and fed,
I sat in her lap, the performing self
Who, as they say, had a vocabulary—
Petal and *oar*, *bubble* and *wand*, each
Dipped into the font of her approval,
Each come at last to be submerged in what
It was, my belief, my whole erotic life.

Like a letter pushed under the future's
Door, that dress can be packed back up
In the case. Pull out this Venetian mask,
A character called Sintomo, and assume
Beneath the marbled-paper complexion
His phalloid nose, his leering eye-slits.
A disguise both mocks and abets whatever
Power wants to pretend is right. The mercurial
Thief steals not to have but to be
Something, his stolen goods a fantasy
Acted out, consumed, controlled by
A self in love with its own images
Bent to the glass where he makes
Himself up, prodigal of conscience,
Outsider "I" of the poem. I ought to know.

And here, shabby as a carpet slipper, is
My old dog-eared Selected Auden. St. Wiz!
Subdued to what you worked in, the foiled
Caresses from which thought is born.
Look to its motive, you taught, and not
The choice love makes. The bald giant
On the runway, whose name is always Need,
Picks at random, his makeshift eye,
His mouth that gives the lie to another
Tongue, his homespun heart worn to rags
On someone else's body—anybody's.
Love builds its house on sand, on ordinary

Swoons and unworthy objects as gladly
As on the motherland with its ricks and sheds,
Or the glided idolized imaginings
We wander through. Love is analogy,
What suits. How cannily you moralized
The body, insisted guilt lie down with lust,
Wooed the superior mind with dirty secrets,
And made your prayer that love be not
Perfection but the energy attracting us
Toward it, any longing that fits a god.

And between the pages, pressed to that wound
He'd sent his letter to, a wildflower
Itself now paper-thin, a splayed sun-bow —
Covenant with what memory it was meant
To recall? The boy I was? Or the figure
Of the youth I am in this poem? The future
Sometimes seems former lives, or stages
Of a life, drawing them out of the past,
The flashing moment's hasp snapped up.
The future that boy desired and feared
Depends on our converging, expansive
Recognition of something more than either
The boy or his guardian could in no time
Want to make of it, a past less deviant
Than defiant, struggling to be in touch
With spirit. The lover is an older man
On purpose, inspirer in this pastoral
Of hero-worship, and love's the yearning
Text, best beloved and still puzzled over.
The years come up, the sun goes down
Tonight as if into the case itself
Whose cover is fastened now, and once again
I'll turn to walk downstairs, back
Into the empty house, into the waiting arms.

⊰❖⊱

HONOR MOORE

·

POEM FOR THE END

You leave. I write what happened, type it—onionskin. A romance
        you called it. Save carbons, airmail it: love letter to
                a married man. A year later, standing
            where you and I stood, a woman talks—
                    execution of Basques in Spain,
a photographer who'd seen it, whom she interviewed.
        She leaves him, changes her mind, goes back. "We made
                love—" she talks fast. "We can't give up, must find ways

to nurture men, not lose autonomy—" Alone I've come back
        to heal. Tsvetaeva writes a poem: Death and the loss
                of love, her blond captain, are
            interchangeable. All day, as if waiting, I
                    play records, Beethoven again
and again. A novel of passion. A triangle:
        three women. Intense pain about this thwarted love, writes
                a critic, marks the start of her mature

vision. As if to live completely, one must lose love. As if
        to gain knowledge one must lose the first romance, a blond
                captain. Last night, because of the music,
            in the dark, my own hands, I touched delicately
                    the place between, opening my
thighs, touched as if you, as if filling one's own need were—
        as if easy. Use anger. What has had to be
                translated. Talk about the craziness of

trying to write the ultimate. Music. A sense of place. And
        it rains. Snow sinks inches a day even in sun. I
                still don't have a color photograph: how
            the sun sets here, which colors the snow reflects, and
                    the snow is melting. In a room
across the road, the man I wait for sits with another
        woman. I am waiting as if for a lover
                for a man not my lover. I wait for him

as if he knows I wait, as if for my lover for this
    man I have decided not to love because I love
        someone else. Wait through fatigue for the poem
      about you, feeling like nausea, the craziness,
        my anger. Not at. From. Last night
this: a man—fantasy—comes to my bed. I love him
    as no one else has, mouth him until his eyes half-
        close, till he cannot speak, until he rocks. "We

fucked our brains out," she says. "Makes you understand why men want
    those encounters—short—that freedom." If I were a painter
        working the small area near my mouth:
      In one year this face has learned her most powerful
        emotion is powerless. There's
something new in her. I would want you to know it
    by the mouth. Alone I've come back to this place. This
        is not my normal state. I am a person

with friends. I live in a context. I do not wait for men. I
    do not wait, without interruption, for poems. There is
        someone I love. I rarely work after
      dinner, maybe twice a year. Once I flew to France to
        meet a married man. Just once, for
love. Passion: let a whole moment move through you without
    the fear of being cruel. That's the balance, a perfect
        sunny July day. The actual is

fitful and relentless as March, a final thaw. Often
    passion has had to be translated. "We stood against
        the glass, touching it, watching the late sun
      on the East River, acknowledging its beauty,
        then we made love." But what did you
say that he knew what you wanted? "You don't have to say
    anything." The perfect sunny day. Did you think love
        was a chat at a small table? Was it love

last night, that hand, unexpected, through my hair? Can love be
    a telephone call in which a voice you love, long
        distance, tells you not to be afraid as
      you wait for the poem? Or is love just want. Last night
        I wanted someone. Alone in
a dark room, radio, a piano pure as black
    Eurydice's wild dance, shocking as a full white
        rose, cooling as water, sweet as love or hands

touching that delicate place, scent of hyacinth. I wanted
    so much, wanted someone to want, to come to me wanting
        me. Winter, just a year ago, you, whom
      I loved, were leaving. Perhaps we would never see
        each other again that way, that
passionately, yet we prepare as if we are to
    leave together, I driving through sunset, night, to the
        train. Kissing, you say "I've never understood

kissing at trains," then swiftly, "Goodbye, better this way"—and choose
    a seat behind the only fogged window. The night is
        intensely cold, the moon a harsh orange
      sickle rocking on its back. I have not seen him
        that way again. A voice. A hand
through hair. Such wounds do not heal quickly. Do you think love
    is just a chat at a table? Was it love he looked at
        me with? If I were a painter, I would

work the area near the mouth for days. This woman knows now
    you have some things fleetingly, that's all. Would you know that
        by her mouth? I soothe myself. Honey.
      Hibiscus. And music. An airport terrace at
        Nice. I wait to leave the same man,
frightened I'll miss my flight. He doesn't—won't—speak. I want
    him to say I love you. He won't. Didn't. A woman,
        a stranger, walks toward us, dyed red hair, breasts

heavy, jouncing against a lime green sweater. "Oooh la la! Oooh
    la la, Madame!" This out loud, say you whom I love, not
        in jest, to a woman, a stranger, and
      I leave in minutes. You kiss me, just lightly. We
        certainly will, perhaps never
see one another again. Across the road, a room,
    light. A man sits with another woman. I depend
        on music written by a deaf man dead

two hundred years for sustenance, to get beyond my too
    strong sense of place. What has had to be translated does
        not translate back into one language. I
      wait, with Beethoven. Some fear is gone, you can tell
        in my voice, the poem pasted, three
sheets, white on the wall. I am trying to learn the
    ultimate, and it shows near my mouth. There is no
        photograph, how the sun sets, which colors the snow

repeats. These carbons repeat what happened between us before
you left on that train, try, while lying, to tell truth of
feeling, the truth of a moment, but
dodge facts: marriages, desire. A romance, you
called it. Use anger. Love was
translated. If you were a painter, you might have known it
in my face. At night, a year later, snow extends
this room's light. Future. This out loud: The future.

•

A WINDOW AT KEY WEST

Waking in silence and, through tilted blinds,
the mark of red bougainvillea—pink light tossed
at a white door. Out of sleep, I turn
in a narrow bed, and the sheet tugs after me.
Walls the color of milk, wind dragging leaves
across the courtyard, scraping whispers.
Life is incomprehensible, he'd said
when I asked if he had a theory. Late
dalliance of tropical green,
bromeliad, look of palm bark, and beyond

closed windows, a table set for supper.
In my dream I knock. A woman offers spoiled food
then turns away. Now the sky goes dark
and the breeze stops. Why does she ask for narrative?
You make plans but sit instead on a porch
talking about Nietzsche whom you have
never read—never has sense seemed less
consequential. His skin is very black
against the white chair, his voice honest
and loose in the temperate air. The children

ask to walk, but we sink into the large car,
drive the quiet, small streets of an old town. This is
the shape my life takes around absence
any understanding would flatten. Light in the room,
but the sound is blocked—all that suggests it
is movement of light, shadow
rippling a surface of tawny wicker.
There are certain sentences I can't bear

to speak again: *I can love you less.*
Of course I understand. He brings plates of food—

    green, then red, yellow. A red biplane, tall
glasses for beer, murmurs near a bar in shadow,
        greeting without handshake or embrace;
then today in a room on the ocean, late silver
    light, each chair a distinct bright color. He
        asks only for the present: her face
    behind a language I don't speak, something
    pulling. Beyond a closed window the noise
        of bodies in water, broken
by the talk of children. Her voice in this room

    waylays almost any grief. Standing there
at an ironing board, the dress patterned and torn,
        she burns her wrist: And so there will be
evidence. Later, wind and a raw Sunday heat: whites
    go whiter, blacks blacken and glare until
        eclipsed stripes of blind give actual
        seconds of joy: red bougainvillea
    late light flushes almost blue, blossoms
        folded to the shape of bells so
brilliant now, they seem to tremble and ring out.

·

EDWARD

The car, then he moves, opening door suddenly
heavy, further into the warehouse night, or
perhaps we drive uptown, city darkening, leaving
it all unsaid. You are thinner than ever. We were
children then really, my fast blue car, a beach,
rooms in which you placed objects with a grace
that flattered God. I was watching men, as you were,
swerving an old car out the dirt drive after
you put guests to bed. On your knees in prayer
now, every day, *fingers at the glands in my neck*
like every gay man I know. Tweed and muffler, beard
patterned across a cheek. *I don't know how*
to get past this. In restaurant dark, friends move
through our conversation as if the past were
a bright street. A mime's fingers. *No one makes*

love, and this year there have been so many.
Oh darling, old friend — of beauty, of exuberant
knowledge — turn as you close the door, take me
as you did then, a bouquet of lilac, a waltz.

Days of rain until you can't remember sun,
breath on the mirror, brothers and sisters
around a New England table. I was hungry
for what you gave, awkward in my largeness:
Delicate, you said, like a *Victorian*.
Offshore, low sounds of horns in fog, but the past
comes proudly forward. Who could have told us
it was the present we would find in ruins?
You move across the street like a cello sounding
or like grief — you who travel the places
where the texts were written, cross every floor
like a dancer. There is no wind. I want to hear
your voice, ask how you are. Behind the attic
wall: milk, cookies, late night talk of book
or film. It's as if someone purposely disturbed
this: a brook runs loud in spring, you live here
with a boy who builds paper castles. I wore
silk, you carried French luggage. Who could see
it was our future we would find in ruins?

Don't be ridiculous! How would I phrase it?
Is your blood poisoned? Or: What is it like
to sit in a beautiful room waiting it out?
There are ten of us here, bent, moving, showing
signs of life, and the sky outside is near gray.
Thursdays, they cut the grass. Either I travel
or stay home. Who are we to each other? I mean
when you dream figures on a road, am I ever
one of them? You put the key in a car door,
then drive a hundred as if we are lovers.
That house: stones painted white, the desert, dust
rising from the driveway, a lizard scuttles up
a whitewashed wall, we dine with a blackhaired woman
from Boston. One might argue we knew nothing
of love. Were the trees willows? Yes, and
you showed me plants that grow a hundred years
no matter how dry the ground. What is it I circle
like a plane in weather, or a wooing husband?
You're falling away, darling, aren't you? Slowly.

GIRL IN A FUR-TRIMMED DRESS

Fille à la Fourrure,
TOULOUSE-LAUTREC, C. 1887

It's not a dress, and he hasn't got the lips
right. I'm surprised you sat long enough

that he did you from behind—ostensibly
prim, wearing that orange coat you lied about

losing, which I replaced for you as a gift
and which you sent back to me without a note.

He knew you twenty years before I did—
Oh how I fell for you, swooning beneath

those dizzying fingers, your green eyes wide
with something I thought more than haste.

We met at a small supper outside Paris
one late August. I wore black, you black

and white. By then your gold hair had gone
off, but I could feel your body: They never

understand that, how a woman's flesh holds
a woman lover long past youth.

He never undressed you or your mouth
would not be open, and you never

looked straight ahead—always your eyes darted,
hungering toward the next enthusiasm.

But he got how you sit, those haunches
holding you down, and clipped you at the hip

to please you, though I suspect those days
you found yourself slim enough to welcome

mouth or finger, had we some brothel afternoon
lain like those whores he's so famous for.

But what you lived long before
put you off any touch or so I now believe —

the darkened stair, footfalls, another woman.
Surely your hair has gone dead gray.

I like to think of you looking out windows.
He's got the blue just right and the walls

like bleached fire, orange coat, and creamy
fur encircling your shoulder like meringue.

I am finally now as I was before you
except when I recall — not how you looked

in high middle age or the graze of your hand
but the pitch of your voice — which I turn from

seeking indifference, or a life
whose passions would not have been futile.

EILEEN MYLES

·

AN AMERICAN POEM

I was born in Boston in
1949. I never wanted
this fact to be known, in
fact I've spent the better
half of my adult life
trying to sweep my early
years under the carpet
and have a life that
was clearly just mine
and independent of
the historic fate of
my family. Can you
imagine what it was
like to be one of them,
to be built like them,
to talk like them,
to have the benefits
of being born into such
a wealthy and powerful
American family. I went
to the best schools,
had all kinds of tutors
and trainers, traveled
widely, met the famous,
the controversial, and
the not-so-admirable
and I knew from
a very early age that
if there were ever any
possibility of escaping
the collective fate of this famous
Boston family I would
take that route and
I have. I hopped
on an Amtrak to New
York in the early

'70s and I guess
you could say
my hidden years
began. I thought
Well I'll be a poet.
What could be more
foolish and obscure.
I became a lesbian.
Every woman in my
family looks like
a dyke but it's really
stepping off the flag
when you become one.
While holding this ignominious
pose I have seen and
I have learned and
I am beginning to think
there is no escaping
history. A woman I
am currently having an affair with said
You know you look
like a Kennedy. I felt
the blood rising in my
cheeks. People have
always laughed at
my Boston accent
confusing "large" for
"lodge," "party"
for "potty." But
when this unsuspecting
woman invoked for
the first time my
family name
I knew the jig
was up. Yes, I am,
I am a Kennedy.
My attempts to remain
obscure have not served
me well. Starting as
a humble poet I
quickly climbed to the
top of my profession
assuming a position of
leadership and honor.

It is right that a
woman should call
me out now. Yes,
I am a Kennedy.
And I await
your orders.
You are the New Americans.
The homeless are wandering
the streets of our nation's
greatest city. Homeless
men with AIDS are among
them. Is that right?
That there are no homes
for the homeless, that
there is no free medical
help for these men. *And women.*
That they get the message
—as they are dying—
that this is not their home.
And how are your
teeth today? Can
you afford to fix them?
How high is your rent?
If art is the highest
and most honest form
of communication of
our times and the young
artist is no longer able
to move here to speak
to her time . . . Yes, I could,
but that was 15 years ago
and remember—as I must—
I am a Kennedy.
Shouldn't we all be Kennedys?
This nation's greatest city
is home of the business-
man and home of the
rich artist. People with
beautiful teeth who are not
on the streets. What shall
we do about this dilemma?
Listen, I have been educated.
I have learned about Western
Civilization. Do you know

what the message of Western
Civilization is? I am alone.
Am I alone tonight?
I don't think so. Am I
the only one with bleeding gums
tonight? Am I the only
homosexual in this room
tonight? Am I the only
one whose friends have
died, are dying now?
And my art can't
be supported until it is
gigantic, bigger than
everyone else's, confirming
the audience's feeling that they are
alone. That they alone
are good, deserved
to buy the tickets
to see this Art.
Are working,
are healthy, should
survive, and are
normal. Are you
normal tonight? Everyone
here, are we all normal?
It is not normal for
me to be a Kennedy.
But I am no longer
ashamed, no longer
alone. I am not
alone tonight because
we are all Kennedys.
And I am your President.

•

MAXFIELD PARRISH

Often I turn on people
in rather strange &
inexplicable ways.
The source of
the irritation
escapes me.

It always has.
Sometimes
my heart just
opens and
all the lions
get called
back to some
other corner
of the cave.
You'd probably
laugh at the
flowers I
bought tonight.
Bluish purple
& they don't
even have
a name. "Name?"
pronounced the
man at the
fruit stand
he shook
his head
& laughed.

These purple
flowers have
no name. &
no smell. But
the room
smelled & looked
different when
I brought them
in with me.
For instance
I was gentle
with their
stems while
I thought
about how
many lovers
have told
me I'm
rough. These
are hearty

thick stems
yet I slipped
the elastic
off their
limbs as
if I were
a servant
undressing
the president's
child. Just
thinking of her
for once. Oddly
alive & being
touched by
me in this
practical way.
The whole thing's
off-kilter the
way my purple
flowers grow.
Something that
makes sense
in February.
I have enough sense
to buy flowers
now. But such
strange ones.
Sprayed. Their
eerie color
is not real.
At least not all of it.
Maybe none of
it. The eerie
little branches
from which
piney green leaves
grow & I guess
that's real. But
the 287,
no I mean
thousands
of faintly blue bells
I can hardly see
I must be getting old

up close they make me feel dizzy
the fineness, the wealth of this pseudo-life
tiny balls, pale blue
with a sliver of a tongue
sticking out or sometimes
everything's teeny & sexual
it's sort of like underpants
a cover or a case
that's purple & the little
ball is blue.
I don't know why this wave
of a plant belongs in my vase.
I needed something fake to
start me up. Something
I could be gentle
with just to try.
Looking hard I say Baby
I don't know why I can
give you everything
& I'm dazzled by your frown.

.

MERK

There's too much light in my life
there that's better
the street people recommend
don't let your brother fling his
leg & arm around you like
you're his girlfriend. Humpin your
kneecap, stuff like that
the vilest smell of all tonight
is human food
it's November when the moons switch
places. White is bad
black is good. Food stinks.
Carrying their buckets of soup
to their stupid abodes
furs around their necks, beasts.
What do humans eat? Dogs, more or less.
Ripping fruit from the vine
snipping the crop
maybe vegetables would like to

let their baby be too
and never never eat the human
that is a crime. Push my machine
to see what nazi called
me. Go out and kill her with my teeth
I'm a bored outsider
the season is cold
everywhere doors are slamming
and look who you're in the
room with now. Someone to eat
I hope. Think of Goethe
Werner Goethe with his leg
flung up on a rock in
Italy. Take a bite
of that fat calf.
He's like a big posing gondola
what's the idea
every poet I know is a partial artist
the lucky ones are dead
naturally incomplete
but look at everyone you think of
hanging on to some misapprehended
particle of modernism, all
plumped up with pillows
there's nothing
after a modern idea
for poets. All they do
is think & eat. If you call
that making something
& I don't, I don't call that art.
We must offer ourselves
up as food or eat
someone. If you can make there
be less of someone else
or someone could take
a bite out of you
then you could join in the incompletion
or excess of your age
I'm sick of seeing dunces celebrated
that's the job
someone that looks
good in ribbons
someone surrounded
by their editor's

arms. Love object
of a lesbian
but not being
one. Particle board
potential screen
play, plastic
hair, translates
well, millions will hold
you on the train
bite me now
bite me forever
in your two strong

o eat me read
me something

I am the daughter
of substitution
my father fell
instead of the dresser
it was the family
joke, his death
not a suicide
but a joke

how could I accidentally
get eaten
slipping into your
sandwich or refrigerator
sort of a dick
that crawls
up from the bottom of your
ice cream cone

it's too late for some
of us, but for others
it's never late
enough. Tonight
when they moved
the lights and everything
looked completely
horrible for
a change
I was looking

for sympathy
and you asked
me for the menu

I have escaped the
unseemly
death of the alcoholic
yet I keep my ear so close
to the ground & I know
what they know
I begin to smell
funny, another fate

it was as if I was falling
last night
but I imagined
myself a bit
of food
& I was safe
in your mouth
& I would
never die

it is the legacy
of my family
to change in the air
& smash as
something new

not a woman
but a chair
full of flowers

not a poet
but a donut
or a myth

go up there
& get me a cracker
darling
& proudly
I walked.

SLEEPLESS

I came in tonight and my building sighed.
It was a beautiful woman stretching in
the morning. All blue and blonde and
gauzy white. My dreams of you are always
softer than you are. My dreams
must need a goddess and it seems she has
your face. And so you may stay awhile
in my heart. My image of your languorous
arms and fists slowly stretching through
the early day as if Monday were another
sleepless woman's body. Two of you
to make the universe complete.
The embrace of you makes my day
so sweet because I am the author
of this sport. The other woman is dark
and green and curly, full of rocks
and sauce and dark lights hanging

in the sky. She's the sound of a
yawning cave. She pulls me down
and makes me whisper evil and
violent wishes, makes me spank
her with a whip and fierce
rules and fond names to cage
her in. How could everything
shrink so—these women dancing
in my mind. What holds the world together
for anyone else—blind women, white
men, frightened Chinese boys. I guess I
have a hunger that's stronger than
toast, I wouldn't say most
because the shapeless woman hanging
over my shoulder says I mustn't.
She shows me with her eyes which are water.
She tells me with her breath, incredible,
a hurricane, a disaster.
Her teeth are sparkling
ruin, her tongue a poison
snake, her throat
an endless fall
onto a meadow of warm sushi.

And lakes of blood and
green birds swooping
and singing.

And dawn, a dawn
that's unrecognizable.
It's there I finally
stopped in your
midnight arms.

What could lead
me this way,
what furry
balconies await me. What amber
yawns what plentiful breasts
diving between the legs
of God to see a mirror
an amazing pond, a one-eyed
man inside you cleaning
the kitchen with a sparkling
knife. I step on his face
and snap his back in two
with my finger and
you reward me with
heartthrob and
I never do come back.
I want you home with
me. I want you alone
with me. I wish you
would get lost
so I could walk the world
with my women.
I would call your name
everywhere. Wouldn't
that be enough, even
better. There is a woman
in the flower. Millions
of women hiding in the trees.
You will never miss me.
There is a universe
of color for you to
feed from. Before

I leave you I will
open its legs
with my sword.

．

SCHOOL OF FISH

Everything's equal now. Blue leash blue bike
blue socks covering my ankles today
what about my friend: "I never wear socks"
for a week or two she lived in the streets &
it was such an illumination. What's this human
addiction to light. One morning I dreamt about
homelessness, joked about it. Life reduced
or expanded to getting doggie her very
next can. Dog's inexcusable addiction to
eating. At the bottom of the sea, David said,
the fishes are inexcusably addicted to light.
Same day I and my dog were left on the street.
No home, no keys, streams of pouring grey
rain. Now what is this grey, in relationship
to blue. Ask some painter is it less light
or is it what. What kind of hat should
I have worn yesterday in my crisis.
The dog's blue leash was gone. My feet reaching
over the bounds of the sidewalks, its curbs
and waves, pavement splashing up
hard and grey. Where did I see that man?
Someplace so human they even had one of *them*.
In a dark blue teeshirt, laughing. There is nothing
to my anecdote, my predicament, my color
crisis. There is nothing but blue & grey.
A glint hits the golden key, and it's a bad one
not the original and I kept turning and turning
there were copies everywhere in the neighborhood
that's what I am trying to say. I simply walked
and the apologies kept coming streaming in
and I said I simply walked and the tree
turned, no the key and the bottom of the sea
is flooded with light, we just get used to it
the deeper and deeper we go and the harder
it is to turn the key and eventually we

go and it is very very dark
we just get used to the light
but the blues and the greys and the feelings
of lostness, it's like home, it's like family.

LETTA NEELY

·

MULTIPLE ASSAULTS

*Multiple generations of the same race on two continents are
being infected. In sub-Saharan Africa and in Harlem, we have
women, men, and children dying together in the same house.*

multiple generations of the same race on two continents are
being infected. In your crib and my crib, on Amsterdam Avenue
and on Times Square, on Christopher Street and on Fulton Street, we
gots women, men, and children dying together in the same house.

the shit b funky

can you hear the base
can you hear the base
1 2 1 2 3 1 2 3 4 7 9 21
times   can you hear the base of his skull
hit the baton
hit the ground
can you hear the base of his skull
hit the ground you walk on sometimes

are you in tune with the groove
can you see the groove of her soul dancing
red through the glass shards he hit her with cuz
his skull hurt

can you get the rhythm of
over and over   and over and over
again and again and again
of the groove and the base

"it's strictly base now," he said
"only freebase
cuz needles in yo arms give you diseases that faggots got
and they need them so they can die . . ."
can you feel the base   can you get the groove now

freebasin gon kill yo ass too
and dead is dead is dead

and what if when you were down, i picked you up
i gave you my hand to grasp cuz i am strong
what if i fed you when you were hungry
and let you cry on my shoulder when your womon left
what if after all that we've been through,
what if i am a faggot
would you kill me then
would you say i manipulated you and touched you funny
would you get mad and kill me cuz i didn't tell you
you were crying on a faggot's shoulder cuz a
shoulder is a shoulder and a tear
is a tear
would you get mad and kill me cuz i didn't tell you
that you eating off a plate that i eat off too

and what if sistahs, what if i am a dyke
what will you do now
cuz before you might have said my hair is nappy cuz i wanna b a man
but now that it's down to be black again and perms
don't define all that we are
now sistahs, what would you do to me if i am a dyke
would you not speak to me in the streets
would you hug your man extra tight when i walk by
what would you do on that late night when i offer you a ride home
to your home and we start to talk
and we to go to my home and talk all night and when dawn comes up
you see audre's picture on my wall and jump up to leave
like ah'm bout to pounce on you
and you say, "why didn't you tell me, i wouldn'tna got in a car with you
bitch"
and you say, "why didn't you tell me, i wouldn't come up in your crib,
bitch"
and it didn't come up cuz all night we was talkin bout
lynching and burnings and povertys and revolt and what the fuck didn't
come up last night,
sistah

what would you do
if your little brother, your big sistah
yo uncle, yo mama, yo auntie, or your best friend from
way back when

came up to you
and said, i'm dyin, i'm dyin, i got AIDS, won't you give me some
aid?
would you say: faggot, get out my face
would you say: bulldagger, get out my way
would you say: sistah, brother, father, mama

move

.

RHONDA, AGE 15, EMERGENCY ROOM

> . . . Yeah, I been to juvee, what about it?
> I was up at Spofford—they got legends
> bout me—thought they wasn't gon git
> rid a' me, but yo' I had to git de fuck up
> outta dere, they had hoes that murder
> people in that piece
> and
> I'm baaad and all but I ain't never
> murdered nobody yet and I try not
> to fuck up nobody too much less
> they mama cain't recognize 'em
>
> Last night, my man Ray-Ray, he 23
> and built better than buster douglass
> well anyway, we was over to his
> crib and he was tryin' to git on
> for some
> but he been locked up for 4 months
> and I dont know what that nigga
> been doin—shit, I know what
> I was doin up in Spofford—
> so when I tole him I was having my
> menstruals, he decided to get plexed.
> He smoked a blunt and wouldn't
> take me home and den the nigga
> went n' fell asleep.
> I was like damn, here I am
> at Ray-Ray's crib and I got
> a motherfuckin curfew and a
> math test tomorrow (I'm tryin
> to do good in school for probation

and dis lady who teach English
say I got potential—which I did
look up in the dictionary. It mean
I gots mad promise if my ass don't
end up in jail).

So I'm lookin for a pencil,
anything to write on which,
when I find it, is a paper towel
and thinkin that Ray-Ray ain't
helpin me none and he must
be a stupid nigga to boot cuz
he ain't got no paper and I
had to sharpen the pencil
wit a knife. I starts to think
bout findin me a new man.

Me and my math problems
plexin each other to death,
when Big Mac come knockin.
He Ray-Ray's cousin
so I let him in. He say,
          where Ray-Ray?
I'm like he sleepin, he blunted out—
          Ah, he say, *you wanna watch a movie*

I look at the napkin, crunch it
up, make a perfect 3 pointer and
follow Big Mac to the living room.
He put in the tape and turn off the
light. Then the movie come on
and at first I'm fixin to git up cuz
this ain't my kind of movie—girls
in all kinds of crazy positions suckin
white boys off, bitches lettin em
whip they ass and tie em up. That's
at first, cuz the next thing I know
I'm feelin crazy shit go through me:
          cunt juice drippin down
          my leg and I'm freakin
          myself out cuz i thought
          that shit only happen at
          Spofford. Cuz I'm imaginin
          I'm stompin all the

white boys. Walkin up to
em while dey whippin dem
girls and I'm stickin .45s in
dey backs — but that ain't all.
I'm thinkin after I kill em,
de ladies gon want to fuck
me, and yeah, that's the part
I'm trippin on, that I want them
to fuck me and that Ray-Ray
didn't never make me feel like
the cuties in juvee.

And I look over at Big Mac to see
if he know yet by the look on my face that
I'm a fuckin homo. Cuz if he don't know yet
I want to fix my face before he guess.
And when I look at him I'm like
I know this nigga done lost his mind cuz
the bitch is sittin there with his dick
outta his pants and his hand movin all
fast n shit and he stop when he see me,
den he start talkin real deep bullshit
he say

    Rhonda, come here, Why don't you
    do me. Come on Rhonda do me.
    Ray-Ray ain't gonna mind. I ain't
    gonna tell him.

He reach over and
touch my titty and me, ms. bad ass
all of a sudden cain't move
I'm frozen, I mean I couldn't move
    damn you cute
    girl, I wanna git my groove
    on wit you, I always . . .
The nigga
stop talkin then.
He all grunts and shit and I'm
imaginin I'm on another planet
tryin to think about the math test
and that lady teacher I got
and I feel all that POTENTIAL
running the fuck away
cuz I won't claw this nigga to death
cuz I cain't even believe it's happenin

cuz he Ray-Ray's cousin and
cuz I ain't never felt no pain like this
so I don't feel it/I/think/bout/this/
time/I/beat/this/bitch/so/bad/she/lost/
6/teeth/and/got/scars/to/this/day/
from/the/box/cutter/I/slashed/cross/
her/face/

I guess he done cuz he start to say
somethin
     don't worry girl, I know you . . .
And I don't hear the mothafucka
finish cuz I'm outta the room and
shakin Ray-Ray so hard he think
it's a earthquake in Bed-Stuy.
I make
that nigga
git up
and take
me home
in his mama's
raggedy-ass hoopty.

And I start cryin
when I see my projects
and commence to tellin
Ray-Ray everything.
First thing he do is say,
     hell naw, you my bitch,
     ah'm a take care of this shit.
Den he tell me to take a bath
and he gon call me after he settle
this shit.
Then he leave.
I let myself in and hope mama ain't wake.
She ain't.
I go to de bathroom,
flick de light on,
watch de roaches git
de fuck out my way,
and set the water to run.
I wuz gonna take a real
hot bath, but I

membered too
late we ain't got
no hot water right now.
So, I pullt the drain
and went to bed.
But all I'm thinkin
bout is my test
and my potential—
how ahm gon git it back—
so I find the damn book
and jist study and study and study
till round bout 7:30 when
I'm still wide awake and
fixin to go to the school.

For the first time I'm gon
make first period.
I'm steppin out the door and I see
Ray-Ray walkin up,
he look real mad.
I don't feel nothin but
good cuz I know I can
pass. He git closer and I
smell malt on him. He say,
  I see you like them clothes, bitch
and I member right
then that I ain't changed
he say it again,
  yeah, you like the fuck smell on dem clothes.
I go
  you crazy nigga, I ain't like shit about yo cousin
he like,
  you lyin cunt, Big tole me de
  whole story. He say you wanted to fuck him,
  He say you come over to him while he
  tryin to watch a movie and put
  your hand on his dick and
  He say he told you he wasn't gon
  disrespect me like that but you kept
  touchin on him and I cain't blame the nigga
  for goin for his. I cain't believe you did that
  shit, Rhonda. You spose to be my girl and you
  go fuckin my cousin.

He got me backed up in
the corner in the lobby. People
see us and don't nobody say shit.
I don't say shit again cuz ahm in
shock and de only thing I'm thinkin

is bout how
to figure $x = y^2$
when he say,
      You ain't got nothin to say, bitch?

the way to solve $x = y^2$ was
still runnin through my mind
when he hit me and I fell down
and I felt him kickin math answers
out my head.
I got sad cuz I wasn't gon' make
first period and my POTENTIAL
act like it ain't never comin back.

·

8 WAYS OF LOOKING AT PUSSY

1.

enter here and find your home
your bathwater run already
the sun setting in the distance
heat on the horizon of your clit

2.

swollen pussy
all laid out and relaxed,
says to everyone in the room
"I have been to mecca and back
and it ain't nuthin compared to what you
done did"

3.
when you're wet and waiting
I could be lost six
universes away without a map
and sniff my way home

4.
baby, baby, hold still
my dreads are underneath
your thigh

5.
with those three brown fingers inside,
you impregnate me with desire
I grow wide and wild
my water breaks,
this dam gives and we are tossing on the rapids
tossing on the rapids
overturning canoes,
water races out and over your arm
warm cum shoots out
races up your
arm, you put
your mouth
over this geyser

6.
I love like the ocean at first light
the waves coming in to meet the edges
of earth; running up and back like tiny orgasms
high tide the explosion
of you
on my
tongue

7.
my teeth on your nipple tastes sweet
I clench harder bite down on sensations
like acupuncture—I feel energy rising
connecting from
one hand/nearly elbow deep in your pussy
one hand over your mouth
your sister and my boy cousin
so close they can smell but
they snore instead you giggle
I bite harder taste past skin
you giggle again

8.
venus flytrap
eats me alive
everytime

ACHY OBEJAS

·

LIFES

I.
The lives of my mother fit in one name,
typed on envelopes cut open like fish bellies.
She makes them dance, like she does.

On her night table she keeps a few photographs,
black & white, of someone she knew:
a familiar woman with simmering coal eyes
on the arm of a gent in white linen;
their long-ago poses are exotic, ordinary.

Today my father falls asleep,
his dry muscles soft before the hum of the TV screen.
She complains (she complains),
hiding the trace of comfort trailing her words.

The thirty-odd years tumble
into a thimble on the sewing table
where she keeps gay embroidery,
store-bought patterns.

In the garage, he keeps every nail, every screw, every pin
according to size, length and weight;
little jars catalogued like a library,
never used.

They wear pajamas,
cotton synthetic blends of extraordinary softness,
the kind that sprout tight little beads of fuzz
around the elbows, belly worn.
They hold each other all night.

Thirty-odd years and in the morning
he silences a cough, unknots the blankets
and sheets, brings her coffee.
With an impulse she might spill it,
but it's too long in the same cup.

II.
Sometimes I swallow glass,
but no one names me against my will.
It's never planned,
but I make my own calling.

These are familiar lives in foreign languages,
intimate tongues.
(My mother refuses to read the subtitles;
she acknowledges nothing.)

These are sharp, salty loves.
Death on the first kiss.
She has a question:
How long can you keep your head under water?
(My mother is amphibian,
a lizard whose tail will grow a new head.)
She says she'd rather not know.

My chest is tight, bursting.
Death on every first kiss.
(My mother is immortal,
posthumous nails grow on the cadaver.)
These photographs are different.
She avoids them.

III.
I tell her
in my glove compartment
there's another brand-name envelope
swollen with nearly instant photos;
they were processed overnight.

But my mother wants to hire a professional,
a photographer who will shoot me
in black & white at family occasions.
She'll wait for days and sometimes weeks
for memory's return,
enlarged and pinned like dried flowers to the page.

This is her calling.
My mother wants to be annihilated
with happiness.
She wants to take me with her

to be a happy hell
where there's never the individuality of pain.

•

THE PUBLIC PLACE
(AFTER OLGA BROUMAS)

I have been watching her for a long time. I have been watching
this woman, this small frame on the grass in a public place. I
have been watching the long dark hair fall like a web on her
shoulders, the neck, the fine slender arms, the way she senses
I'm here watching her. I am a spy. I am exploring, mouth open,
the hard ribs of her body, the hips hidden in denim, the creases,
the creases, the muscles that stretch under dark blue jean
patches so tight. I am a pirate, my tongue the ship (a fantasy)
that rises with the storm of each movement I am inside her I'm
watching inside her from behind the brown iris I'm spying. I do
not know her I am her lover I do not touch her she rises she
stands in the grass in the public space she is barefoot soft feet
unaccustomed to being so naked those feet white feet moving away
from the grass the public place the imprint of her still fresh on
the grass the public place taking the intersection against the
light with a vengeance a dare in her white step she is barefoot I
am her lover I am the woman she goes to, going home.

•

DANCING IN PARADISE

You lean against me
as we dance, the soft huddle
of our heads together,
our breaths clean steam in the blue
smoke, rapid, exhausted.
We mix margaritas, because
I like the name, a
woman you love. You're older.
I'm willing, drunk, unbuttoned.
You lead, peeling layer after
wet layer, a heap
of sweaters, shirts and precious
metals. Your breast is
slick with sweat, hands agile,

242 • THE WORLD IN US

eels in glass waters.
When you scoop me up, I twist
in your lap, a thick
needle thrust through my tongue. Later,
you give me a reading list,
blank journals, your mother's
recipes. You take
what you need, knowing there's no
autonomy of the
senses, those five carnivores
in their own essential
food chain. What survives is memory,
twin jewels, the blade of
a pelvic bone. Instinctively,
we keep our eyes open,
ears keen, for marine smells,
salt, the plexus of light,
sound, water.

•

SUNDAY

Love set them going, our mothers,
tiny little wind-up toys
as shiny and urgent as pearls;
later dull and slow, like late-model cars,
something bloated about their design.

Love set them going, directed
their noses to the clean cosmetic,
the innocent films.
They married one man;
they made love only once.

It was love that gave them careers,
new wares, made them
dark-haired girls sifting rice,
checking magazines for quick tests titled:
"Do you know your lover?"
"Is your marriage happy?"
Everyday the air of nitrous oxide.

They never told the fathers about us,
the daughters standing with arms akimbo.
We were the open secret,
as beautiful and repellent as tattoos.

Now they see themselves the snail on the tank.
We are stone nymphs come to life,
brilliant betas,
too many things at once.

I tell you, if you whisper to me, woman,
it goes no further.
Pain or peace, I cannot take it to them.
If you touch me, your albuminous kiss,
that is between you and me.

It is love, casuist love, a twisted Gabriel
who turns them away:
Our mothers, black veils, votive, orthodox,
gravely whispering to men
misdemeanor sins.

They light dripless, traceless,
invisible candles for penance,
sing prayers like insurance,
dream crashes in station wagons, family cars.
Year after year, the missal for breakfast.

When we become them, a little taller perhaps,
buddha women late in life,
will we be like them,
with our steeples and postulates,
trembling?
Tell me, here, with a tremor of a different sort,
our eyes lidless, your breath cool,
about our mortality.

GERRY GOMEZ PEARLBERG

·

THINK BACK

Agnes Moorehead, Hedy Lamarr,
Edith Head, and a smirky beautician
named Madge are in a low-cut car
heading toward the headlands, the outback, the margins.

Heads in the clouds, gloved hands on the wheel,
they're heady with the thrill of an all-girl
American adventure circa 1950-something.
Why not? Life's short.

"Life's short," croons Agnes.
She should know, but that comes later.
Right now everything that matters is in that car.
The breeze is blowing through the front-seat hair
of Edith Head and Hedy Lamarr.
Four single girls on the road for a drive.
Madge's manicured hand riding Agnes' thigh.

Edith leans forward to adjust her tie
and imagines a film that hasn't been
made yet, a movie called *Thelma and Louise*.
Madge and Agnes laugh her off, and Hedy joins in,
roaring as she freshens her face in the rearview mirror.
One eye on the road, she guides the lipstick sprocket
along the pocket of her lips, doesn't miss
a beat driving that stop sign red
around the sarcastic octagon of her mouth,
fully aware of Madge eyeballing her
from the back seat, flooding
with desire, a full tank of gas
sidling up to an easy match.

A girl can't help noticing how
another girl applies her makeup.
Vantage point is everything.

Years from now, Madge will take advantage
of *her* vantage point, sit everyone down around
a crystal ball of blue water, and inform them that
they're "soaking in it."
They'll be appalled, might even shrink back
from imagining too vividly the infamous
Moorehead deathbed scene—two rival lovers (both
bombshell legends) in the hospital room
mopping her brow, pondering the will,
recalling the taut infusions of lipstick,
mascara, and eau de cologne on the sheets
and pillowcases of other, non-deathbed beds.
Yes, they, like everyone else, are "soaking in it."

But all that comes later.
Right now is its own cliff-hanging time and place,
its own quickly driven moment,
with a Continuity Lady called Today
and a Script Girl named Mañana.

.

MARIANNE FAITHFULL'S CIGARETTE
FOR L.

It was on the floor, being X-ed out by her long
black heel, infinite and doomed. I had to have it.

Her lips had been around it. Lipstick left on it.
I had to have it. I asked you to get it.

She was raking her fingers through her thin blonde hair.
Glancing up at the ceiling, chain-smoking.

The academics around her were talking, talking, talking.
She gazed up at the ceiling—bored, exhaling.

She rolled her eyes, then looked at us and smirked, you said.
I missed that, pondering the acropolis of fallen cigarettes at her feet.

How they looked like smoldering ruins—toppled, scattered.
Broken haloes of a calcified Atlantis.

Pondering chain-smoking. What a beautiful word.
I missed the look she gave us, bemused and bored.

I was thinking about the ring of lipstick on the filter.
I was thinking about the brand, and where she might've bought it.

Watching her light up was like seeing the Messiah.
Or Buddha's burning moment under leaves of cool desire.

·

SAILOR

The girls go by in their sailor suits
They catch my eye in their sailor suits
Big or slight they all grin like brutes
In steam-ironed pants and buffed jet boots
They saunter right up my alley.

I study their easy, confident strides
Crew cuts and white hats capping decadent eyes
They shiver the pearl on night's oystery prize
They shiver me timbers, unbuckle me thighs
This alley was made for seething.

From the sweat of a street lamp or lap of the sea
A smooth sailor girl comes swimming to me
Says she wants it right now and she wants it for free
Clamps her palms to my shoulders, locks her knees to my knees
This alley was made for cruising.

Her face is dark coffee, her head has no hair
Her cap shines like neon in the bristling night air
She pins her brass medals to my black brassiere
Tucks her teeth like bright trophies behind my left ear
This alley is very rewarding.

She tosses her jacket and rolls up her sleeve
On her arm's a tattoo of an anchor at sea
She points to the anchor and whispers, "That's me."
And the wetter I get the more clearly I see
This alley was made for submersion.

Her fingers unbutton my 501's
This girl's fishing for trouble and for troubling fun
She slides off her gold rings and they glint like the sun
Then she smirks, rubs her knuckles, and spits out her gum
This alley was made for swooning.

Now she's pushing her prow on my ocean's sponge wall
Uncorking my barnacle, breaking my fall
And there's pink champagne fizzling down my decks and my hall
As she wrecks her great ship on my bright port-of-call
This alley was made for drowning.

•

LOOP-THE-LOOP IN PROSPECT PARK (1905)*

I.
The early evening hill is a lantern's lamp
nightly relumed with a golden match.

From here I watch the families traverse
the Long Meadow paths like ants

with empty picnic baskets and wide black prams,
scurrying home before the oncoming dark.

They barely notice me reclined upon this hill
observing their departures amidst a spreading quietude,

at once random and precise: it stills the park
benches, the lily pond, the lindens and the elms—

and the rowboats hitched to the silver firs
that batten down Swan Boat Lake's shore,

hull clanking hull as if to entice the by-the-hour
and half-day renters—even the Lullwater

*This poem was inspired by a photograph in George Chauncey's *Gay New York: Gender, Urban Culture, and the Making of the Gay Male World, 1890–1940*, in which Chauncey writes: "[A] female impersonator from a poor neighborhood in Brooklyn where he was known as Loop-the-loop, a suggestive play on the name of a popular ride at Coney Island, reported to a doctor in 1906 that he regularly plied his trade 'chiefly for the money there is in it.' Loop-the-loop often worked in his neighborhood as well as in Prospect Park, where, he reported, he and the other prostitutes paid off the patrolmen so that they could wear dresses" (pp. 68–69).

Creek that feeds the lake subdues
its anxious murmurings

in deference to the tranquilizing night.
In the evening some things vanish

and other things grow clear. Succulent aromas
Impinge on air: night-blooming trees

repeal the scent of frankfurters and beer.
That's when we appear,

emerging from what conceals
and thus releases us: wood glens

dark as apothecary phials, dense hydrangea
fortresses that wreathe the fields

in folded maps of powder blue—the fountains
in the Vale Cashmere, the Vale's blurred

hedge of rose and bittersweet and rose,
the glade of bamboo slivers that skirts the Nethermead,

and the cattails that eclipse the marsh's bank,
obscuring the limits of its amphibious border,

its miracles of ambidextrous reach.
At these apertures of dusk, we wait.

II.
I've paid those cops quite handsomely
to let me be while wearing this dress,

this purse, these fine white women's gloves.
I've paid them handsomely

to be a fairy in Prospect Park at dusk
in my dress, hat, stockings, gloves.

The boys call me "Loop-the-loop" like the Coney Island ride—
ten times the thrill at a somewhat higher price.

III.
Our joke is that they call it "Prospect Park" because it's here
the trade is best: older gentlemen stroll the open fields

with Bungalow Bar or pipe in hand, lingering
by benches: patient, well-mannered, self-possessed,

eager to purchase what the poor-but-pretty will purvey—
though too many come with illusions of finding love for free.

Me? I've got love at home—a charm-school faun,
dreamy boy whom I adore.

This is business, like those swan boats for hire
waiting in the shallows for the chance

to guide or be guided into deeper waters.
But beyond the money that's in it,

there's pleasure too, when a moan
is delivered into the dark

or a sigh to the ear like an envelope.
Inside the tunnel of the Endale Arch

stir nightly echoes of delirium's touch
that even terror of disgrace cannot disarm.

IV.
I remember one warm October night
meeting an uncommonly handsome man

by the swell of purple ironweed near Music Island
where the wealthy take in after-supper shows:

the sky seemed extra-wide—a vagrant shield of sky—
into which darkness exhaled all its glistening stars:

it was one good night: soft sentiment
alighting like dragonflies

before money passed from hand to hand.
Long after money, there's memory's romance:

it pleases me to think of all the men who'll think of me
on lonely nights beneath the spread of other, less compelling skies.

V.
Morning dew, I've learned here, isn't *morning* dew at all —
it falls at night, while meteors fall.

I can't begin to count the stars that I've watched glide
across Brooklyn's endless sky — nor the nights

I've lain in the arms of men — some lovely, some tender,
some grudging — on grassy beds incandesced

by dew as night's cool astronomy lays low
and the horse-drawn carriages begin their ride

through the park's dim carriage roads, and the
trolley-cars plunge the hill to Flatbush

Avenue on steel scars re-incised
by morning's light. By that awakening world

beyond the margins of this park,
we mark our time. Soaked like nymphs

and Neptunes, we compose ourselves and rise
from the foamy smell of semen

like the Coney Island tide, when the sun tosses out
her first white net, and the schools of fish,

still sleeping, are confounded by the light.
It's then, before returning home

to the faun's warm, rumpled bed
that I stroll back to this hill to watch

my loose, unchartered club of men
drift like inky phantoms from the park —

past the Comfort Stations where the east and west
drives meet, beyond the Doric Shaft,

Monument to Sailors and Soldiers,
dispersing at last at Grand Army Plaza,

baptized by the shadow of its high, Triumphal Arch.

.

DOG STAR

How that girl can move
on this white-hot
San Francisco day's high noon
I'll never know.
Treeless, blunt savannah air
bends like clumps of batter
in my wire-whisking stare.
Today it's like a desert here.

Her millet-colored van's a secret cave.
She always enters from the rear.
Her slow crawl toward the dashboard
is a choppy filmstrip, sand and white,
scratched up by the trickle of her clean blade knife
and glare that alternately shows and fades
the paper bag of bones between her teeth,
her hind legs flexing in the spotted shade.

She's a brass hyena uncaking a cool dirt den,
a wild mutt muscling her way from a wire pen.

The sun throws constellations
on the hood and rearview mirror of her van.
She curls against the window pane —
bleached hair, tan shirt and
sandy cheeks like native relics under glass,
and finally in the mashing heat she sleeps,
a tough glazed donut in the driver's seat.

Tethered by bright chains of canine dreams,
she twitches, growls, and snaps at each.

I watch her, straining at my leash.

ROBERT E. PENN

·

MORNING SONGS

It is December.
Sunrise.
Already seventy degrees Fahrenheit.
The curtains drawn,
wooden jalousies closed.
Frying falafel smells
rise up the inner courtyard,
waft through my
fifth story suite windows.
Breakfast preparation.
The penthouse.
Middle of town.
City center.
Main square.

I climb to the roof.
The plaza below yawns.
Flesh of dense pedestrian traffic
in brown, black and fair people ripples.
Exoderm of old cars, packed buses and
aging lorries stretches, then wrinkles
as town inhales its first breath,
chokes on exhausts.

Minaret across
medians, rotary, bus stops and
mosaic tiled buildings dominates.
Now it sings.
Imam.
Morning prayers.
Come to them.
Call for them.
My first morning in Islam.
Call to prayer.

"Allahu Akbar"

Skin of crowded city relaxes.
Three by five foot patches,
Band-Aids, appear
on the surface of metroanatomy.
Prayer rugs now clothe the square.
Men kneel on swatches
of color and design.
Women are nowhere to be seen,
hidden beneath thick veils
and ground skirting robes.

> "Allahu Akbar
> Allahu Akbar
> Allahu Akbar
> Allahu Akbar
> Ashhadu an la ilaha illa-llah illa-llah
> Hayya ala-s-sala
> Hayya ala-l-falah
> Hayya ala-l-falah
> Allahu Akbar
> Allahu Akbar
> La illaha illa-lah
> As-salatu khairun min-an-naum
> As-salatu khairun min-an-naum
> As-salatu khairun min-an-naum."

This is very different
from church sounds of childhood.
Where dark music was suppressed,
reserved for only the appreciative.
Bouncing sanctitude
not shared in the lilywhiteburbs.
At least not by many.
When visiting there,
dare not share a love for gospel.

Do not speak of drums.
Primitive.
Exorcise African rhythm and
root from your soul.
Let them evolve into spirituals,

which many can understand and love.
Keep it within the community
or it will be challenged
and an existence,
tenuous at best,
will suffer yet another blow.
Which might turn out to be
that famous straw.
The one that breaks our collective back.

Alive Arab-African pride.
Living.
A sound of color that
no one had taught me to despise.
No one debased in media,
in convention's classroom
or in colonists' histories.
No one told me to distance
myself from this sound
in order to achieve
the American dream.

Morning song that does not need
to struggle for acceptance.
Needs neither deceptive packaging
for commercial success
nor a white face
to make it mainstream.
Nasal chant unashamed.
Rich voice from throat or gut,
unaware of a perceived need
to spring from diaphragm.
Raspy, deep toned,
rich, dark.
Free.

June.
Another part of African Islam.
A small hotel room
with efficient bath.
Single window and glass door
to prefab balcony
over interior garden and
outdoor restaurant.

Imported blinds rotate up.
The scent of fresh mangoes
sneaks under the sill.
Air conditioner drones too loudly
but fends off
Red Sea–drenched air.

Predawn ritual.
Developed by reading from
the four corners,
the four elements,
the seven continents
and seven directions,
unity of spirit.
Cross-legged silence
before flowers open
to accept the sun's heat
and synthesis.
Nothingness.
Peace.

> "*Om shakti, om shakti*
> *om shakti, om*
> *Namu amida Buttsu*"
> Evil is not real
> and does not stain
> There is no God but God
> Thy will not mine be done
> The light has come
> I have forgiven myself
> The light has come
> I have forgiven the world
> In the name of the father,
> the son and the holy ghost
> Amen."

Ramadan.
Holy month.
Light peeps over the horizon.
Loud hum overpowers the A/C.
Amplified.
Anachronistic.
Incongruous with
this sandy town

of soil streets.
Scratchy recurrence
breaks the meditation.
Record.
Call to prayer.
Recorded.
Classical Arabic.

"Allahu Akbar. . . ."

Sounds.
Chant.
Call for them.
No need to
take it wholesale.
Not an interruption
to selected ceremony.
Don't take offense.
It intertwines.

"Spirit am I
Allahu Akbar
Free of all limits
Ashhadu an la ilaha
Safe and healed and whole
illa-llah illa-llah
Free to forgive
La illaha illa-lah
And free to save the world
As-salatu khairun min-an-naum."

This song flows across
morning treetops.
Awakens believers
throughout the sector.
Renews their hearts
and hopes.
Brings joy and abundance,
insha'Allah.

Leaves unfurl.
Flowers quiver,
dogs stir,
men kneel,

women, behind curtains,
pray together alone.
Welcome this awakening.
Blessing is free.

·

HAND

She has a full beard when I first meet her. She is masculine. She is
wonderful. We are romantic. We are secretive. We stroll along beaches.
We walk beside lakes arm in arm. We ignore the ridicule. This is how we
met:

I was a 1950s dog paddling in the water of a cool Ontario lake. She
was an 1890s French damsel distressed by a failed love affair, jilted. I was
prancing and jumping with the waves. She leapt from the Eiffel Tower. I
saw her through a gap in time, heard her scream regret as she fell, saw her
recognize no silly man was worth her life, and flew to her assistance high
above the lake surface.   When we touched somewhere mid-air between
our continents, time and space altered. I became a man, she changed into
a post–World War II suffragist: strong, willful, and crafty. She could spit
blood if needed. She fell madly in love with me and never asked but knew
I was grateful at last to be a man in love with her.   We settled in
Montreal, where she plucked each hair from her beard and wore provincial
black, and I learned to speak French. I succeeded at business, became a
member of the board, and was respected in the community. Most people
feared her.

After 45 years of marriage, her strength was falling but she still trudged
to the office to collect me after work for our customary Friday evening
stroll home. The other spouses awaited their husbands patiently, but she
knocked on the door when the board meeting ran two minutes late and
exhaled blood to make her point.   I came out to console her. We sat
with the wives. One remarked that my wife had a hair on her chin. I said,
"No, it's a little beard." My wife agreed. The other woman was more
provincial and quite shocked. I laughed, "Once she had a full beard," and
told the story of my wife's landing from the French sky direct from the
Crystal Exposition.   All the women remarked what an imagination I
had.   The other board members came out of our chamber. I stood with
my wife, who was very weak. "Sit down," I suggested. "No," she said, "we
are from here. We will stroll tonight as we always do. As Quebecquois do.
Don't worry." She released me and went with the chairman. I did worry.
(And I regret that I cannot write down my sadness because this is her story.)

I went to the bathroom. There was a hip hop kid there. The age of my
grandson . . . if I had one. Very handsome, a little arrogant. My hand

brushed against his shoulder when I reached for a paper towel. He scowled at me. I was frightened but pretended to ignore him.   When I returned to the waiting room, there were several other Black kids dancing to urban sounds coming from a boom box. Not loud but very hip. One or two kids were only toddlers. A janitor was wiping up blood I thought mother had spit earlier. I sensed her absence.   The boy from the bathroom came and stood next to me, very close. "See her," he indicated a girl of four. "She's the best. A little while ago this song about following leaders was on. When the rapper talked about following, she danced a bandwagon and got on. When the rapper talked about the leader selling drugs, she danced herself off the bandwagon."

I smiled at him and he took my hand. It was my wife's hand.

CARL PHILLIPS

·

COTILLION

Every one of these bodies, those in drag, those
not, loves a party, that much is clear. The blonde
with the amazing lashes — lashes, more amazingly,

his own — tells me it is like when a small bird
rises, sometimes, like the difficult thing is not to.
I think he is talking about joy or pain or desire

or any of the several things desire, sweet drug,
too sweet, can lead to. I think he means moments,
like this one, sudden, when in no time I know that

these lashes, the mouth that could use now more
painting, these hairless, shaven-for-the-event arms
whose skin, against the shine of the gown, a spill of

blood and sequins the arms themselves spill from,
glitters still, but dully, like what is not the
main prize does always — I know this man is mine,

if I want him. Meanwhile around us, the room fairly
staggers with men, and an aching to be lovely, loved,
even. As in any crowd, lately, of people, the heavy

corsage of them stepping in groups, the torn bloom
that is each taking his own particular distance,
I think the trick is one neither of joining or not

joining, but of holding, as long as I can, to some
space between, call it rest for the wary, the slow
dragging to nowhere I call heaven. I'm dancing

maybe, but not on air: this time through water.

THE KILL

The last time I gave my body up,

to you, I was minded
briefly what it is made of,
what yours is, that

I'd forgotten, the flesh
which always
I hold in plenty no

little sorrow for because — oh, do
but think on its predicament,
and weep.

We cleave most entirely
to what most we fear
losing. We fear loss

because we understand
the fact of it, its largeness, its
utter indifference to whether

we do, or don't,
ignore it. By then, you
were upon me, and then

in me, soon the tokens
I almost never can let go of, I'd
again begin to, and would not

miss them: the swan
unfolding
upward less on trust than

because, simply, that's
what it does; and the leaves,
leaving; a single arrow held

back in the merciless
patience which, in taking
aim, is everything; and last,

as from a grove in
flame toward any air
more clear, the stag, but

this time its bent
head a chandelier, rushing
for me, like some

undisavowable
distraction. I looked back,
and instead of you, saw

the soul-at-labor-to-break-its-
bonds
that you'd become. I tensed
my bow:

one animal at attack,
the other—the other one
suffering, and love would

out all suffering—

.

AS FROM A QUIVER OF ARROWS

What do we do with the body, do we
burn it, do we set it in dirt or in
stone, do we wrap it in balm, honey,
oil, and then gauze and tip it onto
and trust it to a raft and to water?

What will happen to the memory of his
body, if one of us doesn't hurry now
and write it down fast? Will it be
salt or late light that it melts like?
Floss, rubber gloves, a chewed cap

to a pen elsewhere—how are we to
regard his effects, do we throw them
or use them away, do we say they are
relics and so treat them like relics?
Does his soiled linen count? If so,

would we be wrong then, to wash it?
There are no instructions whether it
should go to where are those with no
linen, or whether by night we should
memorially wear it ourselves, by day

reflect upon it folded, shelved, empty.
Here, on the floor behind his bed is
a bent photo—why? Were the two of
them lovers? Does it mean, where we
found it, that he forgot it or lost it

or intended a safekeeping? Should we
attempt to make contact? What if this
other man too is dead? Or alive, but
doesn't want to remember, is human?
Is it okay to be human, and fall away

from oblation and memory, if we forget,
and can't sometimes help it and sometimes
it is all that we want? How long, in
dawns or new cocks, does that take?
What if it is rest and nothing else that

we want? Is it a findable thing, small?
In what hole is it hidden? Is it, maybe,
a country? Will a guide be required who
will say to us how? Do we fly? Do we
swim? What will I do now, with my hands?

•

IN THE BLOOD, WINNOWING

I.
Before the dumb hoof
through the chest, the fine hair
of wire drawn over the head, snapping
free the neck's blue chords,

before the visionary falling away
from a body left mumbling to itself,
consigned to the damp sling
of tropic circumstance,

there was this morning now,
in the shower, when you know
you are dying,

you are dying and your body—
a lozenge or a prayer, whatever goes
slim and unimportant when the tongue
has grown overly zealous—

contracts under the steam,
under the light that shows up on your skin
as a deep red the shower's curtain
alone can't account for.

II.
What is it but
yours, the one hand
drawing the scrotum (no longer
yours) back upon itself?
When you come
into the other hand, it's like
spitting on death's breast, on
her spectator shoes
to distract her.
Trembling in the water,
in the stick of yourself,
you watch the talisman's shadow,
already twisting, diminished against
the tiles, to the pig's-tail stump
of conclusion,

all it ever was.

III.
Stones do not matter.
You are twenty-nine for no reason,
or thirty-seven, your favorite prime.
Perhaps you are precisely that age
when a writer means, finally,
all that he says, a cubed square
of cell after cell containing
all the hounds of childhood,
with their hard buckles and hot
irons, their pins for under

your fingers. Dreams
are of falling
asleep at locked windows,
you are all the stones
that keep missing the glass.

IV.
Nothing stops
for you admiring the hair
that has sprung late
at either shoulder,
for you crushing your face
into the shirts that bloom
like cutaway views of old
lovers from your wall of closet.
It is any morning when the train
rattles over birdsong, the suggestion
of blades coming dry
from the night; brilliantly,
shaft after shaft, the sun passes
over the shit and bone and feather
of yours and other lives on earth,
the canted row-houses, children
in their crippled victory gardens,
throwing knives in the air,

and you tell yourself (already
growing hard again over the train's
crosstown difficulties)
that everything counts:

the correct tie,
the bit of skin between sock
and cuff, the man beside you,
strange and familiar as a tattoo
the hand wakes to and keeps
wanting to touch,
refusing to believe
in that part of the world
where things don't wash off.

UNDRESSING FOR LI PO

Li Po,
the moon through the vertical blinds
is laying its bars down,
I see black, tapered lives, and
the paler ones in between, all the sticks
of my life left to mend.
Fingering the two flat prayers
at my chest, one pierced with a gold ring,
the other rouged with a broken wedge
of mouth-paint,
I'm remembering your fondness
for wine, Li Po, you desiring your own
reflection, or the moon's, the same thing,

and dying from it.
At the mirror, to the man I love
too much, I am trying to say
that I have no need
for his tattooed body, his
hands at my wrist, the cicatrix
of woes tilting down
from beneath the belly—

that I'm tired
of flesh tumbling over the dwindling sword
of itself,
something like joy . . .

Li Po, Li Po,
the moon is picking its way
over used swabs and razors, pots of cream,
my face where I left it, on the dressing table.
I am thinking
mountains,
good wine,
plash of exile,
letters to nowhere, the poems,
untrimmed affection,
distance, boats coming
more still than the water
in their wandering.

Li Po, last night,
drunk again, I stood naked downstairs,
just dancing, dancing . . .
I watched my feet recover and lose again
their apricot, moving in and out from
the moon's light,
watched my body lose all particulars
save clean grace, what I'd forgotten.
I imagined dancing with a man seven feet tall,
the moon making a small planet of his face,

I thought of you again, Li Po.

─❬ ✦ ❭─

D. A. POWELL

·

[TRIPTYCH]

once	we kissed	the world
goodbye	aware	that it
was dying	of all	contained
within	these lines	I'll keep
two breaths	and you	to one side
of me	laughing	on the nightstand

·

[STUDS AND RINGS: FAVORS OF THE PIERCING PARTY]

. . . and so he dug a hole deep in the ground, and went and whispered in it what kind of ears King Midas had.
—OVID

studs and rings: favors of the piercing party
hole in the head.   you got your rightwrongright ear
sent out in a press release: post self disclosure

boys admired your jewels.   for a time
you liked getting stuck.   and advertised

when did you close your legs: no openings
available you whisper like a tease.   but rumors
trail behind you in the reeds: "golden boy
has suggestive ears."   you still can hear them

·

[ALWAYS RETURNING: HOLIDAYS AND BURIALS.
NOT EVERY WEEK]

always returning: holidays and burials.   not every week
has had its good friday.   except that lately latches
left unfastened for me.   biscuits rise in the piesafe
a dark suit smells less like mothballs: chrism

and condolences.   calendars come gaily from the florist
accounts receivable.   time and the supplier of easter
lilies: collusion.   we sit cozy in the parlor together
a cenotaph of cousinry.   unexpected guests do drop in

·

[MY FATHER AND ME MAKING DRESSES:
TOGETHER]

my father and me making dresses: together
we debutantes.   cruel in lace bodices

we swoon to saxophones and rich husbands.   late
afternoon: shots of brandy in our cocoa

aren't I blessed with a young father firm
and flouncy: giggling in his petticoats

the other boys sigh when he mows the lawn
they fumble with their pockets and blush

while we two chums.   in a workshop of taffeta
never tire of chat: rugby or crushes or appliqué

I put my knee in his back.   I cinch and cinch
as preparing for an antebellum barbecue

where an ashley might fill with regret.   and atlanta
explodes in flames: a host of scarlet poppies

•

[YOU'RE THIN AGAIN HANDSOME. IN OUR LAST]

you're thin again handsome.   in our last
hour together I'll be dabbing gravy off
your lip: stuck out.   an infirmary stoop

how can anything perplex us more than words
the pause in which we chew: parapraxia
I feed you lines.   you're a poor actor now
flubbing the bit part.   indignant us both

I'll want better for you than institutional
lunch in white paper.   pee stained underwear
a brief brief career as the delicious romantic lead

•

[THE MINOTAUR AT SUPPER: SPARE THE NORITAKE AND THE SPODE]

the minotaur at supper: spare the noritake and the spode
from these ungular hands.   goblet stems scattered at my hoofs

a spattering of color on my hide.   remnants of one youth
another impaled on my horns: I must say grace over his thighs
for there may be no path back to him.   the way is dim and twists

myself am halfboy.   am beauty and the end of same: a hungry thing
hunts me also: through which passageway do my nostrils sense blood
what aperture brings me air salted with cries of an ancient corrida

MINNIE BRUCE PRATT

·

ELBOWS

Cover your arms.
Don't let your elbows
show.

That's what my neighbors
down in Alabama tell
their daughters
so no elbow
plump or thin
tan or pink
will entice others
to passion.

But if I thought
my scrawny, two-toned
elbows would lure you

if I thought
my skinny, sharp-boned
elbows could secure you

I'd flap my arms
like a chicken
like a peafowl
like a guinea hen

when next I saw you
honey
I'd roll
up my sleeves and
sin
sin
sin.

POEM FOR MY SONS

When you were born, all the poets I knew
were men, dads eloquent on their sleeping
babes and the future: Coleridge at midnight,
Yeats' prayer that his daughter lack opinions,
his son be high and mighty, think and act.
You've read the new father's loud eloquence,
fiery sparks written in a silent house
breathing with the mother's exhausted sleep.

When you were born, my first, what I thought was
milk: my breasts sore, engorged, but not enough
when you woke. With you, my youngest, I did not
think: my head unraised for three days, mind-dead
from waist-down anesthetic labor, saddle
block, no walking either.
                              Your father was then
the poet I'd ceased to be when I got married.
It's taken me years to write this to you.

I had to make a future, willful, voluble,
lascivious, a thinker, a long walker,
unstruck transgressor, furious, shouting,
voluptuous, a lover, a smeller of blood,
milk, a woman mean as she can be some nights,
existence I could pray to, capable of
poetry.
          Now here we are. You are men,
and I am not the woman who rocked you
in the sweet reek of penicillin, sour milk,
the girl who could not imagine herself
or a future more than a warm walled room,
had no words but the pap of the expected,
and so, those nights, could not wish for you.

But now I have spoken, my self, I can ask
for you: that you'll know evil when you smell it;
that you'll know good and do it, and see how both
run loose through your lives; that then you'll remember
you come from dirt and history; that you'll choose
memory, not anesthesia; that you'll have work
you love, hindering no one, a path crossing

at boundary markers where you question power;
that your loves will match you thought for thought
in the long heat of blood and fact of bone.

Words not so romantic nor so grandly tossed
as if I'd summoned the universe to be
at your disposal.
                  I can only pray:

That you'll never ask for the weather, earth,
angels, women, or other lives to obey you;

that you'll remember me, who crossed, recrossed
you,
            as a woman making slowly toward
an unknown place where you could be with me,
like a woman on foot, in a long stepping out.

·

CRIME AGAINST NATURE

1.
The upraised arm, fist clenched, ready to hit,
first clenched and cocked, ready to throw a brick,
a rock, a Coke bottle. When you see this on TV,

robbers and cops, or people in some foreign alley,
is the rock in your hand? Do you shift and dodge?
Do you watch the story twitch in five kinds of color

while you eat Doritos, drink beer; the day's paper
sprawled at your feet, supplies bought at the 7-11
where no one bothered you? Or maybe he did. All

depends on what you look like, on if you can smile,
crawl, keep your mouth shut. Outside the store,
I, as usual, could not believe threat meant me, hated

by four men making up the story of their satiated
hot Saturday night and what they said at any woman
to emerge brash as a goddess from behind smoky glass,

how they won, if she would not bend her eyes or laugh,
by one thrusting question, broke her in half,
a bitch in heat, a devil with teeth for a cunt.

What's wrong with you, girl? the grin, gibe, chant.
What's the matter? (Split the concrete under her feet,
send her straight to hell, the prison pit fire,

blast her nasty self.) *You some kind of dyke?*
Sweating, damned if I'd give them the last say,
hissing into the mouth of the nearest face, *Yesss,*

hand jumped to car door, metal slam of escape
as he raised his hand, green bomb of a bottle,
I flinched, arm over my face, split-second

wait for the crash and shards of glass. His nod
instead, satisfied he'd frightened me back down
into whatever place I'd slid from. Laughter

quaked the other men. At me, a she-dog, queer
enough to talk? At him, tricked by a stone-face
drag woman stealing his punch line, astonished

as if a rock'd come to life in his hand and slashed
him? He dropped his hand, nodded like he'd won.
Slammed into my car, I drove away, mad, ashamed.

All night I seethed, helpless, the scene replayed,
slow-motion film, until I heard my *Yes,* and the dream
violence cracked with laughter. I was shaken out

on the street where my voice reared up her snout,
unlikely as a blacksnake racing from a drain, fire-
spitting, whistling like a siren, one word, *yes,*

and the men, balanced between terror and surprise,
laugh as the voice rolls like a hoopsnake, tail
in her mouth, obscure spinning blur, quiet howl,

a mouth like a conjuring trick, a black hole
that swallows their story and turns it inside out.

For a split second we are all clenched, suspended:
upraised fist, approving hoots, my inverted ending.

2.
The ones who fear me think they know who I am.
A devil's in me, or my brain's decayed by sickness.
In their hands, the hard shimmer of my life is dimmed.
I become a character to fit into their fictions,
someone predictable, tragic, disgusting, or pitiful.
If I'm not to burn, or crouch in some sort of cell,
at the very least I should not be let near children.

With strangers, even one with upraised fisted hand,
I blame this on too much church, or TV sci-fi, me cast
as a mutant sexual rampage, Godzilla Satan, basilisk
eyes, scorching phosphorescent skin, a hiss of words
deadly if breathed in.
                          But what about my mother? Or
the man I lived with years? How could they be so
certain I was bad and they were not? They knew: the girl
baby fat and bloody from the womb, the woman swollen
stomached with two pregnancies. My next body shift:
why did it shake them? Breasts full for no use but
a rush of pleasure, skin tightened, loosened, nipples,
genitals gleaming red with unshed blood.
                                            I left
certainty for body, place of mystery. They acted
as if I'd gone to stand naked in a dirty room, to spin
my skin completely off, turn and spin, come off skin,
until, under, loomed a thing, scaly sin, needle teeth
like poison knives, a monster in their lives who'd run
with the children in her mouth, like a snake steals
eggs.
       I've never gotten used to being their evil,
the woman, the man, who held me naked, little and big.

No explanation except: the one who tells the tale
gets to name the monster. In my version, I walk
to where I want to live. They are there winding
time around them like graveclothes, rotten shrouds.
The living dead, winding me into a graveyard future.

Exaggeration, of course. In my anger I turn them
into a late-night horror show. I've left out how

I had no job for pay, he worked for rent and groceries,
my mother gave me her old car. But they abhorred me:

my inhuman shimmer, the crime of moving back and forth
between more than one self, more than one end to the story.

3.
The hatred baffles me: individual, doctrinal, codified.
The way she pulled the statute book down like a novel

off the shelf, flipped to the index, her lacquer-red
lips glib around the words: *crime against nature*, and yes,

he had some basis for threat. I've looked it up to read
the law since. Should I be glad he only took my children?

That year the punishment was: not less than five nor more
than sixty years. For my methods, indecent and unnatural,

of gratifying a depraved and perverted sexual instinct.
For even the slightest touching of lips or tongue or lips

to a woman's genitals. That means any delicate sip,
the tongue trail of saliva like an animal track quick

in the dew, a mysterious path toward the gates, little
and big (or *per anum* and *per os*), a pause at the riddle,

how tongue like a finger rolls grit into a jewel of flesh,
how finger is like tongue (another forbidden gesture),

and tongue like a snake (*bestial* is in the statute)
winding through salty walls, the labyrinth, curlicue,

the underground spring, rocks that sing, and the cave
with an oracle yelling at the bottom, certainly depraved.

All from the slightest touch of my lips which can
shift me and my lover as easily into a party on the lawn

sipping limeade, special recipe, sprawled silliness,
a little gnawing on the rind. The law when I read it

didn't mention teeth. I'm sure it will someday if
one of us gets caught with the other, nipping.

4.
No one says *crime against nature* when a man
shotguns one or two or three or four or five
or more of his children, and usually his wife,
and maybe her visiting sister. But of the woman
who jumps twelve floors to her death, no I.D.
but a key around her neck, and in the apartment
her cold son in a back room, dead on a blanket:

Some are quick to say she was a fraud hiding
in a woman's body. Some pretend to be judicious
and give her as an example of why unmarried sluts
are not fit to raise children. But the truth is
we don't know what happened. Maybe she could not
imagine another ending because she was dirt poor,
alone, had tried everything. Or she was a queer
who hated herself by her family's name: *crooked*.

Maybe she killed the child because she looked
into the future and saw her past. Or maybe
some man killed the boy and pushed her, splayed,
out the window, no one to grab, nothing to hide
but the key between her breasts so we would find
the child and punish the killer. The iron key
warm, then cooling against her skin, her memory,
the locked room. She left a clue. We don't know
her secret. She's not here to tell the story.

5.
Last time we were together we went down to the river,
the boys and I, wading. In the rocks they saw a yellow-
striped snake, with a silver fish crossways in its mouth,
just another one of the beautiful terrors of nature,
how one thing can turn into another without warning.

When I open my mouth, some people hear snakes slide
out, whispering, to poison my sons' lives. Some fear
I'll turn them into queers, into women, a quick reverse
of uterine fate. It took only that original slightest
touch of Y, of androgen, to alter them from girls.

Some fear I've crossed over into capable power
and I'm taking my children with me. My body a snaky
rope, with its twirl, loop, spin, falling escape,
falling, altered, woman to man and back again, animal
to human: And what are the implications for the political
system of boy children who watched me like a magic
trick, like I had a key to the locked-room mystery?
(Will they lose all respect for national boundaries,
their father, science, or private property?)

In Joan's picture of that day, black, white, grey
gleaming, we three are clambered onto a fist of rock,
edge of the river. You can't see the signs that say
Danger No Wading, or the water weeds, mud, ruck
of bleached shells from animal feasting, the slimy
trails of periwinkle snails. We are sweaty, smiling
in the sun, clinging to keep our balance, glinting
like silver fishes caught in the mouth of the moment.

6.
I could have been mentally ill or committed
adultery, yet not been judged unfit. Or criminal
but feminine: prostitution, passing bad checks.
Or criminally unnatural with women, and escaped,
but only if I'd repented and pretended
like Susan S., who became a convincing fiction:

Rented a two-bedroom, poolside apartment, nice,
on Country Club Road, sang in the choir at Trinity,
got the kids into Scouts, arranged her job to walk
them to school in the morning, meet them at 3:00 P.M.,
a respected, well-dressed, professional woman
with several advanced degrees and correct answers
for the psychiatrist who would declare her *normal*,
in the ordinary sense of the word. No boyfriend
for cover, but her impersonation tricked the court.
In six months she got the children back: *custody*.
It's a prison term, isn't it? Someone being guarded.

I did none of that. In the end my children visit me
as I am. But I didn't write this story until now when
they are too old for either law or father to seize
or prevent from hearing my words, or from watching
as I advance in the scandalous ancient way of women:

our assault on enemies, walking forward, skirts lifted,
to show the silent mouth, the terrible power, our secret.

•

RED STRING

*The more I studied the situation, the more I was convinced that the
Southerner had never gotten over his resentment that the Negro was no
longer his plaything, his servant, and his source of income. The federal laws
for Negro protection passed during Reconstruction times had been made a
mockery by the white South where it had not secured their repeal. . . . It
seemed horrible to me that death in its most terrible form should be meted
out to the Negro. . . . For all these reasons it seemed a stern duty to give the
facts I had collected to the world.*

—IDA B. WELLS-BARNETT

At first she thought the lump in the road
was clay thrown up by a trucker's wheel.
Then Beatrice saw the mess of feathers.

Six or seven geese stood in the right-of-way, staring
at the blood, their black heads rigid above white throats.
Unmoved by passing wind or familiar violence, they fixed
their gaze on dead flesh and something more, a bird on the wing.

It whirled in a thicket of fog that grew up from fields plowed
and turned to winter. It joined other spirits exhaled before dawn,
creatures that once had crept or flapped or crawled over the land.

Beatrice had heard her mother tell of men who passed
as spirits. They hid in limestone caves by the river, hooded
themselves inside the curved wall, the glistening rock.
Then just at dark they appeared, as if they had the power
to split the earth open to release them. White-robed, faceless
horned heads, they advanced with torches over the water,
saying, *We are the ghosts of Shiloh and Bull Run fight!*

Neighbors who watched at the bridge knew each man by his voice
or limp or mended boots but said nothing, let the marchers
pass on. Then they ran their skinny hounds to hunt other
lives down ravines, to save their skins another night
from the carrion beetles, spotted with red darker than blood,
who wait by the grave for the body's return to the earth.

Some years the men killed scores, treed them in the sweetgums,
watched a beast face flicker in the starry green leaves.
Then they burned the tree.

Smoke from their fires
still lay over the land where Beatrice traveled.

Out of this cloud the dead of the field spoke to her,
voices from a place where women's voices never stop:

They took my boy down by Sucarnochee Creek.
He said, "Gentlemen, what have I done?"
They says, "Never mind what you have done.
We just want your damned heart." After they
killed him, I built up a little fire and laid out
by him all night until the neighbors came
in the morning. I was standing there when
they killed him, down by Sucarnochee Creek.

I am a mighty brave woman, but I was getting
scared the way they were treating me, throwing rocks
on my house, coming in disguise. They come to my bed
where I was laying, and whipped me. They dragged me
out into the field so that the blood strung across
the house, and the fence, and the cotton patch,
in the road, and they ravished me. Then they went
back into my house and ate the food on the stove.
They have drove me from my home. It is over
by DeSotoville, on the other side in Choctaw.

I had informed of persons whom I saw
dressing in Ku Klux disguise;
had named the parties. At the time
I was divorced from Dr. Randall
and had a school near Fredonia.
About one month before the election
some young men about the county
came in the nighttime; they said
I was not a decent woman; also
I was teaching radical politics.
They whipped me with hickory withes.
The gashes cut through my thin dress,

through the abdominal wall.
I was thrown into a ravine
in a helpless condition. The school
closed after my death.

From the fog above the bloody entrails of the bird, the dead flew
toward Beatrice like the Night crow whose one wing rests on the evening
while the other dusts off the morning star. They gave her such a look:

Child, what have you been up to while we
were trying to keep body and soul together?

But never mind that now. Here's what you must do:

Tie a red flannel string around your waist.
Plant your roots when the moon is dark. Remember
your past, and ours. Always remember who you are.
Don't let those men fool you about the ways of life
even if blood must sign your name.

·

THE OTHER SIDE

Men flirt in the silvered mirror, eyelids, shadow-
wings. The dance-floor red-blue spotlights shine hot
as lantern glow. At showtime, Beatrice works to know
who is a woman. The pumping dancer, gripped naked
by spandex at the crotch, could she hide a resting cock?
Her breasts insist on homage, thrust at every mouth.
Beatrice holds up crisp dollars, twist into cleft, sweat,
is rewarded by a look: *I deserve everything I get.*
A lady with beaded breasts caught under bronze net
lip-syncs a torch song, languid hand full of taxi money
to carry her, still dancing, lanky legs, past boys
idling outside, a fist of baseball bats, to prove her man.

A crowd circles the stage. Dark and pale faces blaze
above what runs fiery toward them, like kerosene spilled
from a kicked-over lantern. The spirit goes this way
and that, like rainwater shifts on a clay dance ground,
stepping from one sunken footprint to another. She watches
their mouths, the people about to kneel and drink their desire.
They will lick burning water from the dirt. They will rise up
bold in a body they have never worn.

*　　*　　*

The emcee jokes:
Get to be as old as me, have to decide if you're a he or she,
scolds her niece-nephew, her nephew-niece, which is Mawu,
which Lisa? One clanks keys from a cinched fighter's belt,
the other flutters hands and lashes.

The unsmiling woman
at her elbow asks Beatrice sideways, *What kind of woman*
are you? Stand here. Answer. Rearing proud head, she shies
at touch, a hand on her rough starched shirt. Yet her voice leads,
low, whispering, *Answer me and live.*

Wanting to taste
her scarred path, to trace with tongue each danger passed.

To meet as if at a dirt crossroads, makeshift altar,
a pile of stones, plastic roses, red ribbon, a sign
with illegible words from a god once there. To kneel and lick
her palm, scraped raw, shoved down on pavement. To walk on,
their tracks stirring the dust in the road.

To enter the lean-to
house and lie down as night rises, fog billowing like smoke
up from the fields. Inside, a fire, the bloody shirt stripped off.

To lie under her, to become the place both are going,
a rhythm like oars in water. The winter begun outside.
The snakes asleep. None to lick her ears so she could
hear an answer, none waiting to steal her words.

On her own
about how to answer, she waits for the unknown woman to ascend
through smoke, past the grinning bouncer, the vending machine.
She waits for her boot clack on the stair, old sound of desire.

Beatrice waits for the woman with eyes that say, *Come with me.*
Into the rain-streaked street of night, the yellow leaves fallen
like golden scars on black asphalt, they walk out their answer
to the riddle, the woman who is not a man, the woman who is not
a woman, following the yellow drift like fire around the corner.

MARIANA ROMO-CARMONA

·

CROWS

How do I know the sound
of stone hitting against stone?
I am lying in bed, trying to sleep
a quilt over my head

I imagine someone clearing a field
to build a wall
I hear metal
I see piles of rock on the back
of a pick-up truck
the stones bang the metal sides
and ring hollow through the trees
but, how do I know that?

When the rain starts, I know that swish
of leaves swept by wind
presaging rain, how *do* I know
and when a sharp caw breaks the vision of
autumn woods in my ears
I see the crow, glistening black
against the trunk of birches
cawing again as the stone truck
drives away
churning up earth
and stirring up ruts in yesterday's mud
I sit up, sleepy and achy, *how do I know?*

When I was a child I knew the sound
of the knife-sharpener's call
pushing a cart and the hum
of his wheel
though I saw neither one.
But when I heard my mother crying
deep and tearing in my sleep

what I knew was more
than stones, metal
rain   wind   black crow
emanating ghostly: this is how
a woman cries
stifled, alone
metal crashing against stone
and *how do I know . . .*

·

SIGNS

In the woods are filaments of light
promising something to the pines.
My oatmeal steams. The blackberries
I picked yesterday rolled off
one by one into the bowl. They've turned red.
On the table
a pamphlet bears the stamp
of a demure matron holding
a Victorian rose.
In languished pose she looks down
her left hand gently brushes
the edges of her collarbone, at her waist
her belt dangles undone. *Your Life Change*
proclaims the title   etched between
a chain of roses
Menopause and Osteoporosis.
The belt undone, the eyes cast down
the black tresses gathered up
reveal a nape of neck, curve of a gentle jaw.
Who invented the tight-waisted dress that slopes
into fullness at the belly?
This is not an illustration that speaks
for the pamphlet   but I'll take
the implication
she has loosened the belt, the woman with a rose
to allow her fuller belly at menopause
to breathe easily at last.

·

FISH

A school of clouds and a bunch
of unknown flowers
assert their ground from the mud
along the reservoir
above the clouds swim swiftly   I blink
sweat in my eyes and a fat squirrel
darts in my path as I run
my forty-ish eyes cannot tell you the kind
of squirrel it was nor the kind
of cloud   only the blur
of memories pressed
in single bubbles at my throat
I miss my son   one bubble rises
and fish, no   clouds
gravitate in winds
I wish they'd clear my throat of this pain
I miss my son
running over leaves I mourn
for each one I did not bend to see   to keep
their colors are a gasp of pleasure
at this stage
even though I miss
even though I am   I live.

·

DAYLIGHT

Daylight changed without you. The weather got colder, it rained, the sun
came out, wet newspapers dried on the street corner, pigeons fluttered
about the park, children squealed on the sidewalk wearing witch faces and
pumpkin heads, half-eaten candy apples melted on their sleeves . . .

Another day went by. Your side of the bed got rumpled, too. I borrowed
your pillow, whispered your name, opened the window and blew at the
dust, tilted the lamp shade, breathed in the twilight . . .

I noticed the sounds of leaves rustling, of trains approaching underground,
of women laughing a little like you, I conjured up your face and traced
your lips in the air, thinking, your absence is different now. There's no

anxiety, only discomfort, a stillness about everything—time doesn't move the same way, my thoughts are quieter.

I thought I'd get more work done without you, I was wrong. I got the mail and paid the bills, flipped the calendar to November, munched on the yellow quince I bought because it smelled like my childhood, but it had no flavor . . .

The weather changed again, the night is restless with warm wind and radios blaring, the sound of car horns bending at the corner. Before I sleep there will be hollow moments of missing you. I know you'll be here tomorrow . . . what frightens me is knowing this is how it would be if you were really gone, leaving my skin slowly, carving out the time, until I finally feel your absence surrounding me like mist, taking shape, like the depth of your eyes and the scent of your body.

—<✸>—

RUTH L. SCHWARTZ

·

POSSIBLE

It is the breast I remember seeing,
the nipple pink and round, the lustrous flesh,
before I saw the woman had no arms
in the locker room. Her teeth were excellent,
tugging her blouse on,

but it is her breast I remember
when I see again how what is perfect
lives beside what is tragic and damaged,
how silence arcs between these two,
each making the other possible.

·

FLAMENCO GUITAR

This music is the country you lost
when you were born,
the café which never closes, the sex which
comes so close your pores are
weeping with longing, and never touches you,
the nights you don't sleep, the hands in their ceaseless
moving like birds, the conversations interrupted
only by dancing, the dancers weeping with their bodies
painted like eyes,
here where black coffee and red wine are the only
waters, where crusty bread and creamy cheese
flecked with oregano and pooling tears of olive oil
are the only foods.
It's the music you strain to hear through all the needy
ordinary days,
the music which will only stop
when you abandon everything to follow it
—because this music lies to you, but it's a gorgeous lie,
full of such craving and entreaty, the chance for nothing
to be ordinary, ever . . .

It's like Conrad's heart of darkness, says the guitarist
later, when you introduce yourself
and learn he has a day job, he's a psychologist,
this isn't Seville, just College Avenue in Oakland,
the passions so much larger than our bodies
are lodged in our bodies, there is nothing we can do
to be rid of them, not the passions, not the bodies,
because whatever you make of your life
the soul keeps turning the other way,
like a child leaning backwards
over a railing toward the water, hanging by its feet,
so this music which is motion itself, you want it
to hold still,
its frenzy fixed so you can look
through its violet scarlet tangerine lens
and glimpse your life there, floating in the colors.

·

CAN PIGEONS BE HEROES?

*A brave pigeon named President Wilson saved the lives of hundreds of
American soldiers during World War I . . . by carrying a message 25 miles
through fog and machine gun fire, wounded in the breast, with one leg
shot away.*
　　—FROM THE PUBLIC ART EXHIBIT *CAN PIGEONS BE HEROES?*

It's their otherness I admire,
their rust-colored eyes, like those of the best china dolls,
which have real lids, and open and shut.
Their bobbing heads, emerald and amethyst-ruffed necks,
scaly red feet which could carry them anywhere,
delicate, impermeable,
and how they live and breed in our landscape, ignoring
or sometimes using us
for their own, purely pigeon ends;
and how like us they finally are,
aggressive, obsequious,
marked by lust . . .
Yet there is also the way an entire flock
can rise as one bird
in some unspoken, instantaneous agreement—
which seems to me much more subtle
and far-reaching than love,

with its clanking of one awkward heart
beside another.
Today, next to the people perched on benches
as if this were Paris, or someplace equally romantic,
the pigeons look sick, unkempt,
ill-cared-for. Of course,
no one cares for them,
it's every bird for himself in this city;
there are greasy, bedraggled feathers,
a limp, an oozing eye;
there's one with a bald tumor, sprung
from its green bright neck
—but the bird still wants to live,
it's carefully fitting its beak between each cracked brick
for any fallen bread.
Meanwhile there are two human lovers
putting lips to each other's ears,
head to a shoulder, hand to hand, as if practicing,
a young man in a baseball cap
wearing stereo headphones and reading,
rocking a little back and forth,
a trio of teenagers with pierced lips and eyebrows
and boldly dyed hair,
a young bike messenger on break
who throws away half a cigarette, still lit,
so the plume of smoke rises up between the pigeons
for minutes afterward like a secret signal.
Now a woman throws crumbs,
delight on her face
as the birds jostle and squirm;
she shifts on the bench, moving closer and closer,
and when the bread is gone she talks
to the pigeons, shows them her empty hands—
then yawns,
as if after love.
Now the lovers are replaced
by a man who looks as if the green
duffel bag he carries
might be everything he has.
He's checking the left-behind coffee cups,
then drinking from them,
and watching him, I want to finish eating my sandwich
and loop the straps of my bag more tightly
around my arm.

That's it. That's it exactly.
The way we turn away from each other,
running and flapping, making a knot
of ourselves —
so that I wonder about heroes, human and pigeon both,
what force there is beyond instinct
or hunger, in any one of us,
flying against machine-gun fire
in our singular bodies.

.

EDGEWATER PARK

Even now, at the end of the century,
when our survival as a species

seems a matter of dumb luck,
our bodies studded with these jewels of tenderness

the way so many dying insects
bead the spider's web —

even now, on the cliffs above the beach,
I see two men who meet for pleasure,

nothing else,
fully clothed, in a cove of bushes,

standing face to face, as if to dance —
but one has both hands on the other's cock

and is pulling at it, tenderly —
and the body, at least, would name this Love,

and who are we to contradict
the pure animal body?

All around us, in expensive houses,
men and women married many years

touch far less joyfully than this,
with less attention to the hunger of it.

And truly, what do we have left
but moments of this gazing, pulling

at each other, at ourselves,
the shells ground finer and finer

under our feet,
making a kind of jagged sand,

the insects we call Canadian Soldiers
rising from the water in great swarms

to mate and die—
on my window they looked like tadpoles,

hundreds of them flooding toward
the light—

and some of them
made their way in,

the whiteness of the ceiling
became their water,

they massed there as full of joy
as if it were the sea.

By morning they were dead,
their many bodies

light and dry,
littering the tabletops.

And the spiders, lucky spiders,
ate for weeks.

⤙ ☼ ⤚

ROBYN SELMAN

•

21 EAST 10TH, 2BR, WBF, EIK

There we were. Two women, who I think still
think of themselves as underage tomgirls,
in one small corner of the terrible,
terribly lovely, uninhabited world.
We were led about by Mrs. Bass,
agent of this terrain, whose piercing glance
pointed—practiced, fiery, divalike—
at the cornices and sprays of evening light,
at the door that simply wasn't French, but with
imagination (pause), sanding (pause), cloth cinched
just so, could be made—her word—*delicate.*
Our heels, all six, clicked over each square inch.
We flicked lights, ran taps, unpacked in our minds
until Mrs. Bass's coughs announced the time.

We'd simply taken too long. We were (pause)
wrong. The right customer (she let us know)
needed no encouragement to sign,
knew prewar from post, could live well in both,
had neither inclinations nor preferences,
came complete with sterling references,
was straight, would ultimately propagate
and then arrange with her to buy more space.
This spelled romance for Mrs. Bass, who (pause),
like Sisyphus, had an ongoing job to do.
Slow and (her word) *different,* we were dismissed.
We walked awhile before tripping the switch
on our surprisingly pregnant with
(pause) ourselves, undaunted old apartment.

•

EXODUS

Open your eyes, O beloved homeland, and behold your son,
Sancho Panza, returning to you. If he does not come back very

rich, he comes well flogged. Open your arms and receive also
your other son, Don Quixote, who returns vanquished by the
arm of another but a victor over himself and this, so I have
been told, is the greatest victory that could be desired.
—CERVANTES, *Don Quixote*

1

And so I went forth, exhilarated,
in uniform: worn-through jeans, muscle tees,
stripped of bras and ancestral history.
Since I had nothing real to take along,

I took along a fig-shaped stone,
a bag of gold buds, a resin-stained bong,
hash oil, in which papers were coated,
and two tabs of four-way blotter acid,

lactose-laced cocaine, cut to average,
a fifth of scotch, which was a parting gift,
a poncho, a guitar, feminist sheet music,
and *Court and Spark*, which I'd tape-recorded.

With all this I'd find someone of my own.
All ill-equipped bride-to-be, I left home.

2

The old man waves to me through iron bars
on his window and I wave back at him.
Ten years back, at a spring semester end,
I went to Greece with three other women.

Joanne, whom I called Joey, my lover then,
was the only woman I knew who'd speak
the word proudly. She worked and was older
and didn't do drugs like I did, or bars.

She even looked what I thought was the part:
hair close-cropped, the top in a boyish mop.
We met in a club called The Other Side,
then fell in side by side later that night

on a futon with psychedelic sheets
that lay in an attic under beamed eaves.

3
An ill-equipped bride-to-be, I left home.
The coke I'd flown with in my underwear
had melted into a yellowish loam.
Cheryl, who'd once caused a fire somewhere

drying her wet shirt in a microwave,
suggested that we lay the gluey high
on the warm radiator to try to save
what stash we could, and I agreed to try.

Moments later, the flakes began to fly
down to the floor like mocking stalactites.
My new roommate looked on, removed, dry-eyed.
She was a grad architecture student

with prefab plans for life in blueprints.
I befriended Mike with the good hash pipe.

4
We lay in her attic under beamed eaves,
then headed to New York from Washington.
My new lover, whom I didn't discover
for weeks was depressed and addicted,

for real, to caffeine and cigarettes,
piloted a Buick big as a hearse.
And when the speed she was sipping kicked in
the car did ninety. I waited for sirens.

We were rushing to a conference on women:
Millet, Morgan, Griffin, Rich, and Steinem.
I asked a woman who wasn't Millet
for her autograph. Mistaken, somewhat

humbler, I returned to Joey in the stands.
They called the next panel "New Lesbians."

5
I befriended Mike with the good hash pipe
and a constant yen for bourbon on ice.
I stayed straight. A consequence of having
no clue how to get that other kind of date.

I wore lavender tops, ankhs, stopped shaving,
carried code books face out though my arms ached,
hoped she'd recognize *Lesbian Nation*,
Millet's *Flying*, poems by Susan Griffin.

As I grew needy, the book chimney grew.
Finally, I turned back to what I knew:
the last of the coke, the dope, me and Mike,
moved in together with the good hash pipe.

He was pretty, but he wasn't a girl.
Next came Bob, but before him I had Phil.

6
They called the next panel "New Lesbians."
I spent the day in the bleachers transfixed.
Joey had to walk off her nicotine fit.
We went to the ladies' (women's) room and kissed.

We were in love, we weren't saying we were.
I wasn't saying that the words I'd heard
were having a druglike effect: gay pride
shot through me, some other blood mixed with mine.

The women I'd known didn't call themselves
lesbians, but winked across tennis courts
in short shorts, and gave slaps in locker rooms
that took the place (psychically) of bedrooms.

Was that sex or athletics? One panelist
asked, "Was sex as much fun with politics?"

7
Next came Bob, but before him I had Phil,
who wore overalls with an unlatched bib
and an army sweater worn at the wrists.
He liked Schumann, Mao, Marx, and Joplin's *Pearl*.

He rarely shaved, he washed infrequently
and spoke with a strong uncorrected lisp
which made him seem younger than twenty-six.
I didn't move in. He broke up with me.

Bob was a prize my mom couldn't resist:
six foot, an accountant-to-be, Jewish,
a hard worker, he'd make love then make coffee.
He took me home on the big holidays.

On weekends, with his parents, we saw plays.
We saw everything except that we were gay.

8
"What did sex have to do with politics?"
Susan, my first, wrestled me to the floor
after her two-set win: six/one, six/four.
She was privileged, both pretty and rich.

Though I wasn't in love with her riches,
the idea that she passed was seductive.
(We escaped the closeted coaches' judgment.)
She was younger, but had already had

stacks of lovers: boys, girls, even a divorced
mother. Both she and her sister lost their
virginity to their older brother.
She said, "*It* had nothing to do with *it*."

I didn't know what *it* she meant, or
pretended I didn't, as I licked and kissed.

9
We saw everything except that we were gay.
Or, I saw everything except the way
around being gay. So I took to bars,
Donna Summer, and Gloria Gaynor.

But I liked the stone butch I met better,
who by day flipped hamburgers and at night
was a chest-taped male impersonator.
Nothing ever happened with her, but I

paid the cover charge again and again
though I didn't speak to any new lesbians.
For cover, I'd take my closeted friends.
We danced shackled together like prisoners.

Eleanor R., Nat, Virginia, or me—
One of us had to be the first to lead.

10
I licked and kissed her in the bathroom stall
as a line of sisters wound down the hall.
Joey's eyes shut against the light green walls.
I drank the warm juices in, swallowing

sips of her like heroin, swallowing
her pride, still unable to summon
any of mine. Months after that kiss
she'd scold me in the Acropolis

for something I'd never heard of that she
loudly termed my *goddamambivalence*.
I snapped back that she was too serious
and imagined leaving her for good right there.

I didn't. I was too in love and scared—
thousands of years up in the chalky air.

11
One of us had to be the first to lead:
Eleanor R., Natalie B., Virginia
Woolf, Elizabeth R., Elizabeth B.,
Hedda and Alla Nazimova,

Debbie Reynolds, Gertrude Stein, Amelia,
Willa Cather, Cheryl, Whitney Houston,
Sylvia Beach, Billie Jean, Martina,
Jodie Foster, Marion Dickerman,

Lisa, Elizabeth Cady Stanton,
Lesley Gore and Susan B. Anthony,
Bessie, Babe Didrikson, Val, Anne Murray,
Barbara Jordan and lifelong companion,

Yourcenar, Colette, Marlene, H. D. —
the minds I admired, the strong-bodied.

12
Thousands of cheers filled the chalky air
in the hot Dalton School gymnasium.
Joey sipped cola and chewed Aspergum.
The speaker railed against the oppression

of gay/straight/white/Latina women.
They called a break. We hit the streets, like a gang, in
our "Sisterhood Is Powerful" buttons.
I was firmly a not-quite believer,

while Joey's button seemed to protect her.
At Sixtieth and Lex, I doubled over.
Outside things were different. I could see
that people could see. But that didn't seem

to bother Joey, whose hand lay on my knee,
a gesture I thought was only about me.

13

The minds I admired, the strong-bodied,
the women who had started my fire,
all in the impregnable closet with me,
shackled together by the same wire.

I was, at the time, just turning twenty
and lacked the mettle to try to unbend
thousands of years of history of women.
And so, like many women before me,

I let other women come out before me.
It wasn't that I had a wicked itch,
for I had long before gladly scratched it,
but I was still afraid of the language.

It was in the closet that the words took form
and with them I went forth in uniform.

14

I thought the gesture was only about me.
We made our way through Greek islands by boat:
Joey in a chair; I, cross-legged and tortured
as Crane, reading his poems on a heap of rope.

I don't remember the other two women
except they were straight and Canadian.
That night after dinner and too much wine
I went to one (with blue eyes?) with the hope

of blurring the line between her kind and mine.
I found Joey walking with a cup of coffee.
I still hear the metronome of her steps,
that morning quiet as our empty bed.

The old man waves to me through iron bars
on his window and I wave back at him.

15
And so I went forth in uniform.
Through iron bars, the old man waved to me.
I left home, an ill-equipped bride-to-be
and lay in an attic under beamed eaves.

I befriended Mike with the good hash pipe.
They called the next panel "New Lesbians."
Then came Bob, but before him was Phil.
What does sex have to do with politics?

We saw everything except that we were gay,
or pretended we didn't, as we licked and kissed.
One of us had to be the first to lead,
thousands of years up in the chalky air.

The minds I admired, the strong-bodied—
I thought the gesture was only about me.

REGINALD SHEPHERD

·

THE GODS AT THREE A.M.

The foolish gods are doing poppers while they sing along,
they're taking off their white T-shirts and wiping the sweat
from their foreheads with them, the gods have tattoos
of skulls and roses on their shoulders, perhaps a pink triangle
above the left nipple, for them there's hope. The gods
are pausing to light cigarettes while they dance, they're laughing
at private jokes while the smoke machine comes on,
one of the gods told you they put talcum powder
in the artificial fog, then walked away, how could anyone
breathe talcum powder, but it makes their skin shine
with sweat and smell of cigarettes and Obsession. Don't try
to say you didn't know the gods are always white, the statues
told you that. The gods don't say hello, and when you ask them
how they are the gods say they don't know, the gods
are drunk and don't feel like talking now, but you
can touch their muscled backs when they pass.

The gods in backwards baseball caps say
free love, they say *this is the time*, and disappear
into another corner of the bar, they're always moving
to another song. The gods with their checked flannel
shirts unbuttoned under open motorcycle jackets,
hard nipples and ghost-white briefs above the waistbands
of their baggy jeans, say *get here*, the gods say *soon*, and you just
keep dancing because you don't know the words, you hope
the gods will notice small devotions and smile, maybe
a quick thumbs-up if you're good. The gods
whose perfect instances of bodies last only
for the instant, or until last call (and then
they disappear into the sidewalk), gods who are splendid
without meaning to be, who do they need
to impress, say *this could be the magic*, they say
live for tonight, and then the lights come on.

NARCISSUS LEARNING THE WORDS TO THIS SONG

I enter this moment in retrospect, already
looking sadly back; I have everything
I need. Strobe lights and sweat compose
the same new song, moving bodies still

in my pessimism of the will and fogged-up
bathroom mirror the morning after of the night
before. *The mirrors would do well
to reflect further.* The man I asked

to dance, the man I was afraid to ask
all night: an expensive spirit in an Armani suit,
pink skin almost translucent under flashing lights,
almost seen through. Those changing tints (blues,

yellows, and reds, melding and alternating) want
to refute mere black and white. Right now I believe
his body's careless promise of pleasure, and also
in its dangers; I am an entire evening

of boredom and credulity leaning against
this metal pillar in a corner. I put that moment here
with other emptiness in the understanding, a man
I'll never hope to be again. (I remember

just how it will be. We were too much
alike.) *Look at yourself in a mirror
all your life and you will see death
at work like bees in a hive of glass.* So I

look to another's tarnished body, and there
will last forever. (I have a condom
in my back pocket, I am a thoroughly modern fable
narrating his own moral: a story that survives

tonight, and all the undressed pictures of desire
corrected into beauty.) Foucault wrote that love
is reminiscence, the shining hour after he leaves
at three or four A.M. (A myth myself, I am familiar

with the other fictions.) Histories of men I haven't met
are waving good-bye from cabs. I author my loss
for the beauty of its afterward, shared hours spent alone
with these glass flowers. I have outlived

my allegory. Send me forget-me-nots.

·

THREE A.M. ETERNAL

You go to my head, the song says: I wouldn't take
so many chances. A small room full of smoke and men,
pale bodies wavering (why should it always be
such pearled white skin—pink, that is—burning paper
making distance? the room's too close), unfinished

phrases, falling orange ashes, off, the words
too blond (*likeness*), too much like words, his hair, merely,
the clouded face crowded with blanks where the
desire should be, filled in too quickly
with all the wrong answers, while the room laughs

at its own joke. *Sentenced again.* As if it were that
easy to start again (lighting another cigarette, effacing
the face), as if you could make something
of it (*night*), the long drunk party,
the bodies hovering, weightless almost (blowing

the smoke up to the ceiling, lowering it), and out
of reach. What a joke. I'd like to talk to you
about it, the room so white, the air so crowded
with the smoke of laughter, I'd like to open
a door, someone, or just to breathe.

EROS IN HIS STRIPED BLUE SHIRT

and green plaid shorts goes strolling
through Juneau Park at eight o'clock
with only a hooded yellow windbreaker
for protection, trawling the bushes after work

while tugboats crawl the darkening freshwater
outlook. Mist coming in not even from a sea, rain
later in the evening from Lake Michigan, a promise
like *wait till your father gets home*. The air

is full of fog and botched seductions, reluctance
of early summer to arrive. It's fifty-five degrees
in June, the bodies can barely be made out
leaning on picnic tables under trees or

set sentinel like statues along the paths (the founder
corrodes quietly on his pedestal, inscription
effaced under FAGGOTS GO HOME). Lips
touched to a public fountain for a passerby

shape clouded breath into a *who-goes-there?*, into a
friend-or-foe?, eyes catching eyes like hooks
cast in a shallow tide. Night pouring in like water
into a lock, the rusted freighter lowered level

to level, banks of the cement canal
on either side, but miles from any dock.

•

THAT MAN

in the green fleece shorts is taking off
his mustard shirt. There's a T-shirt
the same color underneath. Almost the same.

No, not that one.

2.
What I wanted one evening, other evenings:
the trim of honeyed skin between the yellow
and the green; glancing angle
of calf when the right heel pivots
to the left; uneven blue space the mat retains
where he has stretched. I wanted one evening
like another, air free to come and go.

(Imagine myself agraze in that green,
grace of that sexual field a meadow
where I can do no harm, rabbit
or roan oribi hurting grass. But of course
I am a predator, and fail.)

3.
Now he's the world of what happens
happening, flex of thigh or twenty-degree
twist of torso, unclassical
colors still painting the skin
while he extends himself
into the overheated room. Mimesis,
the body mimicking itself, in imitation
of other bodies. Sweat and the chill
of an opened fire door, a rise of skin
where skin can't be seen.

(The branching tree of bones he is.)

4.
A man in motion for once, not parts
to make a man, make up
for him. (Positions his body
assumes and discards, unwilling to be wrong
for long.) Inner of an elbow, back of

a knee (concave where I curl up
with my mirror): wherever the body bends
or turns away.

5.
Soul says nothing
of consequence, over and over, says flesh
repeating itself articulately: waxy rhyme
of salvation, a self identical
with self, reflective sheen
of perspiration:

An ordinary handsome man
improving himself after work.
Thirty-four or thirty-five.
Six o'clock.

6.
The lockers not the same
green as his shorts, stuccoed
with rust, matte walls a blue
when the blue has drained out, pale
and certain as an aging sky.
I'm a visitor in this new city, sky
made of spackle and cement: both of us
naked, only one nude. Then
there is no man at all.

7.
The poem doesn't think of him.

LINDA SMUKLER

·

DAYS INN

It was astonishing to walk into room 233 at the Days Inn   the door open
for us   to turn on the lights and to close the curtains   to see you first
locked into that tan recliner as I sat on the (slightly darker) tan carpet   my
back up against the coarse blue bedspread   to smell disinfectant and to
drink bitter tea   to feel the minutes of our short afternoon slip away into
nervousness and the prints on the off-white walls   then how you lay down
on the bed   and I lay next to you   to kiss   no to talk   to get comfortable
with each other again   we heard raised voices from somewhere   from the
side or overhead   we couldn't figure out where   perhaps a meeting or ten
TVs   screaming children or a gathering of boys to watch the football
game   these were all possibilities as gradually the voices got so loud I called
the front desk to complain   the desk clerk said the voices were coming
from below   something religious for sure   evangelists or a revival
meeting   I told the clerk that I would call her back if we needed to
move   then you asked me to turn off the hard lights and I did and lay
back down next to you and then on top of you and I finally forgave myself
for letting you wait at the train station   I remember you turned me over
and how delirious I became at your touch   and at a certain point I was
overwhelmed with the desire to enter you and all the while beneath us
they called on the Lord   they called for salvation   the desk called and out
of breath I answered and said we were fine and did not want to move and
it was true   the room had become as if lighted by candles and we lay on
a sacred bier accompanied by hosannas and hallelujahs   and the chalice
of your scent   the icon of your face   the idols of your breasts in black
lace   the staff of your finger in my ass and my cock in your cunt   our
coming joined from below by shouts and applause and the exalted blessings
of the possessed

·

TRASH

I stopped home at lunch because I left my cock on the bathroom sink   I
found it there upstairs nested in its harness   condom still on   who did
you think you would fuck that you needed a condom? a   man?   a
woman?   I like that you were ready   a little ashamed that I was not   I

never thought that harness worked very well but it worked perfectly with you
and maybe I don't need a new one after all so I rushed home at lunch
afraid that my lover (or is that what I call you now?) might show up I
looked around for telltale signs in the guest room where we slept shook
out our two pillows and took one downstairs to the master bedroom I know
I'll sleep upstairs again tonight and take that pillow with me to bury my
head where you rested yours I rolled the condom off the cock washed
the pink rubber and put the cock and harness back into their soft cotton
bag I wrapped the condom in one of our Lipton tea bag covers from
last night took it with me into the car and stuffed the package into
the now empty bag of vegetable chips from which you fed me
parsnip yucca ruby taro that one with a drawing inside another that
looked and tasted like potato but which you insisted was not I finished
the chips this morning in the car and it was a way to keep you close taking
that condom still full of you out of its Lipton tea bag cover unrolling a
bit and placing the tip into my mouth I tasted latex and lubricant and I
tasted you and after I was done I rewrapped the condom stuffed the
bundle back into the empty chips bag and put it all into an old brown
paper lunch sack I had to go to the bank so I threw the whole thing out
in the lobby under where one writes deposit slips

·

SIGN

I forgot to tell you about the red sheets my sister bought for us that were
incredibly cheap on sale and that we couldn't replace with the blue sheets
we wanted because the blue sheets are now full price I forgot to tell you
about the reason I wanted to make love last night and instead we had a
fight I forgot to tell you that I came out in sign class a class of twenty
or so under thirty women and one man all from the teaching pro-
fessions all straight from E. Greenbush I forgot to tell you that the
week before the teacher asked me do you have children and I snapped my
fingers together to say no and slapped my hip to say I had a dog she made
me finger spell our dog's name and then the teacher said bring pictures of
your family next week I forgot to tell you that this week I brought pictures
of you and our dog I showed them to the class and when asked I slapped
my hip and gave the sign for dog and pointed to the picture of you and
made the sign for love and person which is the sign for love person or lover
and some of the students looked at me and were very polite some even
smiled it was so easy to say husband and children and all I wanted to say
was lover and dog so I wondered why after all these years I still had to
blush

·

MARRY

The morning I asked you to marry me we were staying at Bob's and I could not say it out loud so I wrote it first   your roses had opened blush pink and were beginning to wilt in the heat   you came out of the shower with cramps and I rubbed your belly and wanted you and thought I'm writing a marriage proposal on a simple yellow pad not even mine how strange I've never asked anyone before   a marriage proposal in Bob's unlived-in apartment while he's in Massachusetts with Peter who has just come down with CMV in both of his eyes   I held you in a brown leather Mies van der Rohe chair and I could have been in my parents' home and thought I am my parents both of them   the way I ask you to marry me cling to me be with me   the walls were white but I do not speak to my parents and they do not speak to me so I could not even tell them and I had one new pimple and so did you   twins I'd say made from our long nights our endless days the stress of our delight   I lay you back over my lap on the van der Rohe chair and entered you   took you   twice   you said yes yes like that and yes and you told me you had never said yes before   then we got dressed and walked out on the streets and am I different   I took your hand so easily but shouldn't it feel different and we walked and I thought how to explain I do not have a ring but I did not say anything   I wanted no yellow bands to fade over time   if at all a circle of straw or perhaps a stem of mint to be changed every day to renew our vows   we accidentally stepped into St. Patrick's because I thought it was St. Thomas's   the air heavy with incense and sanctity   not a place for us so we walked out and started toward the museum our destination but at the last minute I turned around to fix our mistake   we opened the heavy doors to St. Thomas's and found Plexiglas blocking our way into the chapel but the air was clean and clear and look up those windows with stars eye-hurting blue fall down on us as I kissed you standing there inside the church

·

HOME IN THREE DAYS. DON'T WASH.

I am driving to you and I will drive all the way to New York through the long round of the earth   the plains   the wheat   through the hills of Ohio and the darkening cities of Pittsburgh and Philadelphia and Trenton   don't wash   I am listening to music loud   I can't stop   I am driving right into you with my foot my heart my fist   the faster I go the closer I am to you   I only slow down for police cars hidden behind the corners of the highway   behind well-placed trees and planned hillocks   I won the last battle I won in all my short and skinny frame at least 1500 hearts   because of you they saw me   because of you they saw what I have to offer   they cried in ecstasy when I tore off their clothes   they cried when I sliced open their throats   they cried when they saw everything I can give you   they wanted my hardness the curl of my lip   they wanted the murderer in me   don't wash   I want a week's worth of you wet   I want the same underwear   the same sour smell   layers of it thick   the soak and musk of you   I too am acquiring mud and the scum of desire   my cock has not come down yet from thinking about you   through the entire days of battle   don't wash   it's becoming night now   I see pinks and blue   a deer by the side of the road   I'm driving south now into the constant drench of you   the earth on my left shoulder   don't wash   don't wash the books out of your hands   don't wash the telephone you've held between your chin and my mouth   don't wash away the meal you had this morning   the orange juice on your chin   don't wash the history of the breaths you have taken in my absence out of your mouth   I want to know them   all the churches and all the stores smell me as I go by   they smell my desire and the force of my lips   they smell how I hold my breath   the inside of your shoes   that white layer now at the fold where your thigh touches your labia   that punk   your hair matted waiting   wait that long   that much   I want you not to move and therefore not to live except to feel the force of my hand on your forehead   around your jaw   taste my mouth   yellow lines   white lines   a horse in the road   I am not tired   I will drive through the night   I will not eat   the dirt still caked around my fingernails   that is what they want   all of them   they smell what happens with you   that I   a woman   have something to offer a woman   that I have something to take her with   do not wash   you will crawl over me with the mud of your days   with all the slime and smell and wild leaves of them   and I will fill myself on the sourness of your ass and your cunt as they ride between my thumb and forefinger   I will lick you clean   all of that will be mine   I have fasted for days waiting

In the end I will wash you and you will rise out of the bath   sweet smelling   to sleep and wake again   perhaps you will wake to tell me how much I stink because I have not washed even longer than you   you will say: you think you can come in here looking like that?   you think you can come in here with the blood of all those women on your hands?   you think that you can tear apart the world and then come and ravish me?   no   not now   not with your stinking lousy little man self   how small you are   how thin   how unbelievably proud   how wretched   those arms couldn't fuck a pigeon   could they?   those lights that stop sign   this fork in the road   you would have me?   how could you walk into our house this way?

CHERYL BOYCE TAYLOR

·

FOREVER ARIMA
TANTY GIRLIE'S POEM

my Arima mountains closer
my dead twin weaves a pink hibiscus
bouquet for my ankles   welcomes me back
to the house of our birth
a faint steelpan punctuates this calypso
night

ai gurl long time ai eh see yu
yu doh come here for love nor for money
10 years yu away   somebody do yu sometin
i am aroused by the lilt
of my people's voices

the kitchen shelves no longer house
temptations of my childhood
guava jelly   tamarind jam   coconut drops
all replaced by see-thru bottles of curry, jerk
sauce
processed pepper imported from Caracas

the yellow and gold plastic fly cover
keeps the sweet bread insect free
nothing protects me as the memories come
hard and sweet   fragile and scathing

but wait nah, wha yu muder, my sister
sayin bout dat ting on yu head?
she please? . . . OK, me too.

Tantan Rose begins at dawn
gathering provision
yamatoota   tanya   dasheen
sits me down to say . . . -ting change gurl
here com bad jus like America

heat oil in skillet
¼ cup sugar
½ cup chopped garlic

de young people laazzy
doh want to work hard
cussin de parents
well ai never

                    4 cups rice
                    1 cup chopped pig tails

drugs wash away dis place
de neighbor boy, Ms. Martil
'bout 16 years so   on coke
yu remember he?
he iz de one break in de
ole lady house
lord . . . hit she in she head
oh meh lord gawd

                    bowl of spinach
                    bowl of okra

take she Sunday school change
eat she sweet bread
hit she in she head
she nearly dead

                    dash of salt   paprika

yu remember Marcia
6 chiren still no husband
makin de poor muder shame

                    2 cups pigeon peas
                    8 cracked blue crabs

de biggest sister pass
O levels   yes . . . workin
in de Red House   Red House . . .
is like de wite house over there
yeh man Red House

¼ cup bird pepper

de boro lay off de fader
an half de older workmen
shame, shame eh?

¼ cup old oak rum

oh shimps look at de time
yu want som bread an shark
while yu waitin
food nearly finish we gurl

dash som hot pepper on
sip som rum
stir de callaloo
lil curry   lil pepper

chile raisin chiren now eh easy nah
lordy   lordy   gimmie a lil rum
ai glad mine nearly grown

ah   thin   thin   sip ah oak

still smooth gurl —

add lil water tu rice
brown de chicken
sip som rum

so yu come tu see meh
or tu play mas   tell de trut
10 days eh no vacation
yu really americanize yes gurl

mo pepper
lil bit oak

oh mak sure yu tek off dem
gold bracelets before yu go out tonite eh
dey robbin yu in Maxi taxi
in broad daylite
ai tellin yu when de take in 2 rum
any number could play

¼ cup ground ginger
sprig of mint
a pinch of rum
chinke lil bit mo

sweeten up yuh chops gurl
yu doh eat so in America, eh?
Sunday food on Friday
de kitchen smellin nice   nice
   dinner go be good tonite . . .

       brown de chicken
       brown de chicken down
       sip som rum
       brown de chicken
        le we eat

grandma's rocker has the same old squeak
my twin comes close peeks in at me
in the distance Ma Subar fat cock crows
through the open door my aunt's voice

"-nite yes gurl,
but look at meh sister dauter nah
sleep well   til morning eh."

·

'ROUND IRVING HIGH SCHOOL
FOR MALIK TAYLOR

1.
Marijuana joints make circles
hand to hand
like a collection plate
at Sunday service   brother to brother

Brother to brother
how the urban animal bleats
when they meet
shoulder bump shoulder kissing
mouth hiss   hissing

Palms slapping languid days back
back   back into numbness
when i don'tdon'tdon't
give a fuck about no one

They say in New York City
the children carry broken glass
under their fingernails
box cutters in their teeth

2.
My son, you enter tampering with the blues
and even when a deceitful wind blows
messing up your tightly beaded afro curls
nothing shakes you my son
you ignite the riddle
Phife with the blues
hip   hot   hot   jazz

hip   hop   hopping   breaking the
naked sounds of gunshots on Linden Boulevard
notnotnot another stereotypic niggaaa
wid a 40 in his hand

3.
You come skinny and small
all three pounds of you
jumping to da music

Three months old you know to sing
and i'd rather listen to you than James Brown
cause you be loud   black 'n proud
carrying your love way down far
so as only i could see
and i love that sly smile
just like i loved your daddy's

4.
Your hands holding flowers
not guns   and
everything   everything about you
makes me proud to call you mine

PLENTY TIME PASS FAST, FAS DEY SO

1.
i used to kno when mango ripe
an ready to pick
i used to wait for guava
to turn from a hard green ball
when it yellow and creamy ripe wid sun
i'd drag a chair from de gallery
stand up on it and full meh mouth
wid de sweet meat right from de tree
now dat was livin

ah used to kno
if meh grandmudder left hip hurtin
rain comin
an if she right hand damp
it go be sun in de mornin
rain after lunch

dem days chiren would sit out in hot sun
for hours   me din kno notin bout tannin lotion
in we house when it come time for goin out
if you skin did real dark an pretty like mine
man dey shinin it up wid coconut oil
so everybody for miles could see yu comin

an dem nasty ole men
dey seein yu first
dey crocodile eye on yu lil breast
yu eh even kno yu hav yet
an if yu lil chubby huh
de grin gettin more wider
is like de bigger de better
de more de merrier
ting was nice tho

2.

dem days pas   fast   fast   so
we leave an com New York
well   if yu see me up here
in dese people country
ah hav four lock on me door
ah runnin three job ah still cahn see
whey de money goin

Queens geh hard   hard
ah pick up me fas self
an move to Chelsea
Chelsea was a place for Sunday brunch
all you can eat and drink for $13.95
gay   modern   post post modern   and retro

"You don't have $2500 finders fee?
sorry honey—this water closet will be gone
by midday"

Chelsea was a place for hard white cocks
stirring pain my black pussy could never fathom
hard boots   open shirt   pierced nipple
and a lil doggy collar fastened to de cock ring
i got tired of walking behind flat ass
weighted down with money
de damn Gucci backpack bumping
carelessly in meh face

who fader kno this one fader
who kno dat one fader
who runnin de Exxon corporation
dat one is a lesbian avenger
who will proudly use daddy's
gold card to make bail

i'm tired of this fucking, privileged,
politicallycorrectfakedfuckingfreedom
Harlem is still a tourist attraction—

3.
if yu see me in dis place
time pas   fas   fas   fas   so
i eh ha time to study rain
never mind sun
meh left hip hurtin
but it eh predictin notin

i want to hold my friend Letta's hand
at water's edge
transcribe the news waves tell
i want to braid Olga's hair into a tree
fuse her roots backbackback into black soil

i want to play dominoes with Donna and Linda
make soup for Keith when he's sick
draw a bush bath till Billy's fever breaksbreaks
i want my family back

i want to sit and rock you
have my hips predict your coming
sit and rock you back to a time
when we sought respite in each other's breath
i want my family back

i am blown away
in the loose dust that is this city
this house of confusion
these rooms of deceit
we have come to know intimately
i want my family back

in your absence   I am Havana
speaking Spanish to Port-au-Prince
i am Papiamento speaking Wolof to Curaçao
the shrill spaces your withdrawn hands
leave in my body carry dull knives
and cracking trees

at this bewitching hour
i hold out my hands to you
somehow these empty nights
seem the right size for making homes

my tongue is heavy with its own lacks
i hold out my life to you
cause dese days   dese days
duz pass fast   fast so fast
                    so   fas so   fasfas so —

⤙ ✹ ⤚

RICHARD TAYSON

·

FIRST SEX

When we found your father's *Playboys*,
we went into your room and touched
the glossy tanned breasts of the naked
woman on the beach, you pressed
her unblemished skin against the milk-
white flesh of your twelve-year-old
body, I kissed my virginal
lips to your lips and your father
walked in. I don't remember, now,
who had his pants down or who was
lying like a seed in the center
of the photos leafed around him,
all I remember is your father
stood in the doorway, shapely
as God, bearded, big-stomached, right
fist clenched, he wanted to eat us.
Yes, I tell you, fathers eat their sons.
I closed my eyes and waited for him
to tear away my best friend's leg
or carve a rib-bone from his
untouched chest, I heard
the voice of my father:
*Are you a girl? Do you know what evil
is? Are you a girl?*
Are you? But my body proved I was
not a girl, if God
was about to send the flood
waters up over us, I must be
Satan, the spermatozoa hatching
like polliwogs in the twin fishbowls
of my testicles, and the kiss
I wanted even then, the work of Satan.
Your father began yelling in his deep
male voice, the earth
shook, I
opened my eyes and thought he would

hit us with the bed or
bury us beneath a wall or two,
but he gave us one final
look and slammed the door
behind him: we were forever
separate from God, father, son, holy
spirit, we faced each other
in the dark and entered manhood.

•

NIGHTSWEATS

When I hear the guttural throatcall,
I tie the line around you, pull it
so you float toward me
like an unconscious swimmer.
I feel the wetness on my arm,
and think you are pissing or I am
sixteen and sleepwalking with a hard-on,
waking in time to see the arc
sluicing against Mother's new rug.
But I am twenty-eight and think you are
peeing on me, I turn to let it
douse my back but feel
the sheets wet and wake
fully and see
the sweat forcing its way
out, your whole skin
coming apart. You shudder
as if your bones have loosened,
I shake you, but you don't want to
leave the underwater lair of sleep,
I pull the blankets
down, remember
how I had lain before sleep
in the hollow bowl of your pelvis
and ribcage, cradled in the black
slime of pubic hairs, deep-sea flora
floating, how we fell asleep like that.
Now the horror in the dark
is the leak, the sweat
greasing your whole

torso, you don't wake
and I turn on the light,
shout, *wake up, it's a bad
dream,* you cry
it hurts I'm scared, and I go
fill the tub because I don't know
what else to do, begging you
to climb into the cool water
before you catch fire, the whole ocean
a burning oil slick, the sweat
spilling on me
like gasoline, hot
wax, the sun
coming up as you climb in
to your chin, I keep
lifting your mouth above water,
crying as you sleep.

.

PHONE SEX

Sometimes I am so lonely the phone
will do.
Sometimes I am so lonely and you are not
dead, you
live in Brooklyn Heights yet I cannot
touch you.
I have spent thirty years trying not to write
this poem.
Sometimes I am so lonely the phone
will do.

*

Under the paper lantern of sleep, the sudden memory: living in Colorado,
pulling on my boots, going out into the blizzard, the snow burning a hole
in my tongue. I am nearly frozen, standing in front of a house unfamiliar
to us both, knowing you will take me in, and we will make angry love in
front of the fire. I let you take not gently the clothes from me. I would
have done anything you wanted: the prosthetic devices, the rope, the food,
I made myself sticky with honey and let you have this and that part of me,
I was stuck like paper to the wall, letting you have me dry, then wet, while
your wife looked on from her photo by the bed.

*

*You will be automatically matched with the next caller or will hear radio
until the next caller becomes available. To speak to somebody else press the
pound key under the 9 on your touch-tone dial.*

*

Black fishnet stockings
clothespins clamped to his nipples
bananas by the bed   bowl
of water   soap   green washcloth
razors   banana in his mouth   he slits
the skin with his teeth   razor
in my hand   his black hairs
come off the blade like scales:

> summer 1970. I am eight,
> Kenny skins the fish
> on the dock, throws the guts
> in the lake, watches
> the heavy blood sink. Skin
> white as buttocks beneath the moon.

He bleeds slowly
never moans
arms and legs
splayed   kindergarten star
banana halfway in him   he arches
his back   two, then
three
then six
then myself

*press the pound key to speak to
somebody else*

eat white banana meat
iron-smell of blood

*press the pound key to speak to
somebody else*

he wants to tell me his fantasy.

*

In Puerto Rico your wife looks at me from across the table. Your two-year-old daughter pees on the floor. The air sticky as pee. I look into your wife's eyes then over at you by the window, your back to us. Your son bounces a red ball into the apartment, sings in Spanish. He called me "Papi Dos" today, put your hand in mine as we walked through the town. That was the moment I trace back to my self-hatred. Your wife looks at me. Sticky sweet of overripe mangoes on the table. She has left Argentina for this. You have told her the truth, or the nearest approximation: *Faeries de Norteamérica, Pájaros de la Habana, Jotos de Méjico, Sarasas de Cádiz, Apios de Sevilla, Cancos de Madrid, Floras de Alicante, Adelaidas de Portugal.* And your wife stares at me from across the table.

*

99 cents per minute, maximum of twenty minutes

I want you to talk dirty to me

Beat your cock against the receiver

*in a glass elevator in a park on a see-saw against a tree
on the edge of a bridge on the hood of my father's car*

press the pound key

tied up, my mouth gagged

Slap it around a little bit

or you will hear radio until the next caller

Finger it

anyone over fifteen is not my style

Slap it around a little bit

under the 9 on your touch-tone dial

I love all men's cocks

Finger it

Slap it.

*

I have spent thirty years trying not to write
this poem.

Who fucked you, how many times, and where?

I knew you were there before I heard your voice
yelling *Bravo!* when the bassoonist finished her concert.
Trying not to look at me.
Your red corduroy shirt flashing
as you left the music hall.
Colorado night, sweet clear summer, sweet clear soul,
we're talking again, outside the music hall.
Nightfall.
Your hand grips my hand.
Soap bubbles in the tub, you want to sleep with me.
Even after I say no you crawl through the window.

Who fucked you, how many times?

You knew I would fall in love that night.

*

*I was ready to finish your letter last night but as usual something happened
and I couldn't. At work, started with vomits, my boss went to the pharmacy
and bought some medicines.*

How many times and where?

*I haven't been feeling well, a lot of stomach ache, and I have some purple
spots on my chest.*

I have spent thirty years trying not to write
this poem.

*

*Don't call every night, you're not rich, save your money to come
to San Juan.*

You said you had a magic phone.
It made free calls.
Don't waste your money, you said.

Call me late, I said.
Call me early, I said.
What about your wife? I said.

*

Every night
I felt your terror
though we had no name for
it.
Purple spots on your legs, arms, belly.
We had no name for
it.

Vomiting, don't call.

*

And when I called
you had a new boyfriend.
Golden boy, body builder, accountant.
Living in Brooklyn, you said.
I have my green card, you said.
We bought a king-size bed, you said.
We use the same toothbrush, you said.

*

Static on the line, the garbled buzz
of jammed signals. I hold out
for the right words
but get the fourth blond 6'2" blue-eyed
muscley twenty-three-year-old tonight
named David.

Under the gummed eyelid of sleep,
the tops and bottoms
become interchangeable, the sounds
melt down to slogans, acronyms, holy
ellipses

until words stick in my throat,
dissolve slowly,
with lessening pleasure
like the gumdrops
Father brought home
then stopped bringing

home. Word:
something to lick, paw,
insert yourself into.
The need to name in a time
of silence
I do not know if sex is an illusion,
says the woman to her lover
across the table. And I row

downriver towards limitless
sleep, float
on a wordless sea
in a bed-shaped raft.
Splinters in my palm
as I stitch your real name
to my crotch for the time
when you will be unable
to speak and I unable
to forget.

"Faeries de Norteamérica, Pájaros de la Habana, Jotos de Méjico, Sarasas de Cádiz, Apios de Sevilla, Cancos de Madrid, Floras de Alicante, Adelaidas de Portugal." From "Oda de Walt Whitman" by Federico García Lorca.

"I do not know if sex is an illusion." From "Dialogue" by Adrienne Rich.

‐<✤>‐

DAVID TRINIDAD

·

THINGS TO DO IN *VALLEY OF THE DOLLS* (THE MOVIE)

Move to New York.
Lose your virginity.
Become a star.
Send money to your mother.

Call pills "dolls."
Fire the talented newcomer.
Have a nervous breakdown.
Suffer from an incurable degenerative disease.

Sing the theme song.
Do your first nude scene.
Wear gowns designed by Travilla.
Become addicted to booze and dope.

Scream "Who needs you!"
Stagger around in a half-slip and bra.
Come to in a sleazy hotel room.
Say "I am merely traveling incognito."

Get drummed out of Hollywood.
Come crawling back to Broadway.
Pull off Susan Hayward's wig
and try to flush it down the toilet.

End up in a sanitarium.
Hiss "It wasn't a nuthouse!"
Get an abortion.
Go on a binge.

Detect a lump in your breast.
Commit suicide.
Make a comeback.
Overact.

•

ANSWER SONG
FOR TIM DLUGOS

Lesley Gore got her rival good
in the smash answer to "It's My Party,"
"Judy's Turn To Cry," when her
unfaithful boyfriend, Johnny, suddenly
came to his senses in the midst
of yet another apparently unchaperoned shindig.
I picture Judy—hot pink mini-dress
and ratted black hair—being swept away
by a flood of her own teenage tears.
In triumph, Lesley rehangs Johnny's ring
around her neck. She has no idea that
the British are coming, that her popularity
will wane and she'll watch her hits drop
off the charts like so many tinkling
heart-shaped charms, and that there she'll be:
a has-been at seventeen. Naturally
she'll finish high school and marry
Johnny. They'll have a couple of kids
and settle down in a yellow two-story
tract house with white-shuttered windows
and bright red flower beds. At the supermart,
Lesley will fill her cart with frozen dinners,
which she'll serve with a smile as the family
gathers round their first color TV.
Week after week, she'll exchange recipes,
attend PTA meetings and Tupperware parties,
usher Brownie troops past tar pits
and towering dinosaur bones. Whenever
she hears one of her songs on an oldie station,
she'll think about those extinct beasts.
She'll think about them too as, year
after year, she tosses headlines
into the trash: Vietnam, Nixon, Patty Hearst.
Then one afternoon—her children grown
and gone—she'll discover a strange
pair of earrings in the breast pocket
of Johnny's business suit. It's downhill
after that: curlers, migraines, fattening
midnight snacks. Or is it? She did,
after all, sing "You Don't Own Me,"

the first pop song with a feminist twist.
What if Lesley hears about women's lib?
What if she goes into therapy and begins
to question her attraction to emotionally
unavailable men? Suppose, under hypnosis,
she returns to her sixteenth birthday party,
relives all those tears, and learns that
it was Judy—not Johnny—she'd wanted
all along. There's no answer to that
song, of course, but I have
heard rumors.

•

FROM EIGHTEEN TO TWENTY-ONE

I

He said his name was Nick; later I learned
he'd crossed the country on stolen credit
cards—I found the receipts in the guest house
I rented for only three months. Over
a period of two weeks, he threatened
to tell my parents I was gay, blackmailed
me, tied me up, crawled through a window and
waited under my bed, and raped me at
knifepoint without lubricant. A neighbor
heard screams and called my parents, who arrived
with a loaded gun in my mother's purse.
But Nick was gone. I moved back home, began
therapy, and learned that the burning in
my rectum was gonorrhea, not nerves.

III

More than anything, I wanted Charlie
to notice me. I spent one summer in
and around his swimming pool, talking to
his roommates, Rudy and Ned. All three of
them were from New York; I loved their stories
about the bars and baths, Fire Island, docks
after dark. I watched for Charlie, played board
games with Rudy and Ned, crashed on the couch.
Occasionally, Charlie came home with-
out a trick and I slipped into his bed

and slept next to him. Once, he rolled over
and kissed me—bourbon on his breath—and we
had sex at last. I was disappointed,
though: his dick was so small it didn't hurt.

V

Tom used spit for lubricant and fucked me
on the floor of his Volkswagen van while
his ex-lover (also named Tom) drove and
watched (I was sure) in the rearview mirror.
Another of his exes, Geraldo,
once cornered me in Tom's bathroom, kissed me
and asked: "What does he see in you?" At a
gay students' potluck, I refilled my wine
glass and watched Tom flirt with several other
men in the room. Outside, I paced, chain-smoked,
kicked a dent in his van and, when he came
looking for me, slugged him as hard as I
could. It was the end of the affair, but
only the beginning of my drinking.

VII

As one young guy screwed another young guy
on the screen, the man sitting a couple
seats to my right—who'd been staring at me
for the longest time—slid over. He stared
a little longer, then leaned against me
and held a bottle of poppers to my
nose. When it wore off, he was rubbing my
crotch. Slowly, he unzipped my pants, pulled back
my underwear, lowered his head, licked some
pre-cum from the tip of my dick, and then
went down on it. As he sucked, he held the
bottle up. I took it, twisted the cap
off and sniffed, then looked up at the two guys
on the screen, then up at the black ceiling.

·

MOONSTONES
FOR JOAN LARKIN

As Eileen unchains her bicycle
from the railing in front of Yaffa,
the clasp on Joan's bracelet breaks
and half a dozen moonstones
scatter at our feet.
We start to collect them, but
they're hard to see:
we keep confusing them
with tiny pieces of glass.
People pass and stare at us
as we stand there, staring
down at the sidewalk.
A drunk appears and slurs
"Whatcha lookin' for?"
"Moonstones," says Joan.
Beer in hand, he happily
joins the search.
Among the four of us,
we find five — the last one
either rolled out of sight
or (Joan begins to think)
fell off before the bracelet broke.
After about twenty minutes,
she's willing to let it go.
It's past midnight, so
she decides to take a cab
home to Brooklyn. We walk
towards 2nd Ave. At the corner,
I look back: the drunk hovers
where we left him, still trying
to locate the last moonstone
on St. Mark's Place.

•

(DOLL NOT INCLUDED)

```
                                    pu re
                                  glamouri
                                  nthespot
              c                    lighta          she
          e       k                 sbarb          adj
        n           l               iesin          ust
          e     a                  gsofbitt         s
              c                  ersweetlov         t
                                 eandteenag         h          lo
                                 eheartachesh       e          ng
          apinks                 erskintigh         s          bl
          carfco                   tglitter         i          ac
          mplete                   knitbl           l          kt
          stheen                    ackf            v          ri
          semble                    orma            e          co
                                    lmov            r          tg
                                    esin            y          lov
                                    toaf   *        m          es
        a c k                     rilloftu          i
       l     k   p   s           lleatthehe         c
       b      u m p            mwithasinglere       r
                              dsatinroseaccent      o
                                                 phonetoth
                                              eproperheight
```

•

FOR JOE BRAINARD

I remember when I met Joe Brainard. My first trip to New York City. October, 1982. Tim Dlugos took me to an art opening and introduced me to Joe in the center of the room. I was so nervous I bumped into him, causing him to spill his drink.

I remember my first crush on another boy. Roy Ruth, who was a year and a half ahead of me at Superior Street Elementary School. Before he graduated, I approached him and asked him to sign my blue autograph book. He looked surprised, but signed his name.

I remember when all the girls in our classroom were invited to a "special" film in the auditorium. I couldn't understand why I wasn't invited too. None of the girls would tell me what it was about. They'd received pink invitations.

I remember when Tommy Merande, our next-door neighbor, told my brother and me that he'd walked into his parents' bedroom without knocking and seen his mother's breasts. She'd slapped him across the face — hard. Long after they'd moved away, we heard that Mrs. Merande had died of breast cancer. I instantly remembered the story Tommy had told us.

I remember during another trip to New York, at a party at Danceteria, snorting coke with Joe in a bathroom stall.

I remember the first time I came. While "fooling around" with Hal Weiland, a blond boy who lived two doors down the street. We were alone in my house, lying on the living room floor. I didn't know what was happening, but he kept rubbing my cock until. . . . It left a faint stain on our brand-new beige carpet, which I prayed my mother wouldn't notice.

I remember Hal and I "fooling around" whenever we could. Mostly just rubbing together, touching each other's cocks. One day his mother came home and discovered us in his bedroom. After that, we never "fooled around" again.

I remember playing strip poker with the other boys in the neighborhood. On summer afternoons. Each time someone lost all of his clothes, he had to do whatever the others wanted. Like bending over and separating his cheeks (or something equally humiliating). I remember one time we played strip poker with an older boy from around the block. Halfway through the game he said, "You guys just want to see my dick, don't you?" He unzipped his pants, pulled down his underwear, and gave us a good look. It was much bigger than any of ours, and had lots of dark hair around it.

I remember a crowded birthday party for Patrick Merla, during a snowstorm, at an apartment on Washington Mews. I remember sitting on the staircase, smoking, and Joe towering over me telling me how attractive I looked in my black sweater.

I remember being afraid of getting a hard-on in the locker room.

I remember two boys wrestling on a gray mat, surrounded by the whole gym class. Suddenly one of the wrestlers "popped a boner." I remember how stunned everyone was. Then the whispers and snickers. I remember how embarrassed I felt for that boy.

I remember sitting through my high school chemistry class with a hard-on. Trying to concentrate on the chart of the elements, rather than the jocks all around me. Hoping none of them would see the bulge in my pants. And that it would "go down" before the bell rang.

I remember receiving a letter from Joe that said, "I'd love to see you when you're in town next month. Can I take you to dinner? And why don't you bring a toothbrush with you and plan on spending the night." I remember how excited and flattered I was, then how disappointed: when I got to New York, Joe had a cold and couldn't keep our date.

I remember standing against a wall at the Club Baths in San Francisco. In 1976. Wearing nothing but a skimpy white towel. I remember a guy walking right up to me, reaching under the towel, and grabbing my cock. I remember how impressed I was by his directness, how I followed him to his cubicle. I remember having sex with him again—once at his place, once at mine. I remember that we sniffed Locker Room when we came.

I remember going on a secret date with my roommate's boyfriend. We drank a bottle of red wine at the beach, then made out on a couch in his sister's apartment. After we'd started having sex, I dramatically stood up, dressed, and left. The next day, he showed up and said, "What shall I call you now? 'Darling'?"

I remember pausing in the middle of sex with a guy to smoke a cigarette. He was insulted. But I needed a rest because our lovemaking was so intense.

I remember giving a reading with Lyn Hejinian at St. Mark's Church. It was a somber, humorless audience (mostly hers). But every time I looked up from my poems, I saw Joe's face in the center of the room, beaming handsomely at me.

TERRY WOLVERTON
·
THE DEAD STEPFATHER

1.
You are already dead when I am told
about your fall on New Year's Eve, skull cracked
like an egg against Detroit pavement, yolk
seeping into gray matter. How it took
six days to find your next-of-kin, daughter
who said, "Pull the plug."
                                        I was your daughter
once; I'm no one now. Thirty-five years since
you brought me red balloons the night you came
to woo my mother, seventeen since we
last spoke. Those years between, a history
of breakage—bones and glass and brittle vows—
the fragile membrane torn, pieces scattered.
No way for me to claim your death; I'm just
the divorced stepdaughter, irrelative.

2.
If there had been a funeral, incense
would have smelled like gunpowder, gasoline,
and gin, pews crowded with barflies, aging
soldiers, used car salesmen, ghosts of children
clutching red balloons. We would have sung "The
One Rose," in lugubrious chorus, then
shared a stiff drink all around.
                                        There was no
service. Three weeks your body stiffened at
the morgue till your daughter found the cheapest
way to burn you, then dispatch your ashes
to a remote grave. Fuck good-byes. In dreams,
I swim with you across a frozen sea,
fathomless blue; we fight the tide, dodge ice
floes white as shells, until you reach the shore.

·

TUBES

There's one called "Wild,"
weird coppery purple
I wore when I first
went blonde, my early
thirties. Wax cylinder
now worn to the rim
of its metal casing,
convex bed of color
I can only scrape out
with a fingernail, but
no one makes this shade
anymore, so I keep it.

"Exactly Red" — same
vintage: mid-1980s,
when platinum and scarlet
accessorized a black
slip and spiked heels.
It's "featherproof,"
guaranteed not to bleed
beyond the lips'
outline into cracks
that sprout like tributaries
from my mouth more
than a decade later.

"Odyssey," the dull plum
bought after I became
a redhead, worn for everyday,
almost a neutral. "Midnight,"
a stain, purchased to replace
the discontinued "Blackberry."
"Media," blood red so dark
it's nearly black (should
have been called "Medea"),
worn with a '90s
snarl, and never
without lipliner,

but too dark for the blonde
I again assumed, hair shirred
to scalp, bleached raw to cheer
myself after my lover's mother
died of cancer. The current crop
includes three purples: "Lust,"
a frosted lavender too
young for me, but I like
how it transports me
to the '60s, my teens,
to Yardley and Carnaby Street,
to Love perfume;

"Grid," blue violet as
metallic as a shield;
and "Epic," a rich grape
about which a stranger
in the checkout line
of the health food store
said to me, *If you're going
to wear purple lipstick,
you better have a sense
of humor.* And I suppose
I do — my face the canvas
of a would-be Dadaist,

never destined for greatness
so all the more willing
to risk. *If you can't be
beautiful, look interesting* —
the motto I've upheld since
fifth grade when I used
my Christmas money
for my first tube, no demure
pink for this ten-year-old,
but "Cherries in the Snow,"
like my mother wore, bright
cerise too old for me.

Even the mistakes amuse:
"Cadeaux," a harsh magenta,

or my Lancome gift-with-purchase,
"Rouge Essential"—let's just say
some people weren't born
to wear orange. And recently
"Mint Sorbet," the pale green
frost I chose at Thrifty's
in the desert, the one
that turns to peach and then
sloughs off in flakes after
a few hours. When people

tell me, *Every time I see you,*
you look different.
I didn't even recognize you,
I grin through lips that might
be flushed with "Dubonnet"
or cooled with "Opaline."
That's the beauty of it:
by day I'm "Hyper,"
by night a "Siren,"
and essence
bows to
mutability.

•

BLACK SLIP

She told me she had always fantasized
about a woman in a black slip.
It had to do with Elizabeth Taylor
in *Butterfield 8.*

She came to my house with a huge box
gift-wrapped with gigantic ribbons.
Inside, a black slip.
Slinky, with lace across the bodice.
She told me how she was embarrassed
in the department store,
a woman in men's pants
buying a black slip clearly not intended for herself,

and about the gay men in line behind herself,
sharing the joke.

She asked me to try it on.
I took it into the bathroom, slipped it over my head.
I stared at myself for a long time
before I came out of the bathroom
walked over to her
lying on the bed.

That was the first time. It got easier.
The black slip was joined by a blue slip
then a red one
then a long lavender negligee, the back slit to there.

I wore them to bed.
In the morning she would smile and say
how much she loved waking up next to a woman in a slip.
The black slip remained our favorite.
We always made love when I wore the black slip.

Once I showed up at her door late at night
wearing a long coat
with only the black slip underneath.

One night I cooked dinner at her apartment
wearing nothing but the black slip
and red suede high heels.

It was always the first thing to pack when we went on vacation.

And she used to make me promise
that if we ever broke up
I'd never wear that slip for anyone else.

I don't know where it is now.

Stripped of that private skin
when we broke up
I never went back to claim it.

I think she must have
packed it
given it
thrown it
away.

On bad days I imagine her
sliding it over the head of some new love
whispering about Elizabeth Taylor
and waking up to a woman in a slip.

Or perhaps
it's still there
draped on the back of the door.

A sinuous shadow.

A moan in the dark.

·

IN CHINA

I was already
descending into flu
when I boarded the flight
to Hong Kong,
familiar ache
across my shoulders,
throat raw, throbbing

Tucked in knapsack,
my scribbled greeting
card: "Flying halfway
'round the world for our
anniversary; *that's* how much . . ."
Eight years. Our first
big trip, so long anticipated

Marcus was dying
fungus conquering his lungs
and Gil so sick, wasted
body barely able to contain

his rage; my guilty
phone call from the airport
promised money

for the funeral, all
I could do over staticky
lines, the loudspeaker
garbling my flight
I dragged my baggage
to the metal hull
fifteen hour night

Landed after sunset
of the following day
Hong Kong as fevered
as my own damp skin,
happy anniversary, your
business done, you greeted
me with duty-free perfume

Poême, because I am
a poet, lavish dinner
I could scarcely swallow,
litany of guidebooks, plans,
all that we would see
I croaked excuses, your eyes
drowned in candlelight

Next day I trudged
with you through fetid
air in clotted
alleyways, climbed
crooked narrow stairs,
laundry flapping thirty
stories up, birds caged

on aerial balconies,
I choked thick
smoke from incense
coils wide as rope
in a red-lit temple.
You were fervid to explore,
I floated underneath

the surface as if
in a dream, drank mango
juice that stung
a swollen throat,
trolled sidewalk stalls,
my temperature soared
until at last, grudgingly

you let me sleep.
On the plane to Beijing
I coughed as if my chest
would fissure, could not
stop, face florid
sputum bloody, you turned
your grimace to the sky

Beijing airport Muzak
rendered "Yesterday"
one note and halting, a child's
music box wound down,
relentlessly repeated; endless
yesterday mocked us
all through Customs

In that ancient city,
I stayed in our "deluxe"
hotel, stared through grimy
windows as streams
of cyclists rolled past,
watched Asian MTV,
B-movies while you toured

alone the Great Wall,
the Summer Palace. Was
it here that our hands
began to unclasp?
A week before, I'd walked
Gil through the maze of AIDS
bureaucracy, his voice

raw from screaming
at indifferent clerks,
his fever spiraled, spent

the last of his scant health
to fight for Marcus,
his vow, a good death.
You were furious

I'd come to China
sick, as if infection
were a trick to undermine
your yearning for
adventure. My scorched
cheeks craved your
skinflint touch

I roamed the streets,
lumbering blonde curiosity
swaddled in scarves
spewing tissues like tiny ghosts,
past vendors peddling
Marlboros, the park where
even in dead winter

barbers offer haircuts
until dark, storefronts
heaped with dusty boxes,
unrecognizable — I could
not read the signs
I counted blocks, hunted
landmarks, did not want

to lose you in this city
where I knew no language,
could not count money. Forty
dollar phone call to L.A.,
my American Chinese
doctor told me, "Grief's
exploding in your lungs"

I figured it was Gil,
bereaved, and Marcus,
dead. I couldn't read
the picture alphabet
each character a map
legible as leafless trees
on Beijing winter streets

stark as the scarlet product
of my lungs staining
a white tissue: your dark eyes
turned to distance
scanning an unknown
horizon, both of us
so far from home

⭤

MARK WUNDERLICH

·

TAKE GOOD CARE OF YOURSELF

On the runway at the Roxy, the drag queen
fans herself gently, but with purpose.
She is an Asian princess, an elaborate wig
jangling like bells on a Shinto temple,
shoulders broad as my father's. With a flick

of her fan she covers her face, a whole
world of authority in that one gesture,
a screen sliding back, all black lacquer
and soprano laugh. The music in this place
echoes with the whip-crack of 2,000

men's libidos, and the one bitter pill
of X-tasy dissolving on my tongue is the perfect
slender measure of the holy ghost,
the vibe crawling my spine exactly,
I assure myself, what I've always wanted.

It is 1992. There is no *you* yet for me
to address, just simple imperative. *Give
me more. Give.* It is a vision, I'm sure
of this, of what heaven might provide—a sea
of men all muscle, white briefs and pearls,

of kilts cut too short for Catholic girls
or a Highland fling. Don't bother with chat
just yet. I've stripped and checked my jeans
at the door. I need a drink, a light, someplace
a little cooler, just for a minute, to chill.

There is no place like the unbearable ribbon
of highway that cuts the Midwest into two unequal
halves, a pale sun glowing like the fire
of one last cigarette. It is the prairie
I'm scared of, barreling off in all directions

flat as its inhabitants' A's and O's. I left
Wisconsin's well-tempered rooms
and snowfields white and vacant as a bed
I wish I'd never slept in. Winters
I stared out the bus window through frost

at an icy template of what the world offered up —
the moon's tin cup of romance and a beauty,
that if held too long to the body,
would melt. If I felt anything for you then
It was mere, the flicker of possibility

a quickening of the pulse when I imagined
a future, not here but elsewhere, the sky
not yawning out, but hemmed in. In her dress
the drag is all glitter and perfect grace,
pure artifice, beating her fan, injuring

the smoky air, and in the club, I'm still
imagining. The stacks of speakers burn
and throb, whole cities of sound bear down
on us. I'm dancing with men all around me,
moving every muscle I can, the woman's voice

mixed and extended to a gorgeous black note
in a song that only now can I remember —
one familiar flat stretch, one wide-open vista
and a rhythm married to words
for what we still had to lose.

·

GIVEN IN PERSON ONLY

Tompkins Square Park's a mess of shopping carts
overflowing with what's been cast off,
and pierced and tattooed punks affecting poses
soon grown into, arms speckling with tracks,
so when a girl extends a blue-nailed hand
I press to her palm the dollar she requests,

not because it will do her, or me, a bit
of good, but because today I am willing
to give myself to anyone, should they ask.

I've just come back from the clinic,
its waiting room a jumble of secondhand plaid
where Lupita drew blood from a forearm's vein

she called the *kind she likes to see.*
Before her on the gunmetal desk
was the blueprint questionnaire mapping
my sexual history, the penciled dots
a constellation of what I wanted and what
I got. I know I've spent too much time

leaning against walls in bars, chewing ice
from an overpriced drink while shielding an ear
from some techno beat, the bass vibration
in the rib cage the sound desire makes.
There have been back rooms where
I didn't know to whom the hands belonged

or how many, pure surrender. Then
there were the ones *with* names —
the man who bicycled through the snow,
stood in my living room and cried,
our bodies laboring to extinguish
some common flame, or the one

whose shirts still hang in my closet, limp torsos
washed out with use. I don't regret
the hunger that drove me to dark rooms,
stairwells, steam rooms or beaches,
park benches, parked cars, locker rooms
or clubs — locations that give shape

to my notion that sex is like faith —
at its center, it is always the same, unwavering.
I won't apologize for the want and urge,
veiled in daylight as a curtain hides a stage,
no matter what Lupita will have for me
when she splits open her envelope's

folded white wings. In Chelsea the boys skate,
shirtless in late summer, brown thighs
and unflinching faces rolling by like gods.
It's muggy again, the way Manhattan

always seems in my dreams, and above
the water towers and angled roofs, the sun

insists on disrobing through the clouds.
I'll remake myself once again, shed
rapture and sweet release, and replace it
with something equally consummate and strange.
So let the city do as it must and break us down
to dust and skeletons. I'm just beginning.

•

THE TRICK

I made love with a man—hugely muscled, lean—the body
I always wished for myself. He kept pulling my arms
up over my head, pinning them there, pressing me down

with his substantial weight, grinding into me roughly,
but then asked, begged, in a whisper of such sweetness,
Please kiss me. Earlier that evening, he told me

he'd watched a program about lions, admired
how they took their prey—menacing the herds at the water hole
before choosing the misfit, the broken one.

What surprised him was the wildebeests' calm
after the calf had been downed, how they returned to their grazing
with a dumb switching of tails. Nearby the lions looked up

from their meal, eyed the hopping storks and vultures,
before burying their faces, again, in the bloody ribs.
As a teenager, I wished to be consumed,

to be pressed into oblivion by a big forceful man.
It never happened. Instead I denied myself nourishment—
each unfilled plate staring back satisfied me, deprivation

reduced to a kind of bliss I could lie down in
where I remained unmoved, untouched.
Early on I was taught that the body was a cage,

that illness was a battle fought with chaos,
the viruses themselves unnatural; that sex lived
in some pastel chamber that gave way to infants,

first cousins, the handing down of names.
No one ever mentioned being taken in the dark,
or wanting to be broken open, pushed beyond words,

tongue thickening in another human mouth,
or how a person could be humiliated and like it.
To my surprise, I found myself struggling under this man,

pushing my chest up against his chest, arms straining
against the bed, until some younger, hungrier
version of myself lay back on top of me and took it—

the heaving back, the beard, the teeth at the throat.

•

AUBADE

All day I've been searching for omens, flimsy as they are, and the cat
who crossed my small yard, mornings, was the easiest.

Nor my dreams, certainly—last night's scene of endless rollerblading
speeding at a velocity it's not difficult to imagine as erotic,

and fading this morning like the cologne of someone who's just left
the room. And when I turned over the letter you'd sent and I'd lost months ago

it was as if I'd just heard the lock click as you left for the morning,
my own day clear and solitary, waiting for your return. I think of the body's

imprecision, the dull tongs of your legs, the unasked question
of each upturned palm, how over coffee I noticed first your hands,

gripping a newspaper between forefinger and thumb,
then your eyes hurrying on to the next word, the next period.

It's night here. The cat hasn't been seen for days, and I pretend
not to notice. Pretend I'll tell you when he fails to come home.

•
CONTINENT'S EDGE

The surf washed up its rows of green
and the debris scattered its fractured narrative —

a woman's shoe, purple ribbons, a gull's
battered carcass, countless plastic bags, and nets

the clammers use to cart home what their spades turn up,
the hollow shells of trilobites, the crusted thorax of a crab —

all of it rinsed and tilted landward to the beach.
Up the sand crest of dune along trampled paths

are the dished clearings worn of sawgrass
where humans pressed themselves against each other.

Left behind are the telltale markers —
empty tubes of lubricant, the flaccid sacks of condoms

and their silvery wrappers, fluttering tissues gummed with sand.
Once on West Street, where the Hudson grinds out to sea

I watched the she-males flock the cobblestones,
all feathers and leatherette, sequins and razor stubble,

stepping up to slow-turned car windows. I am secretly in league
with them — their nocturnal ministering and bodily commerce,

though there's no ignoring how a car's dark interior
could compromise their tenuous elegance. Somewhere

between the clavicle's arc and swell of calf these givers
offer the succor of mouths and hands, the john's forward thrust

piercing gender's blur and entering the shadowy inner circle
pleasure casts like the compass of the sling-back's spike heel.

Through the confusion of lace and corset stays
and the zipper's small teeth, sex offers up

its one heedless moment, some bifurcated taste
compelling a man to want a man who looks like a woman,

a scaffold of artifice separating desire
from the shaved and perfumed figure beneath the dress.

I have learned to appreciate a man's muscles
for their individuation, carved and unsubtle as reliefs

of Greek soldiers naked and locked in a symmetrical war.
Bound to this musculature is my desire to see myself

in the man I am fucking, albeit a new version—
the crude tattoo I never allowed, the uncut organ

or unlined face. Perhaps the johns want
a man gentler or more graceful than they know themselves

to be, the exchange making possible the quiet
well-appointed rooms of the imagination, just as I

want someone powerful enough to pin me to myself for a while.
Here among the dunes and sexual debris, the waves

give me nothing but what's done for,
the sand shifting with each wave's assault,

sometimes gentle, sometimes hard, the way a hand
draws back an undone shirt.

·

EAST SEVENTH STREET

I love to ride the D train just to emerge from the tunnel
and see the sun dipping, toxic, into New Jersey's petroleum shimmer,
beyond the yellow mass of taxis that cruise the streets like sharks.
When I think of Manhattan, I think of the baby carriage

on Second Avenue cradling a man's small family—
two dogs, a cat, and a goose in a milk crate, craning
her neck like some dangerous flower. All January
they worked the line at the cash machine, ankle deep

in a littler of receipts, clicking the security lock to the Avenue's
petulant slur. I spent my first winter here, five stories up,

smoking, at a hobbled kitchen table, laying out postcards
of cities I'd never live in, an imagined map of disappointments,

paper ghosts. One floor below a thin young man was being burnt down
to an essence. I was neither keeper nor witness to it. We never spoke.
Once I dreamed I leapt from the window ledge, spread crude wings
and flew like the newspaper angels that ride the City's

air current whips. Below me, the streets were made luminous
as I pitched across valleys the buildings carve
through soot-particulated air, before I set down
on a rain-darkened, black-cobbled street. In 7-D

the young man died. No relatives came. Only medics
sterile with masks, their gurney chroming in the dim hallway,
to usher his cooling body to the street. For three days
his apartment door swung open while neighbors sifted

through his things in a city where someone's always poor enough
to covet what's been cast off, and where the mirror
I took from the apartment reflects my face instead of his.
Outside, today, the season tightens into its more contemplative notes,

breaking from summer's excess, while locusts
cut their last swaths through the park's unmowed field.
in the subway tunnel, the arriving train carries with it
a whisper of smoke. Somewhere underground a fire is burning.

<svg>⟨✴⟩</svg>

PERMISSIONS AND ACKNOWLEDGMENTS

Mark Bibbins "Whitman on the Beach," "Bluebeard," "Geometry Class," "Mud," and "Counting" are reprinted from *Swerve* © 1998 by Mark Bibbins, as published in *Take Three: 3* (Graywolf Press, 1998), by permission of the author.

Olga Broumas "Etymology," "Tryst," "The Masseuse," "Landscape with Next of Kin," and excerpts from "Caritas" (#1; "Erik Satie . . ." and #3 "With the clear . . .") from *Rave* © 1999 by Olga Broumas, reprinted by permission of Copper Canyon Press, P.O. Box 271, Port Townsend, WA 98368.

Cheryl Burke "Motor Oil Queen" © 1998 by Cheryl Burke is reprinted from *Motor Oil Queen!* (By the Seat of Your Pants Press, 1998), by permission of the author. "Lizzie" © 1999 by Cheryl Burke.

Regie Cabico "Check One" and "Gameboy" are reprinted from *Aloud: Voices from the Nuyorican Poets Cafe* (Henry Holt, 1994); "Mango Poem" is reprinted from *Columbia 1998*; "Antonio Banderas in His Underwear" is reprinted from *I Saw Your Lover Behind the Starbucks Counter* by Regie Cabico (Big Fat Press, 1997); "Art in Architecture" is reprinted from *The Badboy Book of Erotic Poetry* (Badboy, 1995); all © by Regie Cabico, by permission of the author.

Rafael Campo "Belonging" and excerpts from "Song for My Lover" ("Our Country of Origin" and "A Medical Student Learns Love and Death") are reprinted from *The Other Man Was Me* © 1994 by Rafael Campo, by permission of Arte Público Press. "What the Body Told" and excerpts from "Ten Patients, And Another" ("Kelly," "Manuel," and "Jane Doe #2") are reprinted from *What the Body Told* © 1996 by Duke University Press. Reprinted by permission of the publisher. All rights reserved.

Cyrus Cassells "A Courtesy, a Trenchant Grace" and "Marathon" from *Soul Make a Path Through Shouting* © 1994, and "New Song of Solomon" and "Beautiful Signor" from *Beautiful Signor* © 1997 by Cyrus Cassells. Reprinted by permission of Copper Canyon Press, P.O. Box 271, Port Townsend, WA 98368.

Justin Chin "Why a Boy," "Cocksucker's Blues," and "Ex-boyfriends Named Michael" are reprinted from *Bite Hard* © 1997 by Justin Chin, by permission of Manic D Press. "Undetectable" © 1999 by Justin Chin, by permission of the author.

Chrystos "I Suck," "I Bought a New Red," and "You Know I Like to Be" are reprinted from *In Her I Am* (Press Gang Publishers) © 1993 by Chrystos, by permission of the author. "The Okeydoekey Tribe" is reprinted from *Dream*

On (Press Gang Publishers) © 1991 by Chrystos, by permission of the author. "I Bring You Greetings: How" © 1999 by Chrystos.

Cheryl Clarke   "Passing," "Make-up," and "A Poet's Death" are reprinted from *Experimental Love*, copyright © 1993 by Cheryl Clarke, by permission of Firebrand Books, Ithaca, N.Y. "Palm Leaf of Mary Magdalene," "Stuck," and "Vicki and Daphne" are reprinted from *Living as a Lesbian*, copyright © 1986 by Cheryl Clarke, by permission of Firebrand Books, Ithaca, N.Y.

Jeffery Conway   "Hangover" is reprinted from *Blood Poisoning: Poems* (Cold Calm Press) © 1995 by Jeffery Conway, by permission of the author. "Weight Belt" is reprinted from *Plush: Selected Poems of Sky Gilbert, Courtnay McFarlane, Jeffery Conway, R. M. Vaughan & David Trinidad* (Coach House Press) © 1995 by Jeffery Conway, by permission of the author. "Marlo Thomas in Seven Parts and Epilogue" is reprinted from *B City* © 1994 by Jeffery Conway, by permission of the author. "Modern English" © 1999 by Jeffery Conway.

Dennis Cooper   "Teen Idols" is reprinted from *Idols* (Sea Horse Press) © 1979 by Dennis Cooper, by permission of the author. "After School, Street Football, Eighth Grade," "David Cassidy Then," "In School," "10 Dead Friends," "Poem for George Miles," and "Dreamt Up" are reprinted from *The Dream Police: Selected Poems 1969–1993* © 1995 by Dennis Cooper, by permission of Grove/Atlantic, Inc.

Alfred Corn   "A Marriage in the Nineties" and "To Hermes" are reprinted from *Present* © 1997 by Alfred Corn, reprinted by permission of Counterpoint Press, a member of Perseus Books, L.L.C. "Long-distance Call to Gregg . . ." is reprinted from *The James White Review* © 1998 by Alfred Corn, by permission of the author. "Kimchee in Worcester (Mass.)" © 1999 by Alfred Corn.

Mark Doty   "My Tattoo" and "Lilacs in NYC" from *Sweet Machine* by Mark Doty, copyright © 1998 by Mark Doty, reprinted by permission of HarperCollins Publishers, Inc. "Homo Will Not Inherit," "Michael's Dream," and "New Dog" from *Atlantis* by Mark Doty, copyright © 1995 by Mark Doty, reprinted by permission of HarperCollins Publishers, Inc.

Beatrix Gates   "Triptych" is reprinted from *In the Open: Poems* by Beatrix Gates (Painted Leaf Press) © 1998 by Beatrix Gates, by permission of the author.

Elena Georgiou   "A Week in the Life of the Ethnically Indeterminate," "The Space Between," and "Talkin' Trash" are reprinted from *Mercy Mercy Me* by Elena Georgiou (Vanishing Point Press) © 1999 by Elena Georgiou, by permission of the author. "Intimate Mixture" and "From Where I Stand" © 1999 by Elena Georgiou.

Robert Glück   "Invaders from Mars" is reprinted from *Family Poems* (Black Star Series) © 1979 by Robert Glück, by permission of the author. "Pasolini" and "Burroughs" are reprinted from *Reader* (The Lapis Press) © by Robert Glück, by permission of the author. Excerpts from "The Visit" © 1999 by Robert Glück.

Melinda Goodman   "Cobwebs" is reprinted from *Middle Sister* by Melinda Goodman (MSG Press) © 1988 by Melinda Goodman, by permission of the author. "February Ice Years" is reprinted from *Conditions*; "Lullabye for a Butch" is reprinted from *The Persistent Desire: A Femme-Butch Reader* (Alyson Publications, 1992); "New Comers" is reprinted from *The Arc of Love: An Anthology of Lesbian Love Poems* (Scribner, 1996); "Open Poem" is reprinted from *Outweek* #71 (1990), all © by Melinda Goodman, by permission of the author.

Marilyn Hacker   "Going Back to the River," copyright © 1990 by Marilyn Hacker, from *Selected Poems: 1965–1990* by Marilyn Hacker; reprinted by permission of the author and W. W. Norton & Company, Inc. "Year's End," from *Winter Numbers* by Marilyn Hacker, copyright © 1994 by Marilyn Hacker; reprinted by permission of the author and W. W. Norton & Company, Inc. "The Boy," "Invocation," and "Squares and Courtyards," from *Squares and Courtyards: Poems* by Marilyn Hacker, copyright © 2000 by Marilyn Hacker; reprinted by permission of W. W. Norton & Company, Inc.

Eloise Klein Healy   "Changing What We Mean" is reprinted from *Outweek* © 1990 by Eloise Klein Healy, by permission of the author. "Changing the Oil," "What It Was Like the Night Cary Grant Died," and "From Los Angeles Looking South" are reprinted from *Artemis in Echo Park*, copyright © 1991 by Eloise Klein Healy, by permission of Firebrand Books, Ithaca, N.Y. "Louganis" © 1999 by Eloise Klein Healy.

Melanie Hope   "Sixth Grade" is reprinted from *The Paris Review*, no. 148, © 1998 by Melanie Hope, by permission of the author. "Bare Floors," "Only Days," "INRI," and "Sacrifice" © 1999 by Melanie Hope.

Michael Klein   "The Tides," "Letters from the Front," "Guardian Life," and "Scenes for an Elegy" are reprinted from *1990* by Michael Klein (Provincetown Arts Press) © 1993 by Michael Klein, by permission of the author. "The Range of It" © 1999 by Michael Klein.

Wayne Koestenbaum   "Tea Dance" from *Ode to Anna Moffo and Other Poems* by Wayne Koestenbaum, copyright © 1990 by Wayne Koestenbaum, reprinted by permission of Persea Books, Inc. "1977," "1980," and "1992" (excerpted from "Erotic Collectibles") from *Rhapsodies of a Repeat Offender* by Wayne Koestenbaum, copyright © 1994 by Wayne Koestenbaum, reprinted by permission of Persea Books, Inc.

Joan Larkin   "Housework" is reprinted from *Housework* (Out & Out Books) © 1975 by Joan Larkin, by permission of the author. "Origins" and "Good-bye" are reprinted from *A Long Sound: A Book of Poems* (Granite Press) © 1986 by Joan Larkin, by permission of the author. "Beatings," "Inventory," "My Body," "Legacy," and "Cold River" are reprinted from *Cold River* (Painted Leaf Press) © 1997 by Joan Larkin, by permission of the author.

Michael Lassell   "How to Watch Your Brother Die" is reprinted from *Poems for Lost and Un-lost Boys* (Amelia) © 1985, by permission of the author.

"Kissing Ramón" is reprinted from *The Hard Way* (Richard Kasak/Masquerade Books) © 1995 by Michael Lassell, by permission of the author. "Brady Street, San Francisco" is reprinted from *The Name of Love: Classic Gay Love Poems* (St. Martin's Press) © 1995 by Michael Lassell, by permission of the publisher. "Sunset Stripping: Visiting L.A." and "Three Poems" are reprinted from *A Flame for the Touch That Matters* (Painted Leaf Press) © 1998 by Michael Lassell, by permission of the author. "Going to Europe" © 1999 by Michael Lassell.

Timothy Liu   "Vox Angelica" and "Mama" are reprinted from *Vox Angelica* (Alicejamesbooks) © 1992 by Timothy Liu, by permission of the publisher. "The Size of It" and "Reading Whitman in a Toilet Stall" from *Burnt Offerings* © 1995 and "Strange Fruit" from *Say Goodnight* © 1998 by Timothy Liu. Reprinted by permission of Copper Canyon Press, P.O. Box 271, Port Townsend, WA 98368.

Jaime Manrique   "My Night with Federico García Lorca (as told by Edouard Roditi)" and "Barcelona Days" are reprinted from *My Night with Federico García Lorca* by Jaime Manrique (Painted Leaf Press) © 1997 by Jaime Manrique, by permission of the author. "Baudelaire's Spleen" and "Tarzan" © 1999 by Jaime Manrique.

J. D. McClatchy   "First Steps" is reprinted from *Stars Principal* by J. D. McClatchy (Macmillan, 1986), copyright © 1986 by J. D. McClatchy, by permission of the author. "My Mammogram" and "Late Night Ode" are reprinted from *Ten Commandments* by J. D. McClatchy, copyright © 1998 by J. D. McClatchy, by permission of Alfred A. Knopf, Inc.

Honor Moore   "Poem for the End" is reprinted from *Memoir: Poems* by Honor Moore (Chicory Blue Press) © 1988 by Honor Moore, by permission of the author. "A Window at Key West" is reprinted from *Paris Review*, Winter 1998–99, © 1998 by Honor Moore, by permission of the author. "Edward" first appeared on-line, on *Slate*, October, 1999, © 1999 by Honor Moore, by permission of the author. "Girl in a Fur-Trimmed Dress" first appeared in *Kunpipi* (U.K.), © 1999 by Honor Moore, by permission of the author.

Eileen Myles   "An American Poem" is reprinted from *Not Me* by Eileen Myles (Semiotext(e)) © 1991 by permission of the author. "Maxfield Parrish" and "Sleepless," © 1995 by Eileen Myles; reprinted from *Maxfield Parrish: Early & New Poems* with the permission of Black Sparrow Press. "Merk" and "School of Fish," © 1997 by Eileen Myles, reprinted from *School of Fish* with the permission of Black Sparrow Press.

Letta Neely   "Multiple Assaults," "Rhonda, Age 15, Emergency Room," and "8 Ways of Looking at Pussy" are reprinted from *Juba* (Wildheart Press) © 1998 by Letta Neely, by permission of the author.

Achy Obejas   "Lifes" © 1984 by Achy Obejas. "Dancing in Paradise" © 1991 by Achy Obejas. "The Public Place" and "Sunday" © 1998 by Achy Obejas. Reprinted by permission of the Charlotte Sheedy Literary Agency.

Gerry Gomez Pearlberg "Think Back," "Marianne Faithfull's Cigarette," "Sailor," "Loop-the-Loop in Prospect Park (1905)," and "Dog Star" are reprinted from *Marianne Faithfull's Cigarette* (Cleis Press) © 1998 by Gerry Gomez Pearlberg, by permission of the publisher.

Robert E. Penn "Morning Songs" and "Hand" © 1999 by Robert E. Penn.

Carl Phillips "As from a Quiver of Arrows" is reprinted from *From the Devotions* © 1998 by Carl Phillips, by permission of Graywolf Press. "Cotillion" is reprinted from *Cortège* © 1995 by Carl Phillips, by permission to Graywolf Press. "The Kill" is reprinted from *Pastoral* © 2000 by Carl Phillips, by permission of Graywolf Press. "In the Blood, Winnowing" and "Undressing for Li Po" are reprinted from *In the Blood* © 1992 by Carl Phillips, by permission of Northeastern University Press.

D. A. Powell "[triptych]" is reprinted from *explosions and small geometries* by D. A. Powell (Norton Coker Press, 1991); "[always returning: holidays and burials. not every week]" is reprinted from *The James White Review*; "[studs and rings: favors of the piercing party]" is reprinted from the *Iowa Journal of Cultural Studies*; "[my father and me making dresses: together]" is reprinted from *Denver Quarterly*; "[you're thin again handsome. in our last]" is reprinted from *Puerto del Sol*; "[the minotaur at supper: spare the noritake and the spode]" is reprinted from the *Iowa Review*, all © by D. A. Powell, by permission of the author.

Minnie Bruce Pratt "Elbows" is reprinted from *The Sound of One Fork* (Night Heron) © 1981 by Minnie Bruce Pratt, by permission of the author. "Poem for My Sons" and "Crime Against Nature" are reprinted from *Crime Against Nature*, copyright © 1990 by Minnie Bruce Pratt, by permission of Firebrand Books, Ithaca, N.Y. "Red String" and "The Other Side," from *Walking Back Up Depot Street* by Minnie Bruce Pratt, © 1999; reprinted by permission of the University of Pittsburgh Press.

Mariana Romo-Carmona "Crows" and "Signs" are reprinted from *13th Moon* (SUNY Albany) © 1999 by Mariana Romo-Carmona, by permission of the author. "Daylight" is reprinted from *Speaking Like an Immigrant* (Latina Lesbian History Project) © 1999 by Mariana Romo-Carmona, by permission of the author. "Fish" © 1999 by Mariana Romo-Carmona.

Ruth L. Schwartz "Possible," from *Accordion Breathing and Dancing* by Ruth L. Schwartz, © 1995, reprinted by permission of the University of Pittsburgh Press. "Flamenco Guitar," "Can Pigeons Be Heroes?" and "Edgewater Park" © 1999 by Ruth L. Schwartz.

Robyn Selman "21 East 10th, 2BR, WBF, EIK" and "Exodus," from *Directions to My House* by Robyn Selman, © 1995. Reprinted by permission of the University of Pittsburgh Press.

Reginald Shepherd "Three A.M. Eternal," from *Some Are Drowning* by Reginald Shepherd, © 1994; reprinted by permission of the University of Pittsburgh Press. "Eros in His Striped Blue Shirt," "Narcissus Learning the

Words to This Song," and "The Gods at Three A.M.," from *Angel, Interrupted* by Reginald Shepherd, © 1996; reprinted by permission of the University of Pittsburgh Press. "That Man," from *Wrong* by Reginald Shepherd, © 1999; reprinted by permission of the University of Pittsburgh Press.

Linda Smukler "Sign" is reprinted from *Normal Sex*, copyright © 1994 by Linda Smukler, by permission of Firebrand Books, Ithaca, N.Y. "Days Inn," "Trash," and "Home in Three Days. Don't Wash." are reprinted from *Home in Three Days. Don't Wash.* © 1996 by Linda Smukler, by permission of Hard Press. "Marry" © 1999 by Linda Smukler.

Cheryl Boyce Taylor "Forever Arima" " 'Round Irving High School," and "Plenty Time Pass Fast, Fas Dey So" are reprinted from *Raw Air* (Fly By Night Press, in association with A Gathering of Tribes) © 1997 by Cheryl Boyce Taylor, by permission of the author.

Richard Tayson "First Sex," "Nightsweats," and "Phone Sex" are reprinted from *The Apprentice of Fever* © 1998 by Richard Tayson, reprinted by permission of the author and Kent State University Press.

David Trinidad "Things to Do in *Valley of the Dolls* (The Movie)," "Answer Song," "Moonstones," "(Doll Not Included)," and excerpts from "Eighteen to Twenty-One" are reprinted from *Answer Song* (Serpent's Tail/High Risk Books) © 1994 by David Trinidad, by permission of the author. "For Joe Brainard" © 1999 by David Trinidad.

Terry Wolverton "Black Slip" is reprinted from *Black Slip* (Clothespin Fever Press) © 1992 by Terry Wolverton, by permission of the author. "The Dead Stepfather" is reprinted from *The Jacaranda Review* © 1996 by Terry Wolverton, by permission of the author. "Tubes" is reprinted from ZYZZYVA © 1998 by Terry Wolverton, by permission of the author. "In China" is reprinted from *The Stinging Fly*, no. 2 © 1998 by Terry Wolverton, by permission of the author.

Mark Wunderlich "Take Good Care of Yourself," "Given in Person Only," "The Trick," "Aubade," and "Continent's Edge" are reprinted from *The Anchorage: Poems* (Amherst: University of Massachusetts Press) © 1999 by the University of Massachusetts Press. "East Seventh Street" © 1999 by Mark Wunderlich.

<⟫☼⟫>

ABOUT THE CONTRIBUTORS

MARK BIBBINS lives in New York City. His first collection of poems, *Swerve*, appears in *Take Three: 3* (Graywolf Press, 1998). Other work has been published in such anthologies and journals as *Poetry*, *The Paris Review*, and *The Yale Review*. He received an MFA from the New School for Social Research, where he now teaches poetry workshops. In 1999 he was nominated for a Pushcart Prize.

OLGA BROUMAS was born in Greece in 1949 and came to the United States in 1967 to attend college. In 1977 she won the Yale Younger Poets Award, the first non-native speaker of English to be so distinguished. She has received Guggenheim, NEA, Witter Bynner, and state arts fellowships and has published seven major collections of poetry and three translations from the Greek of Nobel Laureate Odysseas Elytis, most recently his *Eros, Eros, Eros: Poems Selected and Last* (1998) and her own *Rave: Poems, 1975–1999*, both from Copper Canyon Press. She is a bodywork therapist in Brewster, on Cape Cod, and poet-in-residence and director of creative writing at Brandeis University.

CHERYL BURKE (a.k.a. Cheryl B.) is a writer and spoken-word performer. She was born in Staten Island, New York, in 1972 and currently lives in Brooklyn. She is the author of three chapbooks, including *Ripe* (Night & Day Productions, 1996), *Motor Oil Queen!* (By the Seat of Your Pants Press, 1998), which is now in its second printing, and *Nameless*, also from By the Seat of Your Pants, 1999. Her prose and poetry have appeared in *Revival: Spoken Word from Lollapalooza 94* (Manic D Press, 1995), *Excursus Literary Arts Journal*, *Driver's Side Airbag*, *Poetry Nation* (Vehicule Press, 1998), and the London 'zine *Rising*. She has performed her work extensively throughout New York and the Pacific Northwest, as well as in London.

REGIE CABICO is the winner of the 1993 New York Poetry Slam, a Road Poet on Lollapalooza, and the opening act of MTV's Free Your Mind Spoken Word Tour. He is coeditor of *Poetry Nation: An Anthology of North American Spoken Word & Written Poetry* (Vehicule Press, 1998). His two poetry chapbooks are *The Petting Zoo* (IKON, 1994) and *I Saw Your Ex-lover behind the Starbucks Counter* (Big Fat Press, 1997). His work appears in numerous anthologies, including *Aloud: Voices from the Nuyorican Poets Cafe* (Henry Holt, 1994), *The Name of Love* (St. Martin's Press, 1995), and *On a Bed of Rice: An Asian American Erotic Feast* (Anchor Books, 1995). Spoken-word compilations in which his work appears include *Grand Slam: Best of the National Slam, vol. 1* (Mouth Almighty, 1994) and *Relationships from Hell* (Caroline, 1994). Cabico has been featured at Joe's Pub (at the Joseph Papp

Public Theater in New York), the Red Barn (Key West), and the Wonaxe Theater (Vancouver). His solo show, "onomatopoeia & a ¼ life crisis in one act," was presented at the Seattle Fringe Festival and the Here Theater (New York). The recipient of a 1997 New York Foundation for the Arts poetry fellowship, he is a cyberjay on the Performance Channel's "GO POETRY. COM," and he curates two reading series, "Writers on the Ledge" at Dixon Place and "Realness & Rhythms" at A Different Light bookstore in New York City.

RAFAEL CAMPO teaches and practices internal medicine at Harvard Medical School and Beth Israel Deaconess Medical Center in Boston. Born in 1964 to immigrant parents, he attended Amherst College and Harvard Medical School. He is the author of *The Other Man Was Me* (Arte Público Press, 1994), which won the 1993 National Poetry Series award; *What the Body Told* (Duke University Press, 1996), which won a Lambda Literary Award for poetry; and *The Poetry of Healing: A Doctor's Education in Empathy, Identity, and Desire* (W. W. Norton, 1997), a collection of essays that also won a Lambda Literary Award, for memoir. His poetry and prose have appeared in many major anthologies, including *Best American Poetry 1995* (Scribner, 1995), *Things Shaped in Passing: More "Poets for Life" Writing from the AIDS Pandemic* (Persea, 1997), *Currents in the Dancing River: Contemporary Latino Fiction, Nonfiction, and Poetry* (Harcourt Brace, 1994), and *Gay Men at the Millennium* (Putnam, 1997), and in numerous prominent periodicals, including *DoubleTake, The Nation, The New York Times Magazine, Out, The Paris Review, The Progressive, The Threepenny Review,* and *The Washington Post.* With the support of a Guggenheim fellowship for 1997–1998, he completed work on *Diva,* his third collection of poems (Duke University Press, 1999). He lives with his partner of fifteen years and "a big butch red Doberman named Ruby" in Jamaica Plain, Massachusetts.

CYRUS CASSELLS's first book, *The Mud Actor* (Holt, Rinehart & Winston, 1982; Carnegie-Mellon, 1999), was a National Poetry Series selection and a finalist for the Bay Area Book Reviewers Award. Named as one of the Best Books of 1994 by *Publishers Weekly,* his second volume, *Soul Make a Path Through Shouting* (Copper Canyon Press, 1994), was awarded the Poetry Society of America's William Carlos Williams Award and was a finalist for the Lenore Marshall Prize for outstanding book of the year. *Beautiful Signor* (Copper Canyon Press, 1997), his third volume, received the 1997 Lambda Literary Award for Gay Men's Poetry and a Sister Circle Award (for African-American literature), and was a finalist for the Bay Area Book Reviewers Award. His fourth book, *Riders on the Back of Silence,* a novel in verse, is forthcoming in 2001.

JUSTIN CHIN was born in Malaysia and grew up in Singapore. He is the author of Bite Hard (Manic D Press), which was a finalist in the Firecracker Alternative Book Awards as well as the Lambda Literary Awards. His solo performances have been presented nationally. Chin has received fellowships and grants from the California Arts Council, the Djerassi Artist Residency, Franklin Furnace, PEN American Center, and PEN Center USA West. He was on the 1995 and 1996 San Francisco National Poetry Slam teams. He now lives in San Francisco, where he teaches poetry at San Francisco State.

CHRYSTOS (Menominee) was born November 7, 1946, off-reservation in San Francisco. In addition to writing, making art, and working as a maid to support herself, she is a grassroots activist on many issues, including Native rights, women's liberation, lesbian battering, and the injustice of the U.S. prison system. She is the author of four books of poems published by Press Gang Publishers in Vancouver: *Not Vanishing* (1988), *Dream On* (1991), *In Her I Am* (1993), and *Fire Power* (1995), as well as *Fugitive Colors* (Cleveland State University Poetry Center, 1995) and the German/English *Wilder Reis* (Orlando, Berlin, 1997).

Her work appears in many anthologies, including *Unsettling America: An Anthology of Contemporary Multicultural Poetry*, edited by Maria M. Gillan (Penguin Books, 1994), and *Reinventing the Enemy's Language: Contemporary Native Women's Writing of North America*, edited by Joy Harjo and Gloria Bird (W. W. Norton, 1997). She has received grants from the NEA, the Lannan Foundation, and the Audre Lorde Foundation, as well as receiving the Barbara Demming Memorial Grant and the Astraea Lesbian of the Year Award. She knew she was a lesbian by age four, she reports, and began her extensive career as "a bossy femme sex maniac" when she turned eighteen. She is self-educated and sober since 1988. She is currently finishing her novel about incest, *Mon Oncle, Mon Amour*, and working on a manuscript of short stories, one of essays, and another of new poems. She lives in Washington.

CHERYL CLARKE is a poet, writer, and educator whose writing has been greatly influenced by black and lesbian-feminist consciousness and Afro-American culture. Her work has appeared in *Home Girls: A Black-Feminist Anthology* (Kitchen Table/Women of Color Press, 1983); *This Bridge Called My Back: Writings by Radical Women of Color* (Persephone Press, 1981); *Conditions; Feminist Studies; The Black Scholar; Belles Lettres; Gay Community News; Outweek; The Advocate; Sojourner; Gay and Lesbian Poetry in Our Time* (St. Martin's Press, 1988); *Bridges: A Journal for Jewish Feminists and Their Friends; Persistent Desire: A Femme-Butch Reader* (Alyson Publications, 1992); *Radical America, Radical Teacher; No More Masks: An Anthology of Twentieth-Century American Women Poets* (HarperPerennial, 1993); *A Formal Feeling Comes* (Story Line Press 1994); *Kenyon Review; Women's Review of Books;* and *African American Review.* Clarke was a member of the Conditions Editorial Collective from 1981 to 1990. She has published four books of poetry, including *Narratives: Poems in the Tradition of Black Women* (Kitchen Table Press, 1983), *Living as a Lesbian* (Firebrand Books, 1986), *Humid Pitch* (Firebrand Books, 1989), and her most recent, *Experimental*

Love (Firebrand Books, 1993), which was nominated for a 1994 Lambda Literary Award. She is currently working on a new manuscript of poems entitled *Corridors of Nostalgia*. She lives and writes in Jersey City, New Jersey.

JEFFERY CONWAY is originally from Southern California and currently lives in New York City. His work has appeared in such periodicals as *The World*, *Brooklyn Review, The James White Review, B City*, and *The Portable Lower East Side*. His poems also appear in the anthologies *Eros in Boystown* (Crown, 1996), *Gents, Bad Boys & Barbarians* (Alyson Publications, 1995), *Plush: Selected Poems of Sky Gilbert, Courtnay McFarlane, Jeffery Conway, R. M. Vaughan & David Trinidad* (Coach House Press, 1995), *Poetry Nation* (Véhicule Press, 1998), and *Queer Dog* (Cleis Press, 1997). He is the author of *Blood Poisoning* (Cold Calm Press, 1995).

DENNIS COOPER is the author of a five-novel cycle: *Closer* (1989), *Frisk* (1991), *Try* (1995), *Guide* (1997), and *Period* (March 2000), all published by Grove Press, as was *The Dream Police: Selected Poems 1969–1993*. His poetry is included in *Postmodern American Poetry*, a Norton anthology (1994), the PBS series *The United States of Poetry*, and *Up Late: American Poetry Since 1970* (Four Walls Eight Windows, 1987), as well as forming the lyrics to songs by John Zorn, Christian Death, and Stephen Prina. In addition to his fiction and poetry, he writes on contemporary culture for *Spin, George, Artforum*, and other magazines. He lives in Los Angeles, where he is currently collaborating on a pornographic photo-novella with the artist Vincent Fecteau, and writing a nonfiction book.

ALFRED CORN's seventh book of poems, *Present* (Counterpoint), appeared in 1997, along with a novel titled *Part of His Story* (Mid-List Press), and a study of prosody, *The Poem's Heartbeat* (Story Line Press). He has also published a collection of critical essays titled *The Metamorphoses of Metaphor* (Viking Press, 1987), and *Stake: Selected Poems, 1972–1992* was recently released by Counterpoint. Fellowships and prizes awarded for his poetry include the Guggenheim, the NEA, an award from the American Academy and Institute of Arts and Letters, and one from the Academy of American Poets. He has taught at the City University of New York, the University of Cincinnati, UCLA, Ohio State University, and the University of Tulsa, and is currently on the faculty of the Graduate Writing Program at Columbia's School of the Arts. A frequent contributor to *The New York Times Book Review* and *The Nation*, he also writes art criticism for *Art in America* and *ARTnews* magazines. He lives in New York City, and, among the possible labels that might apply to his poetry (white, male, American, Christian), he chooses to be called a gay poet as a response to legal sanctions against his sexuality that are operative in half the United States and in many other countries.

MARK DOTY's five books of poems and two volumes of memoir have received the National Book Critics Circle Award, a Lambda Literary Award, the Witter Bynner Prize from the American Academy and Institute of Arts and

Letters, a Whiting Writers' Award, the PEN/Martha Allbrand Award for Non-fiction, and Britain's T. S. Eliot Prize for poetry. A recipient of fellowships from the Guggenheim Foundation and the National Endowment for the Arts, he's taught at Columbia, Sarah Lawrence, and the University of Iowa Writers Workshop. With his partner, the novelist Paul Lisicky, he lives in Provincetown, Massachusetts, and Houston, Texas, where he teaches in the graduate program at the University of Houston.

BEATRIX GATES's *In the Open* (Painted Leaf Press, 1998) was a Lambda Literary Award finalist. She has published two previous poetry titles, *Shooting at Night* (Granite Press, 1980), a chapbook, and *native tongue*, a letterpress limited edition (hopalong press, 1973). She edited *The Wild Good: Lesbian Photographs and Writings on Love* (Anchor Books, 1996), which called on her years of experience as an editor and designer at Granite Press, and her work has appeared in many anthologies. Organizer of A Different Light's Poetry Series (1992–1995), she also served on the Kitchen Table: Women of Color Press transition team (1993–1996). She has worked as an editor and taught writing, literature, women's studies, and book arts in many settings, including New York University, Goddard College, The Writer's Voice, the New York Public Library, and the New School for Social Research. Recent autobiographical prose appears in *A Woman Like That*, edited by Joan Larkin. She has been awarded a Puffin Foundation grant for WHO SAYS! writing workshops for gay/lesbian/bisexual/transgendered/questioning youth in Downeast Maine, and she is currently working on poetry translations from Spanish with Electa Arenal. She lives in Greenport, New York.

ELENA GEORGIOU (coeditor) is the winner of numerous writing awards—most recently, a New York Foundation for the Arts grant, the Astraea Foundation's Emerging Writers Award for poetry, the National Arts Club Award for fiction, and the Academy of American Poets Award. Her poetry, fiction, and oral histories have been published in numerous literary journals and anthologies, including *Soul: Black Power, Politics, and Pleasure* (New York University Press, 1998); *Too Darn Hot: Writing about Sex Since Kinsey* (Persea Books, 1998), and *Poetry Nation* (Véhicule Press, 1998). She holds an undergraduate degree from Hunter College, the City University of New York, and a graduate degree from City College, the City University of New York. She teaches creative writing at Hunter and City Colleges. Her first collection, titled *Mercy Mercy Me*, will be published by Painted Leaf Press in the spring of 2000.

ROBERT GLÜCK is the author of two novels, *Jack the Modernist* (Sea Horse/Gay Presses of New York, 1985; reprinted by Serpent's Tail/High Risk Books, 1995) and *Margery Kempe* (Serpent's Tail/High Risk Books, 1994); a book of stories, *Elements of a Coffee Service* (Four Seasons Foundation, 1983); a number of books of poetry, including *Andy* (Panjandrum Press, 1973); *Metaphysics* (Hoddypoll, 1977); *Family Poems* (Black Star Series, 1979); *La Fontaine* (Black Star Series, 1981), a rewriting of the *Fables* in collaboration with

Bruce Boone; and *Reader* (Lapis Press, 1989). He lives and teaches in San Francisco.

MELINDA GOODMAN is the author of *Middle Sister* (MSG Press, 1988) and teaches poetry in workshop classes at Hunter College in New York City. She was a 1992 winner of an Astraea Foundation Lesbian Poets Award and one of the editors of *Conditions*, the first lesbian literary magazine. Goodman's work has appeared in numerous anthologies in the United States and abroad, including the landmark *Gay and Lesbian Poetry in Our Time* (St. Martin's Press, 1988). She holds an MFA in poetry from Columbia University and an MA in literature from New York University. The poems that appear in this book are from her unpublished manuscript, *Suck My Heart*.

MARILYN HACKER is the author of nine books, including *Presentation Piece* (Viking Press, 1974), which received the National Book Award in 1975; *Going Back to the River* (Random House, 1990), which received a Lambda Literary Award in 1991; *Winter Numbers* (W. W. Norton, 1994), which received a Lambda Literary Award and the Lenore Marshall Award of *The Nation* magazine and the Academy of American Poets, both in 1995; and the verse novel *Love, Death, and the Changing of the Seasons* (Arbor House, 1986; W. W. Norton, 1995). Her *Selected Poems: 1965–1990* (W. W. Norton, 1994) was awarded the Poets' Prize in 1996. Also in 1996, Wake Forest University Press published *Edge*, her translations of the French poet Claire Malroux. Her new book, *Squares and Courtyards*, was published by W. W. Norton in January 2000. She lives in New York and Paris.

ELOISE KLEIN HEALY is the founding chair of the MFA in Creative Writing Program at Antioch University Los Angeles and the associate editor/poetry editor of *The Lesbian Review of Books*. She is the author of *Building Some Changes* (Beyond Baroque Foundation, 1976), *A Packet Beating Like a Heart* (Books of a Feather Press, 1981), *Ordinary Wisdom* (Paradise Press, 1981), *Artemis in Echo Park* (Firebrand Books, 1991), and *Women's Studies Chronicles* (The Inevitable Press, 1998). Her work has been anthologized in *The Zenith of Desire* (Crown Publishers, 1996); *Queer Dog* (Cleis Press, 1997); *Intimate Nature: The Bond between Women and Animals* (Ballantine, 1998); *Blood Whispers: LA Writers on AIDS*, vol. 2 (Silverton Books, 1994): *The Key to Everything: Classic Lesbian Love Poems* (St. Martin's Press, 1995); *Ladies, Start Your Engines: Women Writers on Cars and the Road* (Faber & Faber, 1996); *The Arc of Love: An Anthology of Lesbian Love Poems* (Scribner, 1996); and *Hers: Brilliant New Fiction by Lesbian Writers* (Faber & Faber, 1995). "Artemis in Echo Park/The Women's Studies Chronicles" is available on CD/audiotape from New Alliance Records.

MELANIE HOPE has studied poetry at Oberlin College, the Bucknell Seminar for Younger Poets, and New York University. Her writing has appeared in *The Caribbean Writer, Sinister Wisdom, Essence,* and *The Paris Review,* as well as in such anthologies as *The Key to Everything: Classic Lesbian Love*

Poems (St. Martin's Press, 1995), *The Arc of Love: Contemporary Lesbian Poems about Sex* (Crown, 1996), *Afekete: An Anthology of Black Lesbian Writing* (Anchor, 1995), and *Queer Dog Homo/Pup/Poetry* (Cleis Press, 1997). She lives in New York City with her lover/partner Catherine and their children.

MICHAEL KLEIN is the author of a book of poems, *1990* (Provincetown Arts Press, 1993), which won a Lambda Literary Award, and *Track Conditions: A Memoir* (Persea Books, 1997), which was a Lammy finalist. He is also the editor/coeditor of three books of essays and poems dealing with the AIDS pandemic — most recently, *Things Shaped in Passing: More "Poets for Life" Writing on the AIDS Pandemic* — all published by Persea Books. He has taught at Sarah Lawrence, at Manhattanville, for the New York Public Library, and in the MFA program at Goddard College in Vermont for the past eight years. During the summer, he is on the faculty of the Summer Workshop program at the Fine Arts Work Center in Provincetown, where he was a fellow in 1990. A native New Yorker, Klein currently curates the Homotext reading series at Dixon Place and also freelances as a voice-over artist. His newest writing will be a book called *The End of Being Known*.

WAYNE KOESTENBAUM is the author of three books of poetry, all published by Persea Books: *Ode to Anna Moffo and Other Poems* (1990), *Rhapsodies of a Repeat Offender* (1994), and *The Milk of Inquiry* (1999). He has also written three books of criticism: *Double Talk: The Erotics of Male Literary Collaboration* (Routledge, 1989); *The Queen's Throat: Opera, Homosexuality, and the Mystery of Desire* (Poseidon Press, 1993), which was nominated for a National Book Critics Circle Award; and *Jackie Under My Skin: Interpreting an Icon* (Farrar, Straus & Giroux, 1995). He also wrote the libretto for the opera *Jackie O* (music by Michael Daugherty). He is a professor of English at the Graduate School of City University of New York and has received a Whiting Writers' Award.

JOAN LARKIN's collections of poetry are *Housework* (Out & Out Books, 1975), *A Long Sound* (Granite Press, 1986), and *Cold River* (Painted Leaf Press, 1997). Twice winner of the Lambda Literary Award for poetry, she coedited the groundbreaking anthologies *Amazon Poetry* (1975) and *Lesbian Poetry* (1980), both with Elly Bulkin, and *Gay and Lesbian Poetry in Our Time* (1988), with Carl Morse. Her recent work includes *The Living*, a play about AIDS; *Sor Juana's Love Poems/Poemas de Amor*, translated with Jaime Manrique; and two books in the Hazelden recovery series: *If You Want What We Have* and *Glad Day*, a book of daily meditations for lesbian, gay, bisexual, and transgender people. She is coeditor of Living Out, a gay and lesbian autobiography series published by the University of Wisconsin Press. She has received fellowships from the National Endowment for the Arts, the New York Foundation for the Arts, and the Massachusetts Cultural Council. A teacher of writing for many years, she has served on the faculties of Brooklyn and Goddard Colleges. Currently teaching at Sarah Lawrence, she lives and writes in Brooklyn, New York.

MICHAEL LASSELL (coeditor) is the award-winning author of three collections of verse: *Poems for Lost and Un-lost Boys* (Amelia, 1985); *Decade Dance* (Alyson Publications, 1990), a Lambda Literary Award winner; and *A Flame for the Touch That Matters* (Painted Leaf Press, 1998), a Lammy finalist; as well as a multiple-genre collection, *The Hard Way* (Richard Kasak/Masquerade Books, 1995); and a collection of short stories, *Certain Ecstasies* (Painted Leaf Press, 1999). He edited two pocket collections of poems — *The Name of Love: Classic Gay Love Poems* (St. Martin's Press, 1995) and *Eros in Boystown: Contemporary Gay Poems about Sex* (Crown, 1996) — and two books of personal essays: *Two Hearts Desire: Gay Couples on Their Love*, with Lawrence Schimel (St. Martin's Press, 1997), and *Men Seeking Men: Adventures in Gay Personals* (Painted Leaf Press, 1998).

Lassell holds degrees from Colgate University, the Yale School of Drama (where he received the John Gassner Prize for Criticism), and California Institute of the Arts, where he later taught in the School of Theater and Division of Critical Studies. For the past fifteen years, he has worked as a journalist: as a theater critic and arts features writer for the *L.A. Weekly* and Los Angeles *Herald Examiner*, as a contributing editor to *The Advocate* and *New York Native*, as the managing editor of *L.A. Style* and *Interview* magazines, as executive editor of *Sí*, and since 1991 as the articles director of *Metropolitan Home*. His poetry, short stories, and essays have appeared in scores of literary journals, anthologies, magazines, and newspapers in this country and abroad, where he has been translated into French, German, Spanish, Dutch, and Catalan.

TIMOTHY LIU was born in 1965 and raised in the suburbs of San Jose, California. After serving as a Mormon missionary in Hong Kong, he received a BA in English from Brigham Young University and an MA in English from the University of Houston. His first book, *Vox Angelica* (Alicejamesbooks, 1992), received the Norma Farber First Book Award from the Poetry Society of America and is now in its third printing. His subsequent books of poems, *Burnt Offerings* and *Say Goodnight*, were published by Copper Canyon Press and were both finalists for a Lambda Literary Award. His work has been widely published, and his journals and papers are archived in the Berg Collection at the New York Public Library. He served as the 1997 Holloway Lecturer at U.C. Berkeley and is currently an assistant professor at William Paterson University. He has also taught workshops at Cornell College, Hampshire College, the Iowa Summer Writer's Festival, the Fine Arts Work Center in Provincetown, and at the Asian American Writer's Workshop in New York City. Contributing frequent reviews to magazines such as *ARTnews, Art Papers, Lambda Book Report, New Art Examiner*, and *Publishers Weekly*, Liu makes his home in Hoboken, New Jersey.

JAIME MANRIQUE was born in Colombia, where his first volume of poems received the National Poetry Award. He is the author of four books in Spanish, including poetry, fiction, and criticism. In English he has published a collection of poems, *My Night with Federico García Lorca* (Painted Leaf Press, 1997), and translated with Joan Larkin *Sor Juana's Love Poems* (Painted Leaf Press, 1997). Among his novels are *Colombian Gold* (Clarkson Potter, 1983), *Latin Moon in Manhattan* (St. Martin's Press, 1992), and *Twilight at the Equator* (Faber & Faber, 1997). In 1999 alone, he published an autobiography entitled *Eminent Maricones: Arenas, Lorca, Puig, and Me* (University of Wisconsin Press), a collection of poems in Spanish called *Mi cuerpo y otros poemas* (Casa Silva), and *Bésame Mucho: An Anthology of New Gay Latino Writing*, which he edited for Painted Leaf Press. He has taught in the MFA programs at Columbia University, Mount Holyoke College, New York University, and the New School for Social Research. He lives in New York City.

J. D. McCLATCHY is the author of four collections of poems: *Scenes from Another Life* (George Braziller, 1981), *Stars Principal* (Macmillan, 1986), *The Rest of the Way* (Alfred A. Knopf, 1990), and *Ten Commandments* (Alfred A. Knopf, 1998), winner of a Lambda Literary Award. His literary essays are collected in *White Paper* (Columbia University Press, 1989), which was given the Melville Cane Award by the Poetry Society of America, and in *Twenty Questions* (Columbia University Press, 1998). He has also edited numerous other books, including *The Vintage Book of Contemporary American Poetry* (1990), *The Vintage Book of Contemporary World Poetry* (1996), and *Recitative: Prose by James Merrill* (North Point Press, 1986). His work appears regularly in *The New Yorker*, *The New York Times Book Review*, *The Paris Review*, *The New Republic,* and many other magazines.

McClatchy has taught at Princeton, Yale, Columbia, UCLA, Rutgers, and other universities; since 1991, he has served as editor of *The Yale Review*. He has also had a prominent role in the world of opera as the writer of four libretti. In 1996 he was named a chancellor of the Academy of American Poets. In 1998 he was elected a fellow of the American Academy of Arts and Sciences and the following year was elected to membership in the American Academy of Arts and Letters. Among his other honors, he has been awarded the fellowship of the Academy of American Poets, and grants from the Guggenheim Foundation and the National Endowment for the Arts.

HONOR MOORE is the author of *Memoir* (Chicory Blue Press, 1988) and *Mourning Pictures* (1974), a play in poetry about her mother's death. She spent twelve years researching and writing *The White Blackbird* (Viking, 1996; Penguin, 1997), a life of her maternal grandmother, Margarett Sargent, a painter and sculptor who was born into Boston Brahmin society and broke out of it, both sexually (extramarital affairs with men and women, including the writer Jane Bowles) and artistically (nine one-woman shows between 1926 and 1932). Poems published in *Memoir* won Moore fellowships from the NEA and the Connecticut Commission on the Arts; *Mourning Pictures* was produced on Broadway and won her an award from the New York State Council on the Arts (and is included in *The New Women's Theatre: Ten*

Plays by Contemporary American Women, which Moore edited for Vintage Books in 1977); and *The White Blackbird* was a finalist for a Lambda Literary Award and the Judy Grahn Award. Moore is currently completing a novel and a new collection of poems. She lives in Connecticut and New York City.

EILEEN MYLES is often named "the last poet of the New York School." She's been reading and performing her work locally, nationally, and internationally since 1974. *School of Fish* (Black Sparrow Press, 1997), her latest volume, won a Lambda Literary Award for poetry. Other titles include *Maxfield Parrish: Early & New Poems* (Black Sparrow Press, 1995), *Not Me* (Semiotext(e), 1991), and a collection of stories, *Chelsea Girls* (Black Sparrow Press, 1994). With Liz Kotz, she edited *The New Fuck You: Adventures in Lesbian Reading* (Semiotext(e), 1995), which also received a Lambda Literary Award. Myles was artistic director of the St. Mark's Poetry Project from 1984 to 1986. In 1992 she conducted a write-in campaign for President of the United States. Currently, she writes about art and literature in *Art in America, The Village Voice, The Nation, The Stranger, Nest, Civilization,* and numerous other publications. She has recently completed a nonfiction novel, *Cool for You.*

LETTA NEELY's work can also be found in the anthologies *Does Your Mama Know?: An Anthology of Black Lesbian Coming Out Stories* (Redbone Press, 1997), *Catch the Fire: A Cross-Generation Anthology of Contemporary African-American Poetry* (Riverhead Books, 1998), and *A Woman Like That: Lesbian and Bisexual Writers Tell Their Coming Out Stories* (Avon Books, 1999). She was a 1995 recipient of a New York Foundation for the Arts fellowship and a Barbara Deming for Money award. In 1997, she received the Pat Parker Award for Artistic Freedom from the Lesbian and Gay Political Alliance in Massachusetts. Originally from Indianapolis, Indiana, she now resides in Dorchester, Massachusetts, where she teaches creative writing, harvests delicious weeds for consumption, and is a part of collective struggle for our liberation. *Juba* — her book of poems — was published in 1998 by Wildheart Press.

ACHY OBEJAS is a cultural writer with the *Chicago Tribune* and the author of *Memory Mambo,* a novel (Cleis Press, 1996), winner of a Lambda Literary Award, and *We Came All the Way from Cuba So You Could Dress Like This?* (Cleis Press, 1994), a collection of short stories. Her poems have been included in such anthologies as *Little Havana Blues* (Arte Público Press, 1996), *Bridges to Cuba/Puentes a Cuba* (University of Michigan Press, 1995), *Stray Bullets* (Tia Chucha Press, 1991), and *Woman of Her Word* (University of Texas, 1983). Her prose has been included in *Latina: Women's Voices from the Borderlands* (Simon & Schuster, 1995), *Dagger: On Butch Women* (Cleis Press, 1994), *Feminisms: An Anthology of Literary Theory and Criticism* (Rutgers University Press, 1995), *Estatuas de Sal* (Ediciones Union, Cuba, 1996), and *Cubana: Contemporary Fiction by Cuban Women* (Beacon Press, 1998), among others. She was born in Havana.

GERRY GOMEZ PEARLBERG is the author of a collection of poems titled *Marianne Faithfull's Cigarette* (Cleis Press, 1998), winner of a 1998 Lambda Literary Award for lesbian poetry. Other recent books include *Queer Dog* (Cleis Press, 1997), winner of a 1998 Firecracker Alternative Book Award, and *The Fetish Papers* (Big Fat Press, 1998). She was the editor of *The Key to Everything: Classic Lesbian Love Poems* (St. Martin's Press, 1995) and *Zenith of Desire: Contemporary Lesbian Poems about Sex* (Crown, 1996). Her work has recently appeared in *Gargoyle, Global City Review, Lesbian Fiction at the Millennium, The Outlaw Bible of American Poetry,* and *The Bark.* She teaches poetry at The Writer's Voice in New York City.

ROBERT E. PENN is the author of *The Gay Men's Wellness Guide: The National Lesbian and Gay Health Association's Complete Book of Physical, Emotional, and Mental Health and Well-being for Every Gay Male* (Henry Holt, 1998). His poetry and prose appear in such anthologies as *Fighting Words: Personal Essays by Black Gay Men* (Avon Books, 1999), *Children of the Dream: Our Own Stories of Growing Up Black in America* (Pocket Books, 1999), *Men Seeking Men* (Painted Leaf Press, 1998), *We Are Everywhere: A Historical Sourcebook of Gay and Lesbian Politics* (Routledge, 1997), *Male on Male Rape* (Insight Books, 1997), *Shade: An Anthology of Fiction by Gay Men of African Descent* (Avon Books, 1996), *Milking Black Bull* (Vega Press, 1991), *Sojourner: Black Gay Voices in the Age of AIDS* (Other Countries Press, 1993), and *The Road Before Us* (Galiens Press, 1991), as well as in magazines including *Essence, Shooting Star Review, Thing,* and *COLORLife,* and such literary journals as *The Portable Lower East Side* and *Arts & Understanding.*

CARL PHILLIPS is the author of four collections of poetry: *In the Blood* (Northeastern University Press, 1992), which won the Morse Poetry Prize; *Cortège* (Graywolf Press, 1995), a finalist for the National Book Critics Circle Award; *From the Devotions* (Graywolf Press, 1998), a finalist for the National Book Award; and the forthcoming *Pastoral* (Graywolf Press). The recipient of awards and fellowships from the Guggenheim Foundation, the Library of Congress, and the Academy of American Poets, among others, Phillips has had his work reprinted in textbooks and anthologies that include *The Best of the Best American Poetry* and *The Pushcart Prize XXXIII.* He has taught at Harvard University and the Iowa Writers' Workshop, and currently teaches at Washington University, St. Louis.

D. A. POWELL received an MA in English from Sonoma State University and an MFA in creative writing from the University of Iowa's Iowa Writers' Workshop. His poems have appeared in *Denver Quarterly, The James White Review,* the *Iowa Journal of Cultural Studies, New American Writing, Boston Review, Pequod, Puerto del Sol,* and *The Washington Post.* He lives in San Francisco, where he serves on the board of Small Press Traffic. Powell has received awards from the Academy of American Poets and the James Michener Foundation. *Tea,* his first full-length collection of poems, was a finalist for the AWP Award in Poetry and was published by Wesleyan University

Press in 1998. He is the author of two chapbooks from Norton Coker Press: *explosions and small geometries* (1991) and, in collaboration with Carol Ciavonne and Patricia Hartnett, *Con Sequences* (1993). His new book of poems, *Lunch*, is due from Wesleyan in 2000.

MINNIE BRUCE PRATT's second book of poetry, *Crime Against Nature* (Firebrand Books, 1990), was chosen as the 1989 Lamont Poetry Selection by the Academy of American Poets, was nominated for a Pulitzer Prize, and received the American Library Association's Gay and Lesbian Book Award for Literature. Pratt's essay "Identity: Skin Blood Heart," now considered a feminist classic, was included in *Yours in Struggle: Three Feminist Perspectives on Anti-Semitism and Racism*, a book that she coauthored with Elly Bulkin and Barbara Smith. Her other books include *We Say We Love Each Other* (Firebrand Books, 1992; Spinsters/Aunt Lute, 1985), *Rebellion: Essays 1980–1991* (Firebrand Books, 1991), and *S/HE* (Firebrand Books, 1995), stories about gender boundary crossing. Her most recent book, *Walking Back Up Depot Street*, from the Pitt Poetry Series (University of Pittsburgh Press, 1999), is a collection of narrative poems about growing up in, and leaving, the segregated South. She lives with author/activist Leslie Feinberg in Jersey City, New Jersey.

MARIANA ROMO-CARMONA is the author of a novel, *Living at Night* (Spinsters Ink, 1997), and *Speaking Like an Immigrant*, a collection of short fiction (Latina Lesbian History Project, 1999). She has published fiction, poetry, and nonfiction in English and in Spanish, and her work has appeared in anthologies such as *Cuentos: Stories by Latinas* (Kitchen Table/Women of Color Press, 1983), *Beyond Gender & Geography: American Women Writers* (East-West Press, New Delhi, 1994); *Mom* (Alyson Publications, 1998), *Queer 13* (Rob Weisbach Books, 1998), *Lesbian Travels: A Literary Companion* (Whereabouts Press, 1998), and *A Woman Like That*, edited by Joan Larkin (Avon Books, 1999). Romo-Carmona lives in New York City and is on the faculty of the MFA program at Goddard College.

RUTH L. SCHWARTZ was born in Geneva, New York, in 1962 and spent her childhood and early adulthood moving around the country. She left home at sixteen, received her BA from Wesleyan University and her MFA from the University of Michigan, then lived for thirteen years in the San Francisco Bay area. For many years, Schwartz made her living as an AIDS educator. Her first book of poems, *Accordion Breathing and Dancing*, won the 1994 Associated Writing Programs Award and was published by the University of Pittsburgh Press in 1996. Her second manuscript of poems, *Survival*, was a 1998 National Poetry Series finalist. Schwartz has received grants from the National Endowment for the Arts and the Astraea Foundation for Emerging Lesbian Writers. Her poems will be represented in the forthcoming anthologies *New Young American Poets* (Southern Illinois University Press) and *American Poetry: Next Generation* (Carnegie Mellon Press). She currently lives in Ohio, where she is an assistant professor of creative writing at Cleveland State University.

ROBYN SELMAN's first book, *Directions to My House*, was published by the University of Pittsburgh Press in 1995. Her poems have appeared in many anthologies, including *The Best American Poetry 1992*, *The Best American Poetry 1995* and *The Pushcart Prize XIX*. She is at work on her second collection of poems, entitled *Essays*. She lives in New York City.

REGINALD SHEPHERD was born in New York City in 1963; he grew up in the Bronx. He received his BA from Bennington College and MFA degrees from Brown University and the University of Iowa. The University of Pittsburgh Press published his first book, *Some Are Drowning*, in 1994 as winner of the 1993 AWP Award Series in Poetry. Pittsburgh published his second book, *Angel, Interrupted*, in 1996; it was a finalist for a 1997 Lambda Literary Award. His third collection of poems, *Wrong* (1999), is also a University of Pittsburgh Press title.

Shepherd is the recipient of a 1993 "Discover"/*The Nation* Award, the 1994–1995 Amy Lowell Poetry Traveling Scholarship, a 1995 NEA creative writing fellowship, and a 1998 Illinois Arts Council poetry fellowship, among other honors and awards. His poems have appeared in *The American Poetry Review, Conjunctions, The Gettysburg Review, The Iowa Review, The Kenyon Review, The Nation, New England Review, The Paris Review, Ploughshares, Poetry*, and *TriQuarterly*, as well as in the 1995 and 1996 editions of *The Best American Poetry*. He was recently appointed assistant professor of English at Cornell University.

LINDA SMULKER is the author of two collections of poetry: *Normal Sex* (Firebrand Books, 1994) and *Home in Three Days. Don't Wash.*, a multimedia project with accompanying CD-ROM (Hard Press, 1996). She was born in Cleveland, Ohio, and studied the visual arts at the Yale School of Art and in the Whitney Museum Independent Study Program. Her work has been widely anthologized, and she is the recipient of numerous awards in poetry and fiction, including the 1997 Firecracker Alternative Book Award in poetry. She has received fellowships in poetry from the New York Foundation for the Arts and the Astraea Foundation for Emerging Lesbian Writers. She currently lives in Tucson, Arizona.

CHERYL BOYCE TAYLOR is a poet and performance artist who was born in Trinidad. Her first book of poems, *Raw Air*, was published in 1997 by Fly by Night Press in association with A Gathering of the Tribes. Her work has been featured in *Catch the Fire!* (Berkeley Publishing Group, 1998), *Chelsea 64* (Chelsea Associates, 1998), *Best Lesbian Erotica 1999* (Cleis Press, 1999), *Longshot* (Longshot Press, 1999), *Poetry Nation* (Vehicule Press, 1998), and *A Woman Like That* (Avon Books, 1999). Taylor teaches poetry writing at the Hamilton Fish Park Branch of the New York Public Library. Her work has been commissioned for Ronald K. Brown's Evidence Dance Company, premiering at Jacob's Pillow and the Joyce Theater in New York City. She appears in *Litany for Survival*, a film on the life of poet/activist Audre Lorde. She holds an MS in education and an MSW.

RICHARD TAYSON's first book of poetry, *The Apprentice of Fever*, won the 1997 Wick Poetry Prize and was published by the Kent State University Press (1998). Other awards include a Pushcart Prize and *Prairie Schooner*'s Bernice Slote Award. His poems have appeared in numerous magazines and anthologies, including *The Paris Review, Crazyhorse, The James White Review, Michigan Quarterly Review, Poetry Nation* (Véhicule Press, 1998), *Things Shaped in Passing: More "Poets for Life" Writing from the AIDS Pandemic* (Persea Books, 1997), *Jugular Defences* (Oscars Press, London, 1994), and *Sleep: Bedtime Reading* (Universe Publishing, 1998).

Tayson's first book of nonfiction, *Look Up for Yes*, coauthored with Julia Tavalaro, has appeared on the bestseller lists in Germany and has been included in *Reader's Digest: Today's Best Nonfiction* in the United States (1998). Finalist for a Books for a Better Life Award, *Look Up for Yes* was released in paperback here by Viking Penguin (1998). Tayson was educated at Colorado State University and New York University and teaches on-line writing workshops for the New School for Social Research in New York City.

DAVID TRINIDAD's books include the forthcoming *Plasticville* (Turtle Point Press), *Answer Song* (Serpent's Tail/High Risk Books, 1994), *Hand over Heart: Poems 1981–1988* (Amethyst Press, 1991), and *Pavane* (Sherwood Press, 1981). His poems have appeared in numerous magazines and have been included in over two dozen anthologies, including *Up Late: American Poetry Since 1970* (Four Walls Eight Windows, 1987), *High Risk: An Anthology of Forbidden Writings* (Dutton, 1991), *The Best American Poetry 1991* (Scribner, 1991), and *Postmodern American Poetry: A Norton Anthology* (W. W. Norton, 1994). He currently teaches poetry at Rutgers University, where he directs the Writers at Rutgers series and is a member of the core faculty in the MFA writing program at the New School for Social Research in New York. Originally from Los Angeles, Trinidad has lived in New York City since 1988.

TERRY WOLVERTON is the author of the novel *Bailey's Beads* (Faber & Faber, 1996), a finalist in the American Library Association's Gay and Lesbian Book Awards for 1997, and two collections of poetry: *Black Slip* (Clothespin Fever Press), a finalist for a Lambda Literary Award in 1993, and *Mystery Bruise* (Red Hen Press, 1999). Her fiction, poetry, essays, and drama have been published in periodicals internationally, including *Glimmer Train Stories, ZYZZYVA, Many Mountains Moving,* and *The Jacaranda Review,* and widely anthologized. She is currently working on a memoir, *Insurgent Muse,* for City Lights Books, and a novel-in-poems, *Embers.* She has also edited/coedited several successful compilations: *Harbinger: Poetry and Fiction by Los Angeles Writers* (Los Angeles Festival, 1990); *Indivisible: New Short Fiction by Gay and Lesbian West Coast Writers* (Plume, 1991); *Blood Whispers: L.A. Writers on AIDS,* volumes 1 and 2 (Silverton Books and the Los Angeles Gay and Lesbian Community Services Center, 1991 and 1994); *His: Brilliant*

New Fiction by Gay Men and *Hers: Brilliant New Fiction by Lesbians*, volumes 1, 2, and 3 (Faber & Faber, 1995, 1997, and 1999); and the forthcoming *Lesbian Fiction at the Millennium* and *Gay Fiction at the Millennium* (Alyson Publications, 2000.)

Since 1976 Wolverton has lived in Los Angeles, where she has been active in the feminist, gay and lesbian, and art communities. In addition to writing, Terry has toured North America as a performance artist and has produced and exhibited audio and video art, as well as installations. She has received ten grants in literature from the California Arts Council, and is the former executive director of the Woman's Building, a public center for women's culture in Los Angeles. For nine years she served as writer-in-residence at the L.A. Gay & Lesbian Center; in 1997, she founded Writers at Work, a center for creative writing in Los Angeles, where she offers several weekly workshops in fiction and poetry. She currently teaches poetry on the faculty of the California Institute of the Arts. She is the recipient of numerous awards for her artistic and community contributions.

MARK WUNDERLICH grew up in Fountain City, Wisconsin, and was educated at the University of Wisconsin and Columbia University. His first book of poems, *The Anchorage*, was published in 1999 by the University of Massachusetts Press. Magazines and periodicals in which his poems have appeared include *Boston Review*, *Poetry*, *The Paris Review*, *Southwest Review*, and *The Yale Review*. Among his awards and honors are fellowships from the Fine Arts Work Center in Provincetown, the Wallace Stegner Fellowship from Stanford University, and the 1997 Writers at Work Fellowship. He lives in California.

BIBLIOGRAPHY

The following is a list of books written or edited by the contributors to
THE WORLD IN US

Mark Bibbins. *Swerve*, from *Take Three: 3* (with Jennifer Barber and Maggie Nelson). Graywolf Press, 1998.

Olga Broumas. *Beginning with O*. Yale University Press, 1977.

——. *Black Holes/Black Stockings* (with Jane Miller). Wesleyan University Press, 1985.

——. *Pastoral Jazz*. Copper Canyon Press, 1983.

——. *Perpetua*. Copper Canyon Press, 1989.

——. *Rave: Poems 1975–1999*. Copper Canyon Press, 1999.

——. *Sappho's Gymnasium* (with T. Begley). Copper Canyon Press, 1994.

——. *Sole Sauvage*. Copper Canyon Press, 1979.

Cheryl Burke. *Motor Oil Queen!* By the Seat of Your Pants Press, 1998.

——. *Nameless*. By the Seat of Your Pants Press, 1999.

——. *Ripe*. Night & Day Productions, 1996.

Regie Cabico. *I Saw Your Ex-lover Behind the Starbucks Counter*. Big Fat Press, 1997.

——. *The Petting Zoo*. IKON, 1994.

——. *Poetry Nation: The North American Anthology of Fusion Poetry* (ed., with Todd Swift). Véhicule Press, 1998.

Rafael Campo. *Diva*. Duke University Press, 1999.

——. *The Other Man Was Me: A Voyage to the New World*. Arte Público Press, 1994.

——. *The Poetry of Healing: A Doctor's Education in Empathy, Identity, and Desire*. W. W. Norton, 1997.

——. *What the Body Told*. Duke University Press, 1996.

Cyrus Cassells. *Beautiful Signor*. Copper Canyon Press, 1997.

——. *The Mud Actor*. Holt, Rinehart & Winston, 1982; Carnegie-Mellon, 1999.

——. *Soul Make a Path Through Shouting*. Copper Canyon Press, 1994.

Justin Chin. *Bite Hard*. Manic D Press, 1997.

——. *Mongrel: Essays, Diatribes, & Pranks*. St. Martin's Press, 1999.

Chrystos. *Dream On*. Press Gang Publishers, 1991.

——. *Fire Power*. Press Gang Publishers, 1995.

——. *Fugitive Colors*. Cleveland State University Poetry Center, 1995.

——. *In Her I Am*. Press Gang Publishers, 1993.

——. *Not Vanishing*. Press Gang Publishers, 1988.

——. *Wilder Reis*. Orlanda (Berlin), 1997.

Cheryl Clarke. *Experimental Love: Poetry*. Firebrand Books, 1993.

——. *Humid Pitch: Narrative Poetry*. Firebrand Books, 1989.

——. *Living as a Lesbian: Poetry*. Firebrand Books, 1986.

——. *Narratives: Poems in the Tradition of Black Women*. Kitchen Table Press, 1983.

Jeffery Conway. *Blood Poisoning: Poems*. Cold Calm Press, 1995.

——. *Plush: Selected Poems of Sky Gilbert, Courtnay McFarlane, Jeffery Conway, R. M. Vaughan & David Trinidad*, ed. Lynn Crosbie and Michael Holmes. Coach House Press, 1995.

Dennis Cooper. *All Ears: Cultural Criticism, Essays, and Obituaries*. Soft Skull Press, 1999.

——. *Antoine Monnier*. Anon Press, 1978.

——. *Closer*. Grove Press, 1989.

——. *Discontents: New Queer Writers* (ed.). Amethyst, 1992.

——. *The Dream Police: Selected Poems 1969–1993*. Grove Press, 1995.

——. *Frisk*. Grove Press, 1991.

——. *Guide*. Grove Press, 1997.

——. *He Cried: Poems and Stories*. Black Star Series, 1984.

——. *Horror Hospital Unplugged: A Graphic Novel* (with Keith Mayerson). Juno Books, 1996.

——. *Idols*. Sea Horse Press, 1979.

——. *Jerk* (with Nayland Blake). Artspace Books, 1993.

——. *The Missing Men*. Am Here Books/Immediate Editions, 1981.

——. *My Mark*. Sherwood Press, 1982.

——. *Period*. Grove Press, 2000.

——. *Safe*. Sea Horse Press, 1984.

——. *The Tenderness of Wolves*. Crossing Press, 1982.

——. *The Terror of Earrings: Poems*. Kinks Press, 1973.

——. *Tiger Beat*. Little Caesar Press, 1978.

——. *Try*. Grove Press, 1995.

——. *Wrong: Stories*. Grove Press, 1993.

Alfred Corn. *All Roads at Once*. Viking Press, 1976.

——. *A Call in the Midst of the Crowd*. Viking Press, 1978.

——. *Autobiographies: Poems*. Viking Press, 1992.

——. *The Metamorphoses of Metaphor*. Viking Press, 1987.

——. *Notes from a Child of Paradise*. Viking Press, 1984.

——. *Part of His Story*. Mid-List Press, 1997.

——. *The Poem's Heartbeat: A Manual of Prosody*. Story Line Press, 1997.

——. *Present*. Counterpoint, 1997.

——. *Stake: Selected Poems, 1972–1992*. Counterpoint, 1999.

——. *The Various Light*. Viking Press, 1980.

——. *The West Door*. Viking Press, 1988.

Mark Doty. *Atlantis: Poems*. HarperCollins, 1995.

——. *Bethlehem in Broad Daylight: Poems*. David R. Godine, 1991.

——. *Firebird: A Memoir*. HarperCollins, 1999.

——. *Heaven's Coast: A Memoir*, HarperCollins, 1996.

——. *My Alexandria: Poems*. University of Illinois Press, 1993.

——. *Sweet Machine: Poems*. HarperCollins, 1998.

——. *Turtle, Swan: Poems*. David R. Godine, 1987.

——. *Turtle, Swan & Bethlehem in Broad Daylight*. University of Illinois Press, 2000.

Beatrix Gates. *In the Open: Poems*. Painted Leaf Press, 1998.

——. *native tongue*. hopalong press, 1973.

——. *Shooting at Night*. Granite Press, 1980.

——. *The Wild Good: Lesbian Photographs and Writings on Love* (ed.). Anchor Books, 1996.

Elena Georgiou. *Mercy Mercy Me*. Painted Leaf Press, 2000.

Robert Glück. *Andy*. Panjandrum Press, 1973.

——. *Elements of a Coffee Service: A Book of Stories*. Four Seasons Foundation, 1983.

——. *Family Poems*. Black Star Series, 1979.

——. *Jack the Modernist*. Sea Horse/Gay Presses of New York, 1985; reprinted by Serpent's Tail/High Risk Books, 1995.

——. *La Fontaine* (with Bruce Boone). Black Star Series, 1981.

——. *Margery Kempe*. Serpent's Tail/High Risk Books. 1994.

——. *Metaphysics*. Hoddypoll, 1977.

——. *Reader*. Lapis Press, 1989.

——. *Saturday Afternoon: An Anthology of Older Writers* (ed.). Small Press Distribution, 1986.

Melinda Goodman. *Middle Sister*. MSG Press, 1988.

Marilyn Hacker. *Assumptions*. Alfred A. Knopf, 1985.

——. *Going Back to the River*. Random House, 1990.

——. *The Hang-glider's Daughter: New and Selected Poems*. Onlywomen Press (U.K.), 1990.

——. *Love, Death, and the Changing of the Seasons*. Arbor House, 1986; reprinted by W. W. Norton, 1995.

——. *Presentation Piece*. Viking Press, 1974.

——. *Selected Poems: 1965–1990*. W. W. Norton, 1994.

——. *Separations*. Alfred A. Knopf, 1976.

——. *Squares and Courtyards*. W. W. Norton, 2000.

——. *Taking Notice*. Alfred A. Knopf, 1980.

——. *Winter Numbers*. W. W. Norton, 1994.

Eloise Klein Healy. *Artemis in Echo Park*. Firebrand Books, 1991.

——. *Building Some Changes*. Beyond Baroque Foundation, 1976.

——. *Ordinary Wisdom*. Paradise Press, 1981.

——. *A Packet Beating Like a Heart*. Books of a Feather Press, 1981.

——. *Women's Studies Chronicles*. The Inevitable Press, 1998.

Michael Klein. *In the Company of My Solitude: American Writing from the AIDS Pandemic* (ed., with Marie Howe). Persea Books, 1995.

——. *1990*. Provincetown Arts Press, 1993.

——. *Poets for Life: 76 Poets Respond to AIDS* (ed.). Persea Books, 1994.

——. *Things Shaped in Passing: More "Poets for Life" Writing from the AIDS Pandemic* (ed., with Richard McCann). Persea Books, 1997.

——. *Track Conditions: A Memoir*. Persea Books, 1997.

Wayne Koestenbaum. *Double Talk: The Erotics of Male Literary Collaboration*. Routledge, 1989.

——. *Jackie Under My Skin: Interpreting an Icon*. Farrar, Straus & Giroux, 1995.

——. *The Milk of Inquiry: Poems*. Persea Books, 1999.

——. *Ode to Anna Moffo and Other Poems*. Persea Books, 1990.

——. *The Queen's Throat: Opera, Homosexuality, and the Mystery of Desire*. Poseidon Press, 1993.

——. *Rhapsodies of a Repeat Offender: Poems*. Persea Books, 1994.

Joan Larkin. *Amazon Poetry* (ed., with Elly Bulkin). Out & Out Books, 1975.

——. *Cold River*. Painted Leaf Press, 1997.

——. *Gay and Lesbian Poetry in Our Time* (ed., with Carl Morse). St. Martin's Press, 1988.

——. *Glad Day: Daily Meditations for Gay, Lesbian, Bisexual, and Transgender People*. Hazelden, 1998.

——. *Housework*. Out & Out Books, 1975.

——. *If You Want What We Have: Sponsorship Meditations*. Hazelden, 1998.

——. *Lesbian Poetry: An Anthology* (ed., with Elly Bulkin). Persephone Press, 1981.

——. *A Long Sound: A Book of Poems*. Granite Press, 1986.

——. *Sor Juana's Love Poems/Poemas de Amor* (trans., with Jaime Manrique). Painted Leaf Press, 1997.

——. *A Woman Like That: Lesbian and Bisexual Writers Tell Their Coming Out Stories* (ed.). Avon Books, 1999.

Michael Lassell. *Certain Ecstasies*. Painted Leaf Press, 1999.

———. *Decade Dance: Poems*. Alyson Publications, 1990.

———. *Eros in Boystown: Contemporary Gay Poems about Sex* (ed.). Crown, 1996.

———. *A Flame for the Touch That Matters*. Painted Leaf Press, 1998.

———. *The Hard Way*. Richard Kasak/Masquerade Books, 1995.

———. *Hollywood, Hollywood: Celebrity Under the Guise of Identity* (with Fred Fehlau, et al.). Pasadena Art Alliance, 1993.

———. *Men Seeking Men: Adventures in Gay Personals* (ed.). Painted Leaf Press, 1998.

———. *The Name of Love: Classic Gay Love Poems* (ed.). St. Martin's Press, 1995.

———. *Poems for Lost and Un-lost Boys*. Amelia, 1985.

———. *Two Hearts Desire: Gay Couples on Their Love* (ed., with Lawrence Schimel). St. Martin's Press, 1997.

Timothy Liu. *Burnt Offerings*. Copper Canyon Press, 1995.

———. *Say Goodnight*. Copper Canyon Press, 1998.

———. *Vox Angelica: Poems*. Alicejamesbooks, 1992.

Jaime Manrique. *Bésame Mucho: An Anthology of New Gay Latino Fiction* (ed., with Jessie Dorris). Painted Leaf Press, 1999.

———. *Colombian Gold*. Clarkson Potter, 1983.

———. *Eminent Maricones: Arenas, Lorca, Puig, and Me*. University of Wisconsin Press, 1999.

———. *Latin Moon in Manhattan*. St. Martin's Press, 1992.

———. *My Night with Federico García Lorca/Mi Noche con Federico García Lorca*. Painted Leaf Press, 1997.

———. *Scarecrow*. Groundwater Press, 1990.

———. *Sor Juana's Love Poems/Poemas de Amor* (trans., with Joan Larkin). Painted Leaf Press, 1997.

———. *Twilight at the Equator: A Novel*. Faber & Faber, 1997.

J. D. McClatchy. *Anne Sexton: The Artist and Her Critics* (ed.). Indiana University Press, 1978.

———. *Bird Poems* (ed.). Everyman's Library/Alfred A. Knopf, forthcoming.

———. *Christmas Poems* (ed., with John Hollander). Everyman's Library/Alfred A. Knopf, 1999.

———. *The Collected Poems of James Merrill* (ed., with Stephen Yensar). Alfred A. Knopf, forthcoming.

———. *Poets on Painters: Essays on the Art of Painting by Twentieth-Century Poets* (ed.). University of California Press, 1988.

———. *Recitative: Prose by James Merrill* (ed.). North Point Press, 1986.

———. *The Rest of the Way*. Alfred A. Knopf, 1990.

———. *Scenes from Another Life*. George Braziller, 1981.

———. *Stars Principal*. Macmillan, 1986.

———. *Ten Commandments*. Alfred A. Knopf, 1998.

———. *Twenty Questions*. Columbia University Press, 1998.

———. *The Vintage Book of Contemporary American Poetry* (ed.). Vintage Books, 1990.

———. *The Vintage Book of Contemporary World Poetry* (ed.). Vintage Books, 1996.

———. *The Voice of the Poet* (ed., poems of W. H. Auden, James Merrill, Sylvia Plath). Random House Audio, 1999.

———. *White Paper*. Columbia University Press, 1989.

Honor Moore. *Memoir: Poems*. Chicory Blue Press, 1988.

———. *The New Women's Theater: Ten Plays by Contemporary American Women*. (ed.). Vintage, 1977.

———. *The White Blackbird: A Life of the Painter Margarett Sargent by Her Granddaughter*. Viking, 1996; reprinted by Penguin, 1997.

Eileen Myles. *Bread & Water: Stories*. Hanuman Books, 1987.

——. *Chelsea Girls*. Black Sparrow Press, 1994.

——. *A Fresh Young Voice from the Plains*. Power Mad, 1981.

——. *The Irony of the Leash*. Jim Brodey Books, 1978.

——. *Maxfield Parrish: Early & New Poems*. Black Sparrow Press, 1995.

——. *The New Fuck You: Adventures in Lesbian Reading*. Semiotext(e), 1995.

——. *1969*. Hanuman Books, 1989.

——. *Not Me*. Semiotext(e), 1991.

——. *Sappho's Boat: Poems*. Little Caesar Press, 1982.

——. *School of Fish*. Black Sparrow Press, 1997.

Letta Neely. *Juba*. Wildheart Press, 1998.

Achy Obejas. *Memory Mambo: A Novel*. Cleis Press, 1996.

——. *We Came All the Way from Cuba So You Could Dress Like This?* Cleis Press, 1994.

Gerry Gomez Pearlberg. *The Fetish Papers*. Big Fat Press, 1998.

——. *The Key to Everything: Classic Lesbian Love Poems* (ed.). St. Martin's Press, 1995.

——. *Marianne Faithfull's Cigarette*. Cleis Press, 1998.

——. *Queer Dog: Homo/Pup/Poetry* (ed.). Cleis Press, 1997.

——. *The Zenith of Desire: Contemporary Lesbian Poems about Sex* (ed.). Crown, 1996.

Robert E. Penn, *The Gay Men's Wellness Guide: The National Lesbian and Gay Health Association's Complete Book of Physical, Emotional, and Mental Health and Well-being for Every Gay Male*. Henry Holt, 1998.

Carl Phillips. *Cortège*. Graywolf Press, 1995.

——. *From the Devotions: Poems*. Graywolf Press, 1998.

——. *In the Blood*. Northeastern University Press, 1992.

——. *Pastoral*. Graywolf Press, 2000.

D. A. Powell. *Con Sequences* (with Carol Ciavonne and Patricia Hartnett). Norton Coker Press, 1993.

——. *explosions and small geometries*. Norton Coker Press, 1991.

——. *Lunch*. Wesleyan University Press, 2000.

——. *Tea*. Wesleyan University Press, 1998.

Minnie Bruce Pratt. *Crime Against Nature*. Firebrand Books, 1990.

——. *Rebellion: Essays 1980–1991*. Firebrand Books, 1991.

——. *S/HE*. Firebrand Books, 1995.

——. *The Sound of One Fork*. Night Heron Press, 1981.

——. *Walking Back Up Depot Street*. University of Pittsburgh Press, 1999.

——. *We Say We Love Each Other*. Spinsters/Aunt Lute, 1985; reprinted by Firebrand Books, 1992.

——. *Yours in Struggle: Three Feminist Perspectives on Anti-Semitism and Racism* (with Elly Bulkin and Barbara Smith). Long Haul Press, 1984; reprinted by Firebrand Books, 1988.

Mariana Romo-Carmona. *Cuentos: Stories by Latinas* (ed., with Alma Gomez and Cherríe Moraga). Kitchen Table Press, 1983.

——. *Living at Night*. Spinsters Ink, 1997.

——. *Queer City* (ed., with Harold Robinson, Ira Silverberg, and Jacqueline Woodson). The Portable Lower East Side, 1991.

——. *Speaking Like an Immigrant*. Latina Lesbian History Project, 1999.

Ruth L. Schwartz. *Accordion Breathing and Dancing*. University of Pittsburgh Press, 1996.

Robyn Selman. *Directions to My House*. University of Pittsburgh Press, 1995.

Reginald Shepherd. *Angel, Interrupted*. University of Pittsburgh Press, 1996.

——. *Some Are Drowning*. University of Pittsburgh Press, 1994.

——. *Wrong*. University of Pittsburgh Press, 1999.

Linda Smukler. *Home in Three Days. Don't Wash*. Hard Press, 1996.

——. *Normal Sex*. Firebrand Books, 1994.

——. *Portraits of Love: Lesbians Writing About Love* (ed., with Susan Fox Rogers). St. Martin's Press, 1997.

Cheryl Boyce Taylor. *Raw Air*. Fly by Night Press, in association with A Gathering of the Tribes, 1997.

Richard Tayson. *The Apprentice of Fever*. Kent State University Press, 1998.

——. *Look Up for Yes* (with Julia Tavalaro). Viking Penguin, 1998.

David Trinidad. *Answer Song*. Serpent's Tail/High Risk Books, 1994.

——. *A Taste of Honey* (with Bob Flanagan). Cold Calm Press, 1990.

——. *Essay with Movable Parts*. Thorngate Road, 1998.

——. *Hand over Heart: Poems 1981–1988*. Amethyst Press, 1991.

——. *Living Doll*. Illuminati, 1986.

——. *Monday, Monday*. Cold Calm Press, 1985.

——. *November*. Hanuman Books, 1987.

——. *Pavane*. Sherwood Press, 1981.

——. *Plasticville*. Turtle Point Press, forthcoming.

——. *Plush: Selected Poems of Sky Gilbert, Courtnay McFarlane, Jeffery Conway, R. M. Vaughan & David Trinidad* (eds. Lynn Crosbie and Michael Holmes). Coach House Press, 1995.

——. *Powerless: Selected Poems 1973–1990*, by Tim Dlugos (ed.). Serpent's Tail/High Risk Books, 1996.

——. *Three Stories*. Hanuman Books, 1988.

Terry Wolverton. *Bailey's Beads*. Faber & Faber, 1996.

——. *Black Slip*. Clothespin Fever Press, 1992.

——. *Blood Whispers: L.A. Writers on AIDS* (ed.). Silverton Books, 1991.

——. *Blood Whispers: L.A. Writers on AIDS*, vol. 2 (ed.). Silverton Books, 1994.

——. *Gay Fiction at the Millennium* (ed., with Robert Drake). Alyson Publications, forthcoming.

——. *Harbinger: Poetry and Fiction by Los Angeles Writers* (ed., with Benjamin Weissman). Los Angeles Festival and Beyond Baroque, 1990.

——. *Hers: Brilliant New Fiction by Lesbian Writers* (ed., with Robert Drake). Faber & Faber, 1995.

——. *Hers 2: Brilliant New Fiction by Lesbian Writers* (ed., with Robert Drake). Faber & Faber, 1997.

——. *Hers 3: Brilliant New Fiction by Lesbian Writers* (ed., with Robert Drake). Faber & Faber, 1999.

——. *His: Brilliant New Fiction by Gay Writers* (ed., with Robert Drake). Faber & Faber, 1995.

——. *His 2: Brilliant New Fiction by Gay Writers* (ed., with Robert Drake). Faber & Faber, 1997.

——. *His 3: Brilliant New Fiction by Gay Writers* (ed., with Robert Drake). Faber & Faber, 1999.

——. *Indivisible: New Short Fiction by Gay and Lesbian West Coast Writers* (ed., with Robert Drake). Plume, 1991.

——. *Lesbian Fiction at the Millennium* (ed., with Robert Drake). Alyson Publications, forthcoming.

——. *Mystery Bruise*. Red Hen Press, 1999.

Mark Wunderlich. *The Anchorage: Poems*. University of Massachusetts Press, 1999.

INDEX OF TITLES

INDEX OF FIRST LINES